THE WORLD'S CLASSICS

ANNALS OF THE PARISH

JOHN GALT was born in Irvine, Ayrshire, in 1779 and was trained for business. At the age of twenty-four he moved to London. He was by turns continental traveller (for a time the companion of Byron), businessman in a variety of ventures, parliamentary lobbyist, colonial administrator in Canada (where his family ultimately settled), and, at all times, an indefatigable writer. He was the author of over forty books but his literary reputation was established and remains based on a series of Tales of the West, novels drawing on his memories of the Glasgow and Ayrshire region in which he grew up. His *Annals of the Parish* (1821), *The Provost* (1822), and *The Entail* (1822) are deeply felt studies of small-town life in eighteenth-century Scotland. He moved, with no great success, to historical fiction, and in 1832 produced *The Member,* the first political novel in English. Though an invalid in his later years, he continued to write, and published a series of novellas. He died in 1839.

The late James Kinsley was Professor of English Studies in the University of Nottingham. He was general editor of two Oxford series, the Oxford English Novels (in which his edition of *Annals of the Parish* first appeared) and the Oxford English Memoirs and Travels. His other work included major editions of the poems of Dunbar, Burns, and Dryden.

THE WORLD'S CLASSICS

———

JOHN GALT

Annals of the Parish

OR THE
Chronicle of Dalmailing
DURING THE MINISTRY OF
THE REV. MICAH BALWHIDDER

Written by himself.

———

Edited with an Introduction by
JAMES KINSLEY

Oxford   New York
OXFORD UNIVERSITY PRESS
1986

Oxford University Press, Walton Street, Oxford OX2 6DP

Oxford New York Toronto
Delhi Bombay Calcutta Madras Karachi
Kuala Lumpur Singapore Hong Kong Tokyo
Nairobi Dar es Salaam Cape Town
Melbourne Auckland

and associated companies in
Beirut Berlin Ibadan Nicosia

Oxford is a trade mark of Oxford University Press

Introduction, Notes, and Bibliography
© Oxford University Press 1967
Chronology © Oxford University Press 1973, 1982

First published 1967 by Oxford University Press
First issued as a World's Classics paperback 1986

British Library Cataloguing in Publication Data
Galt, John
Annals of the parish, or, The Chronicle of
Dalmailing during the ministry of the Rev. Micah
Balwhidder: written by himself.—(The World's
classics)
I. Title   II. Kinsley, James
823'.7[F]   PR4708.G2
ISBN 0-19-281735-3

Library of Congress Cataloging in Publication Data
Galt, John, 1779–1839.
Annals of the parish, or, The chronicle of
Dalmailing during the ministry of the Rev. Micah Balwhidder.
(The World's classics)
Bibliography: p.
I. Kinsley, James.   II. Title.   III. Title: Chronicle
of Dalmailing during the ministry of
the Rev. Micah Balwhidder.
PR4708.G2A8 · 1986   823'.7   85-21550
ISBN 0-19-281735-3 (pbk.)

Printed in Great Britain by
Hazell Watson & Viney Ltd.
Aylesbury, Bucks

CONTENTS

INTRODUCTION

FABLES, says Galt, 'are often a better way of illustrating philosophical truths than abstract reasoning; and in this class of compositions I would place the *Annals of the Parish*.'[1] The minister of Dalmailing writes as a 'witness to the work of a beneficent Providence, even in the narrow sphere of my parish, and the concerns of [my] flock'. This book and its companion, *The Provost* (1822), were not designed as novels; and in their reception as such,[2] to Galt's regret,

> they have both suffered, for neither of them have, unquestionably, a plot. My own notion was to exhibit a kind of local theoretical history, by examples, the truth of which would at once be acknowledged. . . . As stories they are greatly deficient. In the composition of [both] I followed the same rule of art . . . namely, to bring impressions on the memory harmoniously together. . . .[3]

—an application of Aristotle's dictum that literary art is 'something more scientific and serious than history, because [it] tends to give general truths while history gives particular facts'.[4]

Recent critics have given only qualified approval to Galt's attempts at 'local theoretical history'.[5] Ian Jack complains that the *Annals* run on into 'Galt's own observations and

---

[1] *Literary Life* (1834), i. 155-6.

[2] About 1,000 copies of the *Annals* were sold in Edinburgh and London in the first week; of *The Provost*, 2,000 in a fortnight. For comparative sales figures see David Craig, *Scottish Literature and the Scottish People 1680-1830* (1961), pp. 297-8.

[3] *Literary Life*, i. 226, 228.   [4] *Poetics*, ix.

[5] Dugald Stewart had applied the term to a 'species of philosophical investigations . . . *Theoretical* or *Conjectural History*; an expression which coincides pretty nearly . . . with that of *Natural History*, as employed by Mr Hume, and with what some French writers have called Histoire Raisonnée' (*Works*, 1854-60, x. 32-34).

reflections, set down without regard for the limitations of the narrator's understanding'[1]—though you never quite know with ministers. David Craig, on the other hand, objects that Galt shows 'no particular attitude to the way of life he imitates, no effort of art [in] the selection of events'; 'because everything is felt through [the minister's] mentality, all other possible life is diminished to his kind of understanding'.[2] Galt would have regarded this as the more serious criticism. He was born into what Hume had called 'the historical age and . . . the historical nation'; and he was attempting a new kind of history on the ancient complementary principles of instruction and delight.[3] My wish, he said, 'is to be estimated by the truth of whatever I try to represent'; 'if there is any merit in any of my sketches it is in the truth of the meta-physical anatomy of the characters'.[4] The minister himself acknowledges, with gratitude, the limitations of parish life. If it is true, he says—addressing the third Mrs Balwhidder in the tones of Sir Thomas Browne—that 'we live, as it were, within the narrow circle of ignorance, we are spared from the pain of knowing many an evil; and, surely, in much knowledge, there is sadness of heart'. But knowledge of the great world is not a condition of wisdom; and 'I have, in the afternoon of life, been enabled to foresee what kings and nations would do, by the symptoms manifested within the bounds of the society around me', 'for what happened in my parish was but a type and index to the rest of the world'. The human drama of Dalmailing had been an index not only—by a familiar and complacent assumption—to political and social change: '. . . we had intromitted so much with concerns of trade, that

[1] *English Literature 1815–1832* (1963), p. 229.   [2] op. cit., p. 158.
[3] Craig rightly associates Galt with the Blackwood group who were concerned with writing up provincial Scotland and the national character (pp. 156–7, 219, 312–13); but *Annals of the Parish* is also an expression, at a deeper level, of the Scottish interest in institutions and social change. See Gladys Bryson, *Man and Society: The Scottish Inquiry of the Eighteenth Century* (1945).
[4] *Literary Life*, i. 231; letter to Blackwood, 12 April 1826.

we were become a part of the great web of commercial reciprocities, and felt in our corner and extremity, every touch or
stir that was made on any part of the texture'.[1]

It is true that social alterations and national events make
strong, simple, irregular impressions on the minister's mind,
and on that of his parish. The effect may seem superficial to
readers who are accustomed to the much more complex social
novels of the Victorians. But this is just how the recent past
looks to unsophisticated minds in remote places; and events
'are described, alluded to, or ignored, with a near-sighted
lack of perspective that is curiously realistic'.[2] Galt's first
readers were quite persuaded by his minister's account of the
half-century they had lived through. Blackwood's 'worthy
old mother' was angry to discover that the *Annals* was only
a novel, for 'thus it lost all its charms'. A reviewer in 1821
wanted 'the faithful Annals of this homely and veracious
Chronicler' added as an appendix to *The Statistical Account
of Scotland*. Many 'thought the old gentleman very silly to
publish'. Galt carried this public reaction into fiction in *The
Last of the Lairds*: 'That silly auld havering creature, Balwhidder o' Dalmailing, got a thousand pounds sterling, doun
on Blackwood's counter, in red gold, for his clishmaclavers;
and Provost Pawkie's widow has had twice the dooble o't,
they say, for the Provost's life.'[3]

Mr Balwhidder gets a deal of national history as well as
parish events into the *Annals*: agricultural improvement,
industrialization, domestic economy and rural education, kirk
affairs, theological fashions, the Gordon riots, the Irish
rebellion, the American and French wars, 'democracy', and
utilitarianism. But a good deal is left out. In the world of
letters, for instance, the work of the Edinburgh 'literati' may

[1] pp. 137, 175, 186, 197.
[2] Jennie W. Aberdein, *John Galt* (1936), p. 103.
[3] Craig, op. cit., p. 200; Aberdein, op. cit., pp. 104, 107; Galt, *Works* (1936), ix. 14.
There is a dig at Blackwood here; Galt got 60 guineas for the *Annals*, and £300 for
The Provost, Sir Andrew Wylie, and a number of articles (Craig, op. cit., p. 297).

have been beyond the minister's ken; but he ignores the stir made by Burns's *Poems* in the west country in the 1780s;[1] he cannot have been deaf to the theological scandal of McGill's Christology (1786) or to some other local kirk bruilzies;[2] and surely he should have been a contributor to the *Statistical Account* (1791–9). But although the historical content of the book is so much determined by prescription and caprice, Galt exaggerated its formlessness. Its centre is marked at chapter xxvi:

. . . here was an example plain to be seen of the truth of the old proverb, that as one door shuts another opens; for scarcely were we in quietness by the decease of that old light-headed woman, the Lady Macadam, till a full equivalent for her was given in this hot and fiery Mr Cayenne.

The parallel, real enough to the long-suffering pastor, disguises an essential contrast. The first half of the book is a picture of the old, settled world of the landed gentry (Lord Eglesham, Lady Macadam) and tenantry: an idyll marred only by common personal or parochial troubles, or by the familiar incursions of war. The second half introduces new themes (some typified by Mr Cayenne) of industry and urban settlement, religious anarchy, schism and decline, and the 'decay in the wonted simplicity of our country ways'. The minister who had been long accustomed to preach on the smuggling of tea, fornication, the horror of war, 'the helplessness of them that have no help of man', or Antichrist and 'orthodoxy', now finds his arguments—'which were the old and orthodox proven opinions of the Divinity Hall'—confounded; his new themes are 'the evil and vanity of riches', bloody revolution, and the fashionable secular philosophies.[3] It is only in 1807 that he begins to feel a settling of attitudes

[1] 'Old and young, high and low, grave and gay, learned or ignorant, all were alike delighted, agitated, transported' (R. Heron, *Memoir of Burns*, 1797, p. 17).

[2] For McGill, see Burns, *The Kirk's Alarm* (1789).

[3] pp. 128; 44, 98, 129, 137, 143, 147 ff.

and ways, 'really a birth of grace', and that is partly a mark of
oncoming age in himself.

The story is told from the vantage-point of 1810. This
enables Galt to write with an economy and concentration that
would not have been so credible in a fictitious journal; but it
sets him a difficult artistic problem. By 1809 Mr Balwhidder
is, in Galt's words, 'garrulous and doited'. He has so little
self-criticism left that he feels 'better' at preaching now, able
'to hold forth, in an easy manner, often a whole half hour
longer than I could do a dozen years before'. Can Galt maintain the impression of garrulous age; write for the early years
a narrative and dialogue which are vivid without becoming
incredible; and get his minister to show evidence of interior
change? If not, the autobiographical device becomes a burden; the illusion will not work.

The fiction of Mr Balwhidder—old in years, attitudes, and
style—is established in the Introduction, his first account of
the events of 1810. Narrative and sermon here set a standard
style for the book; persuasively, for Balwhidder is a conservative member of a conservative profession, early confirmed
in his ways, resistant to change even in his own calling.[1] He
justifies the clarity of his early annals for Galt, by remarking
that the memory is hazier about the recent past than about the
long ago; and for the later chapters, 'being apt to confound
the things of one occasion with those of another' nowadays,
he has the help of the third Mrs Balwhidder, a woman of
'very clear understanding' and a 'most judicious judgment'.[2]
These devices, sustained by a wonderfully even style, take
Galt a long way towards credible fiction. But he goes further,
and shows his ageing minister, in the annals from 1800 on,
casually aware of his maturity. Mr Balwhidder's first school
apophthegm had been, prophetically, 'Experience teaches

---

[1] He is only half-way through his ministry when he is disconcerted by Willie
Malcolm's new-style preaching (p. 132).

[2] pp. 201, 188.

fools'; he has lately (1802) found his 'experience mellowing
and ... discernment improving'. (This is psychologically true;
a sense of maturity comes slowly to such a man.) He begins
humbly to recognize 'the finger of Wisdom'—his usual term
is 'Providence'—in events. Religious schism, which so much
distressed him, was better than political revolution; his elders
had been right to avoid a head-on collision with Popery—
against which he had preached at the Assembly—'and to this
opinion, now that I have had years to sift its wisdom, I own
myself a convert and proselyte'. Seeing his elders 'set on an
alteration' in kirk discipline, he distrusted his own judgement;
'for they were true men, and of a godly honesty'—a lesson,
this, for what Balwhidder would have called 'prelatic' clergy,
though he is human enough to be a bit prelatic himself towards
those who abandon traditional kirk allegiance. As in discipline,
so now in divinity; he listens respectfully to his 'theological'
elder Mr Siftwell, 'as I have not, at my advanced age, such
a mind for the kittle crudities of polemical investigation that
I had in my younger years, especially when I was a student in
the Divinity-Hall of Glasgow'[1]—the tone and reference,
however, preserving his self-respect!

'It is not ... my design', says the minister, 'to speak much
anent my own affairs'; this would be 'a very improper and
uncomely thing' in a book intended 'for a witness and testimony of my ministry'.[2] But the tension between social annals
and autobiography was recognized from the first in Galt's
draft title, 'The Pastor of his Parish or The Chronicles of
Dunmailing', and indeed the reader is fascinated far less by
events than by Mr Balwhidder's blend of eloquence and
garrulity, pathos and humour, simplicity and sense. The main
merit of the *Annals* lies, as Galt hoped, in the 'metaphysical
anatomy' of the minister.

He displays the necessary virtues of his calling 'to eschew

---

[1] pp. 175, 204, 185, 184, 193, 186.
[2] p. 46.

evil myself, and to teach others to do the same', walking 'in the paths of simplicity within my own parish'. But blameless lives are, in themselves, not often interesting. We are drawn to the minister as to some of the saints, less by his homespun virtue than by the individual and at times eccentric way he exercises it. The enchantment begins in the first chapter, with his induction. He endures the scorn of his people in dignified resignation, 'compassionating their wilfulness and blindness' (and casually noting the 'clash of glar' in Mr Kilfuddy's eye); but prudence also, at the level of property and politics, 'obligates' him to the indignity of going in and out by the kirk window. Balwhidder has a disarming honesty of mind. He admits that he gave up preaching against tea, not only because it turned out harmless enough but also because Mrs Malcolm took to selling it. Writing the first Mrs Balwhidder's epitaph —in English, for the 'worthy woman . . . did not understand the Latin tongue'—was a solemn duty, but designing her monument became 'a blessed entertainment' in the dreary winter nights. He does not suffer much from self-esteem: though he might fairly, on his own account, have resented Lady Macadam's insult, it was 'surely . . . not a polite thing to say to Mrs Balwhidder, my second wife'. He knows that, to the Searcher of Hearts, he is no saint; but he is modest and open enough to record, without giving offence, that Mr Auld defended him as 'a man of a guileless heart, and a spiritual simplicity, that would be ornamental in a child'. He can, however, be as wise as the serpent. Though he admires the business acumen of Mr Kibbock, and is able to give sound tactical advice to the experienced Mr Cayenne, he knows when not to assert his own rights; he gets the real point of a letter into 'a bit nota bene'; he practises the 'quiet canny way' of reform in his parish. He does not know that his Assembly sermon is in an outmoded style; but intuition, rather than humility and insecurity, tells him that it has been a failure.[1]

[1] pp. 95, 5, 20, 26–27; 62, 42, 29; 120, 177, 47, 189, 100.

There are flaws in Mr Balwhidder. His morality is narrow, conventional (even cards are 'thriftless and sinful'); and he is resistant to change. (This is not always, however, an uncritical conservatism. His pastoral experience enables him to see the darker side of Glasgow's new prosperity, and to 'discern something like a shadow' in the 'spirit of improvement'.) The impulse of courage is, in him as in most of us, spasmodic. He is ready enough to sound the trumpet for the Napoleonic war, and he can tell Lord Eglesham with some tact to give up his whore; but he is terrified by the infamous Mr Heckletext, and finds it difficult to face the tantrums of Lady Macadam or rebuke Mr Cayenne's blasphemies.[1] He is, too, casually and engagingly malicious. He passes on the local joke about Lady Macadam and the Douglas cause; vanquished in an unguarded moment by the Enemy, he laughs at the discomfiture of Betty Wudrife 'loud out among the graves'; provoked, he calls Mr Cayenne a 'dying uncircumcised Philistine'; he parodies the schoolmistress. The brazen fornicator Nichol Snipe is humiliated by a bawdy jest *ex pulpito*, which for once does justice to the realism of the Kirk.[2] Yet, despite these capitulations to the Enemy, the minister is patient and charitable towards Mr Cayenne and Lady Macadam, and above all to that 'engine of industry', the second Mrs Balwhidder. Here affectionate tolerance is enriched by pathos and wit:

Often could I have found it in my heart to have banned that never-ceasing industry, and to tell Mrs Balwhidder, that the married state was made for something else than to make napery, and bittle blankets; but it was her happiness to keep all at work, and she had no pleasure in any other way of life, so I sat many a night by the fireside with resignation . . . really a most solitary married man.[3]

The minister's sense of Providence is fundamental to his character; it gives his history a design. Providence brings

---

[1] pp. 58, 137, 179, 105, 64, 78, 118, 144.
[2] pp. 58 and note, 77, 191, 128; 30.   [3] p. 138.

good out of evil, working out the 'destined end' of all things with 'accustomed sobriety' (surely a Presbyterian gloss) and sowing seeds which ultimately yield universal increase. To see in the minister's toothache a divine instrument for the exposure of hypocritical lechery is, perhaps, just within the propriety of this view; but there is improbable and sarcastic parody in 'it pleased . . . Him, from whom cometh every good and perfect gift, to send at this time among us a Miss Sabrina Hookie'—a woman of 'harmless vanity', 'made up of odds and ends'.[1]

The professional gravity of the clergy has been, at least from the Middle Ages, permissible matter for comedy. Preaching perfection, humanity exposes its imperfections; a religious world-view, interpreted by unsophisticated clerical minds, encourages what the world sees as a lack of proportion; and clerical facility in the language of liturgy and Scripture is easily made into an instrument of satire. This kind of comedy runs harmlessly and delightfully through the *Annals*, and sometimes at least—as in the opening parallel drawn between the minister and the king—seems to be within Mr Balwhidder's own perception. But occasionally Galt exaggerates it mock-heroically and, I think, improperly: in, for instance, the minister's notion that 'all things in this world were loosened from their hold, and that the sure and steadfast earth itself was grown coggly beneath my feet, as I mounted the pulpit' for the Assembly sermon; or when he reduces the idea of parish events as a universal 'type and index' to absurdity, seeing parochial harmony as an omen of national preservation but keeping this to himself 'lest it might . . . relax the vigilance of the kingdom'. Mr Balwhidder's literary dream-vision reads like a parody of the *Spectator*, and is out of character.[2] His romantic posturing in chapter v is not incredible in itself ('I was . . . looking at the industrious bee . . .

---

[1] pp. 37, 75, 101; 64, 48, 49.
[2] pp. 97, 182, 142.

and the idle butterfly, that layeth up no store, but perisheth ere it is winter'); it is comic enough, especially in the minister's fancy that 'a connect treatise on the efficacy of Free Grace would be more taking' than a poem on original sin 'like Paradise Lost'; but it is wantonly reduced to farce by his throbs, thrills, and transports.

Like Galt's first readers, we easily accept the *Annals* as a brief memoir, and do not ask for the elaborate statement through character, setting, and event, of the sociological novel. We are content, as in reading a journal, to build on hints and fill out characters who are sketched in outline—especially those close to the minister, resolved not to speak much anent his own affairs. People like Lady Macadam, Sabrina, Mr Cayenne, and the Gaffaws are delineated with remarkable economy and force. But the realization of the three Mrs Balwhidders, almost without description or dialogue, is quite as impressive. Of the first we are told only that she was active in good works, settled the minister in his people's affections, and dwined away after the loss of twelve stone of lint. The second is more dramatically portrayed as a resolute woman and an 'engine of industry', but she appears chiefly at 'the down-lying' or 'the wearyful booming wheel'. The third is the well-bred 'relic' of a Glasgow professor, and a woman of judgement and tact.[1] In fact, our sense of the reality of the three wives grows out of Mr Balwhidder's responses and attitudes; they are almost parts of his character. He married the first 'more out of a compassionate habitual affection, than the passion of love', and in this she quietly died. Then he 'placed [his] affections, with due consideration, upon Miss Lizy Kibbock', and reaped the whirlwind. But if the first Mrs Balwhidder set him in the affections of the parish, the second set him up in the world. He was as dangerously deliberate over the third, bending his brows and looking towards Irville, 'an abundant trone for widows and other

[1] pp. 14, 24; 53, 140; 154, 205.

single women', and carrying out a cautious reconnaissance. A new, unexpected note comes in here, merry if not quite romantic. An understanding is achieved by an indelicate game with chicken legs and 'a kindly nip on her sonsy arm', and a happy old age is assured for Mr Balwhidder. The Glasgow 'relic' is, indeed, the almost silent familiar spirit of the *Annals*; it is unthinkable that the book could have got written during the dominion of the second Mrs Balwhidder. Yet it is one of Galt's subtleties that the woman who most fully engages the minister's feelings is not a wife but the Christian paragon, Mrs Malcolm: she evokes pathetic and even poetical description as none of the three wives does, and remains a romantic, unattainable ideal kept beyond his reach by 'saintly steadiness'.[1]

There is a different kind of romantic feeling in Mr Balwhidder's account of the 'two born idiots' Jenny and Meg Gaffaw. Galt, like Scott, expresses the amusement, affection, fear, and wonder with which his countrymen viewed mental disorder. In what Meg Gaffaw says and does at her mother's death there is pathos, dignity—and a rebuke, unintended but poignant, for the minister who has come out of curiosity and too late: 'What a pity it is, mother, that you're now dead, for here's the minister come to see you. O, sir, but she would have had a proud heart to see you in her dwelling, for she had a genteel turn. . . .' Mr Balwhidder hears this, perhaps defensively, as 'curious maunnering'. But he does see her, Scottishly, as 'a sort of household familiar' with 'much like the inner side of wisdom in the pattern of her sayings', and he takes her admonition over the tythe-boll as prophetic. Meg comes to full stature after her rejection by Mr Melcomb, her last tragic words a kind of ballad poetry:

The worm—the worm is my bonny bridegroom, / and Jenny with the many feet my bridal maid. / The mill-dam water's the wine o' the wedding, / and the clay and the clod shall be my bedding. / A lang night is meet for a bridal, / but none shall be langer than mine.

[1] pp. 9, 31, 154, 156; 46, 154.

'When [Galt] chooses to be pathetic,' said Byron, 'he fools one to his bent.'[1]

Meg is not the only poet in Dalmailing. The minister has his own 'nerve', and an artist's eye for the calm, black-clad figure of Mrs Malcolm 'spinning the finest lint, which suited well with her pale hands'. A preacher of 'moving discourse', he has worked the Bible and the Covenanting tradition into his style: 'we were pre-ordained to fade and flourish in fellowship'; 'where the banner of the oppressor was planted of old, and the war-horse trampled in the blood of martyrs'; 'spinning . . . as if she was in verity drawing the thread of life'; '[this] I made manifest to the hearts and understandings of the congregation, in such a manner that many shed tears, and went away sorrowful'; and (straining our gravity a bit) 'she was removed from mine to Abraham's bosom on Christmas day'.[2] He is addicted to artificial nature-pictures and decorative fancies, in the style of Augustan prose 'meditations'; a poetic simile can bring him to the verge of absurdity. But he has also a natural poetry: 'I saw, as it were, the children unborn, walking in the bright green'; 'it was between the day and dark, when the shuttle stands still till the lamp is lighted'. Sometimes the pattern is complex—made up from peasant speech, Scots poetic tradition, and the language of the preacher—as in the incantations of Meg Gaffaw, or the minister's farewell:

Our work is done . . . and, in the sleep that all must sleep, beneath the cold blanket of the kirk-yard grass, and on that clay pillow where we must shortly lay our heads, may we have pleasant dreams, till we are awakened to partake of the everlasting banquet of the saints in glory.[3]

---

[1] pp. 111-12, 160, 125, 160; Byron to the Countess of Blessington, quoted in Aberdein, op. cit., p. 122. Cf. p. 70, note.

[2] pp. 7; 1, 3, 8, 44, 24.

[3] pp. 28, 46, 56, cf. James Hervey's *Meditations and Contemplations* (1746); 148, 22; 4.

The Scottishness of Galt's style is not fully realized in silent reading. When he is read aloud by a Scot, a distinctive pattern and tone come through—even when, as in the first chapter, the dialect element is slight. This is emphasized by Galt himself. Reviewers had objected that the style of *The Provost* was 'not Scotch, because the words are English,—and not English, because the forms of speech are Scottish'. But, says Galt, 'independently of phraseology, there is such an idiomatic difference in the structure of the national dialects of England and Scotland'—as neat a 'retour' as the phrase 'South Britain'—'that very good Scotch might be couched in the purest English terms, and without the employment of a single Scottish word'.[1] Provost Pawkie records his dialect conversations, but tells his tale in the mannered Anglo-Scots which Galt, in his early essay on John Wilson, calls 'a species of translation'. This is also the minister's basic style, and it makes vernacular phrases and passages in the *Annals* look a bit contrived.[2] Galt was, of course, anxious to sell his work in England, where Burns's 'uncouth dialect' often 'spoiled all',[3] and his Scots is unnaturally light. He uses the vernacular for special effects, and indeed risks weighting it a little in the 1822 edition.[4]

It is 'the common language of the country', says Galt, 'in which [a Scotsman] expresses himself with most ease and vivacity, and, clothed in which, his earliest and most distinctive impressions always arise to his own mind': a vehicle of realism, wit, and feeling. Mr Balwhidder's Scots is marked in his reports of peasant speech and, by a natural extension of the principle, in bits of genre-painting—the portrait of Nanse

[1] Postscript to *Ringan Gilhaize* (1823); *Works* (1936), viii. 325.

[2] Cf. Craig (op. cit., p. 261) on Lady Grippy in *The Entail*, 'often no more than a vehicle for displays of language'.

[3] Cowper to Samuel Rose, 27 August 1787: 'Poor Burns loses much of his deserved praise in this country, through our ignorance of his language. . . . His candle is bright, but shut up in a dark lantern' (*Works*, 1836, vi. 56-57).

[4] See Textual Notes.

Banks, the village's farewell to Charlie Malcolm, and the descriptions of the carlins' secret tea-drinking and the 'pay-wedding'.[1] Dashes of dialect, for Galt and still for Scotsmen with a traditional turn of wit, add comic spice to an 'English' narrative: in, for instance, 'the very parrot . . . was a participator, for the beast gied a skraik that made my whole head dirl'; or in the portrait of the dancing-master, which deserves comparison with the Edinburgh etchings of John Kay. Scots is—and remains today—a ready tool for sarcasm: the 'inditer' of Breadland's Latin epitaph, says Mr Balwhidder, 'could no have been the young laird himself, although he got the credit o't on the stone, for he was nae daub in my aught at the Latin or any other language'.[2] Most important of all, Galt uses the vernacular to evoke strong feeling:[3] in the minister's 'touching discourse' of 1776, the plaint of Nanse Banks, the contrived and unconvincing monologue of the widow Mirkland, and the much truer pictures of the sorrows of Mrs Malcolm and Meg Gaffaw.[4]

1967

[1] Essay on John Wilson (1803); *Annals*, pp. 13, 18, 12-13, 196.

[2] pp. 22, 15, 25.

[3] 'This is perfectly true to the broad Scots for professional pathos which we know to have been used by . . . advocates in court at that time' (Craig, op. cit., pp. 157-8; cf. p. 290).

[4] pp. 81-82, 43, 86-87, 109, 111-12.

NOTE ON THE TEXT

THE text is printed from the British Museum copy of the first edition (12°; 1821), collated with that of 1822. Both editions were published at Edinburgh by Blackwood—and for him, at London, by Cadell. Both were printed in Edinburgh; *21* by James Ballantyne, and *22* by Neill. The title-pages are almost identical. The texts have the same make-up (A1r–S2v; pp. 1–400). In *22*, however, the title-leaf is followed by two new preliminary leaves. The first carries a dedication 'To John Wilson, Esquire, Professor of Moral Philosophy in the University of Edinburgh; as a small expression of the Author's regard for his worth and talents'; the second, an advertisement for two other novels by Galt—*The Ayrshire Legatees* ('lately published') and *The Provost* ('in the Press'). An additional leaf at the end of *22* advertises new books from Blackwood.

A number of substantive alterations were made in *22*. Since the printer was following the paging and lineation of *21*, and had to accommodate these changes, they may be safely ascribed to Galt himself. Some of them eliminate cacophonous repetition or improve the rhythm of the prose; a few show Galt, like Burns in revision, weighting the Scottishness of his language. A larger group of variants corrects obvious errors in printing, and what were apparently misreadings of a difficult manuscript. But although Galt revised his work for *22*, he probably did not read the new edition in proof:[1] it introduces as many new errors (both substantive and accidental) as it corrects, and a number of variant spellings unlikely to be Galt's. I have therefore followed the text of *21*, incorporating changes in *22* which have apparent authority. All departures from *21* are recorded on pp. 211–13.

---

[1] Cf. Galt's second letter to Blackwood, *infra*, p. 207.

SELECT BIBLIOGRAPHY

***

Annals of the Parish, together with *The Ayrshire Legatees*, was reprinted in Blackwood's Standard Novels, 1841 (reissued 1844, 1850, 1854), and by Macmillan in 1895 (1896, 1903). There have been several more recent reprints with introductory essays, notes, and glossaries: notably G. S. Gordon's (Oxford University Press, 1908) and G. Baillie Macdonald's (Everyman's Library, 1910).

COLLECTED EDITIONS (MAIN NOVELS ONLY). *The Works of John Galt*, ed. D. S. Meldrum, introductions by S. R. Crockett, illustr., 8 vols. (Blackwood, 1895); *The Works of John Galt*, ed. D. S. Meldrum and W. Roughead, introductions by S. R. Crockett, illustr., 10 vols. (John Grant, 1936).

BIBLIOGRAPHY. Harry Lumsden, *The Bibliography of John Galt*, Records of the Glasgow Bibliographical Society, ix (1931); B. A. Booth in the *Bulletin of Bibliography*, xvi (1936). See also the books by R. K. Gordon, J. W. Aberdein, Ian Jack and Ian A. Gordon noted below, and W. R. Aitken, 'Bibliographical Notes', in *John Galt* (bicentenary commemorative volume, ed. C. A. Whatley), 1979; Lucien Leclaire, *A General Analytical Bibliography of the Regional Novelist of the British Isles 1800–1950* (Paris, 1954), pp. 31–35.

BIOGRAPHY AND CRITICISM. The primary sources are Galt's *Autobiography*, 2 vols. (1833) and his *Literary Life, and Miscellanies*, 3 vols. (1834). The earliest memoir is by '∆' (D. M. Moir) in the 1841 edition of the *Annals*; modern biographies by Jennie W. Aberdein (1936), Ian A. Gordon (1972), and H. B. Timothy (1977). For early criticism see *Edinburgh Monthly Review*, July 1821; *Quarterly Review*, xxv (1821); *Edinburgh Review*, xxxix (October 1823; by Francis Jeffrey). Modern studies: J. H. Millar, *Literary History of Scotland* (1903), pp. 549–58; G. S. Gordon in *The Lives of Authors* (1950; preface to 1908 ed. of the *Annals*);

R. K. Gordon, *John Galt* (1920; University of Toronto Studies; Philological Series, no. 5); George Kitchin in *Edinburgh Essays on Scots Literature*, ed. H. J. C. Grierson (1933); F. H. Lyell, *A Study of Novels of John Galt* (1942; Princeton Studies in English, no. 28); Lucien Leclaire, *Le Roman régionaliste dans les Iles Britanniques 1800–1950* (Paris, 1954), pp. 30 ff.; Erik Frykman, *John Galt's Scottish Stories 1820–1823* (Uppsala, 1959); David Craig, *Scottish Literature and the Scottish People 1680–1830* (1961), *passim*; Ian Jack, *English Literature 1815–1832* (1963), ch. viii; W. M. Parker, *Susan Ferrier and John Galt* (1965); Marion Lochhead, 'John Galt', in *Maga*, December 1968; Ian A. Gordon, *John Galt: The Life of a Writer* (1972); J. MacQueen, 'John Galt and the analysis of social history', in *Scott Bicentenary Essays*, ed. A. Bell (1973); K. M. Costain, 'Theoretical history and the novel: the Scottish fiction of John Galt', in *ELH* 43 (1976); H. B. Timothy, *The Galts: A Canadian Odyssey*, vol. 1 (1977); Henri Gibault, *John Galt romancier écossais* (University of Grenoble, 1979); C. A. Whatley (ed.), *John Galt 1779–1979* (bicentenary commemorative volume, 1979), which includes C. A. Whatley, '*Annals of the Parish* and History', K. G. Simpson, 'Ironic Self-Revelation in *Annals of the Parish*', J. D. McClure, 'Scots and English in *Annals of the Parish* and *The Provost*'; *Scottish Literary Journal* (John Galt Number), May 1981; P. H. Scott, *John Galt* (Scottish Academic Press, 1985).

revised by Ian A. Gordon 1986

A CHRONOLOGY OF JOHN GALT

Age

1818   *The Appeal: a Tragedy* performed at Edinburgh; prologue by
        J. G. Lockhart, epilogue by Scott. Brief commercial venture at
        Greenock. Galt returns to London in service of Union Canal
        Company   39

1819   Miscellaneous writing, including school books. First acceptance
        by *Blackwood's Magazine*   40

1820   (June) *The Ayrshire Legatees* begins in *Blackwood's Magazine*
        (concluded Feb. 1821). (Dec.) *The Earthquake* (3 vols.)   41

1821   (Feb.) *The Steamboat* begins in *Blackwood's Magazine* (con-
        cluded Dec.). (May) *Annals of the Parish* (translated into French
        1824). (June) *The Ayrshire Legatees*   42

1822   (Jan.) *Sir Andrew Wylie* (3 vols.; translated into French 1823).
        (May) *The Provost* (translated into French 1824). (July) *The
        Steamboat*. (Sept.) 'The Gathering of the West' in *Blackwood's
        Magazine*. (Dec.) *The Entail* (3 vols.; title-page dated 1823.
        Translated into French 1824)   43

1823   Galt leaves Blackwood for Oliver and Boyd for novel publishing.
        (May) *Ringan Gilhaize* (3 vols.). (Dec.) *The Spae Wife* (3 vols.).
        Galt moves to Eskgrove, Musselburgh, Scotland; and meets
        D. M. Moir, his first biographer   44

1824   *Rothelan* (3 vols.). Canada Company founded, with Galt as
        secretary. *Annals* and *Provost* published in French as *Les
        Chroniques écossaises*   45

1825   (Jan.) Galt sails for Canada with other commissioners of the
        Company; returns June. Returns to Blackwood as publisher.
        The Omen   46

1826   Mother dies. Galt sails for Canada in October as Superinten-
        dent for the Company. *The Last of the Lairds*   47

1826–33 Contributions to *Blackwood's Magazine*   47–54

1827   Galt founds the town of Guelph, Ontario   48

1829   Recalled to England; imprisoned for debt July–November.
        Returns to writing for a living   50

1830   *Lawrie Todd; or the Settlers in the Wood* (3 vols.); *Southennan*
        (3 vols.); *Life of Lord Byron* (translated into French, 1836)   51

1830–6 Contributions to *Fraser's Magazine*   51–7

1831   *Lives of the Players* (2 vols.); *Bogle Corbet; or the Emigrants*
        (3 vols.)   52

1832   Founder and secretary of the British American Land Company.
        The Member; *The Radical*   53

1833   John and Thomas leave for Canada (followed by Alexander in
        1834). *Eben Erskine* (3 vols.); *Poems*; *Autobiography* (2 vols.)   54

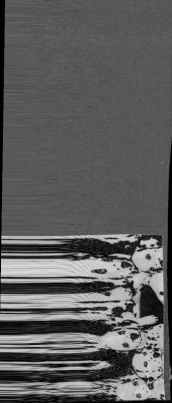

ANNALS OF THE PARISH

INTRODUCTION

IN the same year, and on the same day of the same month, that his Sacred Majesty King George, the third of the name, came to his crown and kingdom, I was placed and settled as the minister of Dalmailing. When about a week thereafter this was known in the parish, it was thought a wonderful thing, and every body spoke of me and the new king as united in our trusts and temporalities, marvelling how the same should come to pass, and thinking the hand of Providence was in it, and that surely we were pre-ordained to fade and flourish in fellowship together; which has really been the case, for in the same season that his Most Excellent Majesty, as he was very properly styled in the proclamations for the general fasts and thanksgivings, was set by[1] as a precious vessel which had received a crack or a flaw, and could only be serviceable in the way of an ornament, I was obliged,[2] by reason of age and the growing infirmities of my recollection, to consent to the earnest entreaties of the Session,[3] and to accept of Mr Amos to be my helper. I was long reluctant to do so, but the great respect that my people had for me, and the love that I bore towards them, over and above the sign that was given to me in the removal of the royal candlestick from its place, worked upon my heart and understanding, and I could not stand out. So, on the last Sabbath of the year 1810, I preached my last sermon, and it was a moving discourse. There were few dry eyes in the kirk that day, for I had been with the aged from the beginning—the young considered me as their natural pastor—and my bidding them all farewell was, as when of

(SAT) 25ᵗʰ OCT 1760

old among the heathen, an idol was taken away by the hands of the enemy.

At the close of the worship, and before the blessing, I addressed them in a fatherly manner, and although the kirk was fuller than ever I saw it before, the fall of a pin might have been heard—at the conclusion there was a sobbing and much sorrow. I said,

'My dear friends, I have now finished my work among you forever. I have often spoken to you from this place the words of truth and holiness, and, had it been in poor frail human nature to practise the advice and counselling that I have given in this pulpit to you, there would not need to be any cause for sorrow on this occasion—the close and latter end of my ministry. But, nevertheless, I have no reason to complain, and it will be my duty to testify, in that place where I hope we are all one day to meet again, that I found you a docile and a tractable flock, far more than at first I could have expected. There are among you still a few, but with grey heads and feeble hands now, that can remember the great opposition that was made to my placing, and the stout part they themselves took in the burly,[1] because I was appointed by the patron; but they have lived to see the error of their way, and to know that preaching is the smallest portion of the duties of a faithful minister. I may not, my dear friends, have applied my talent in the pulpit so effectually as perhaps I might have done, considering the gifts that it pleased God to give me in that way, and the education that I had in the Orthodox University of Glasgow, as it was in the time of my youth, nor can I say that, in the works of peace-making and charity, I have done all that I should have done. But I have done my best, studying no interest but the good that was to rise according to the faith in Christ Jesus.

'To my young friends I would, as a parting word, say, look to the lives and conversation of your parents—they were plain, honest, and devout Christians, fearing God and honouring the King. They believed the Bible was the word of God, and when they practised its precepts, they found, by the good that came from them, that it was truly so. They bore in mind the tribulation and persecution of their forefathers[1] for righteousness-sake, and were thankful for the quiet and protection of the government in their day and generation. Their land was tilled with industry, and they ate the bread of carefulness[2] with a contented spirit, and, verily, they had the reward of well-doing even in this world, for they beheld on all sides the blessing of God upon the nation, and the tree growing, and the plough going, where the banner of the oppressor was planted of old, and the war-horse trampled in the blood of martyrs. Reflect on this, my young friends, and know, that the best part of a Christian's duty in this world of much evil, is to thole[3] and suffer with resignation, as lang as it is possible for human nature to do. I do not counsel passive obedience; that is a doctrine that the Church of Scotland can never abide; but the divine right of resistance,[4] which, in the days of her trouble, she so bravely asserted against popish and prelatic usurpations, was never resorted to till the attempt was made to remove the ark of the tabernacle from her. I therefore counsel you, my young friends, no to lend your ears to those that trumpet forth their hypothetical politics, but to believe that the laws of the land are administered with a good intent, till in your own homes and dwellings ye feel the presence of the oppressor—then, and not till then, are ye free to gird your loins for battle—and woe to him, and woe to the land where that is come to, if the sword be sheathed till the wrong be redressed.

'As for you, my old companions, many changes have we seen in our day, but the change that we ourselves are soon to undergo will be the greatest of all. We have seen our bairns grow to manhood—we have seen the beauty of youth pass away—we have felt our backs become unable for the burthen, and our right hand forget its cunning[5]—Our eyes have become dim, and our heads grey—we are now tottering with short and feckless steps towards the grave; and some, that should have been here this day, are bed-rid, lying, as it were, at the gates of death, like Lazarus[1] at the threshold of the rich man's door, full of ails and sores, and having no enjoyment but in the hope that is in hereafter. What can I say to you but farewell! Our work is done—we are weary and worn out, and in need of rest—may the rest of the blessed be our portion!—and, in the sleep that all must sleep, beneath the cold blanket of the kirk-yard grass, and on that clay pillow where we must shortly lay our heads, may we have pleasant dreams, till we are awakened to partake of the everlasting banquet of the saints in glory.'

When I had finished, there was for some time a great solemnity throughout the kirk, and, before giving the blessing, I sat down to compose myself, for my heart was big, and my spirit oppressed with sadness.

As I left the pulpit, all the elders stood on the steps to hand me down, and the tear was in every eye, and they helped me into the session-house;[2] but I could not speak to them, nor them to me. Then Mr Dalziel, who was always a composed and sedate man, said a few words of prayer, and I was comforted therewith, and rose to go home to the manse; but in the church-yard all the congregation was assembled, young and old, and they made a lane for me to the back-yett[3] that opened into the manse-garden—Some of them put out their hands and touched me as I passed, followed by the elders, and some of them wept. It was as if I was passing away, and to be no more—verily, it was the reward of my ministry—a faithful account of which, year by year, I now sit down, in the evening of my days, to make up, to the end that I may bear witness to the work of a beneficent Providence, even in the narrow sphere of my parish, and the concerns of that flock of which it was His most gracious pleasure to make me the unworthy shepherd.

CHAPTER I · YEAR 1760

*The placing of Mr Balwhidder[1] · The resistance of
the parishioners · Mrs Malcolm, the widow ·
Mr Balwhidder's marriage*

━━━━━━

THE An. Dom. one thousand seven hundred and sixty, was
remarkable for three things in the parish of Dalmailing.—
First and foremost, there was my placing; then the coming
of Mrs Malcolm with her five children to settle among us;
and next, my marriage upon my own cousin, Miss Betty
Lanshaw, by which the account of this year naturally divides
itself into three heads or portions.

First, of the placing.—It was a great affair; for I was put
in by the patron,[2] and the people knew nothing whatsoever of
me, and their hearts were stirred into strife on the occasion,
and they did all that lay within the compass of their power to
keep me out, insomuch, that there was obliged to be a guard of
soldiers to protect the presbytery;[3] and it was a thing that made
my heart grieve when I heard the drum beating and the fife
playing as we were going to the kirk. The people were really
mad and vicious, and flung dirt upon us as we passed, and
reviled us all, and held out the finger of scorn at me; but I endured it with a resigned spirit, compassionating their wilfulness and blindness. Poor old Mr Kilfuddy of the Braehill got
such a clash of glar[4] on the side of his face, that his eye was
almost extinguished.

When we got to the kirk door, it was found to be nailed up,
so as by no possibility to be opened. The serjeant of the
soldiers wanted to break it, but I was afraid that the heritors[5]
would grudge and complain of the expence of a new door, and

I supplicated him to let it be as it was; we were, therefore, obligated to go in by a window, and the crowd followed us, in the most unreverent manner, making the Lord's house like an inn on a fair day, with their grievous yellyhooing.[1] During the time of the psalm and the sermon, they behaved themselves better, but when the induction came on, their clamour was dreadful; and Thomas Thorl the weaver, a pious zealot in that time, he got up and protested, and said, 'Verily, verily, I say unto you, he that entereth not by the door into the sheepfold, but climbeth up some other way, the same is a thief and a robber.'[2] And I thought I would have a hard and sore time of it with such an outstrapolous[3] people. Mr Given, that was then the minister of Lugton, was a jocose man, and would have his joke even at a solemnity. When the laying of the hands[4] upon me was a-doing, he could not get near enough to put on his, but he stretched out his staff and touched my head, and said, to the great diversion of the rest,—'This will do well enough, timber to timber;' but it was an unfriendly saying of Mr Given, considering the time and the place, and the temper of my people.

After the ceremony, we then got out at the window, and it was a heavy day to me, but we went to the manse, and there we had an excellent dinner, which Mrs Watts of the new inns of Irville[5] prepared at my request, and sent her chaise-driver to serve, for he was likewise her waiter, she having then but one chaise, and that no often called for.

But, although my people received me in this unruly manner, I was resolved to cultivate civility among them; and therefore, the very next morning I began a round of visitations; but oh, it was a steep brae[6] that I had to climb, and it needed a stout heart. For I found the doors in some places barred against me; in others, the bairns, when they saw me coming, ran crying to their mothers, 'Here's the feckless Mess-John;'[7] and then when I went in into the houses, their parents would no ask me to sit down, but with a scornful way, said, 'Honest man, what's your pleasure here?' Nevertheless, I walked about from door to door, like a dejected beggar, till I got the almous deed[1] of a civil reception, and who would have thought it, from no less a person than the same Thomas Thorl that was so bitter against me in the kirk on the foregoing day.

Thomas was standing at the door with his green duffle apron, and his red Kilmarnock nightcap—I mind him as well as if it was but yesterday—and he had seen me going from house to house, and in what manner I was rejected, and his bowels were moved, and he said to me in a kind manner, 'Come in, sir, and ease yoursel; this will never do, the clergy are God's gorbies,[2] and for their Master's sake it behoves us to respect them. There was no ane in the whole parish mair against you than mysel, but this early visitation is a symptom of grace that I couldna have expectit from a bird out the nest of patronage.' I thanked Thomas, and went in with him, and we had some solid conversation together, and I told him that it was not so much the pastor's duty to feed the flock, as to herd them well; and that although there might be some abler with the head than me, there was na a he within the bounds of Scotland more willing to watch the fold by night and by day. And Thomas said he had not heard a mair sound observe[3] for some time, and that if I held to that doctrine in the poopit, it would na be lang till I would work a change.—'I was mindit,' quoth he, 'never to set my foot within the kirk door while you were there; but to testify, and no to condemn without a trial, I'll be there next Lord's day, and egg[4] my neighbours to be likewise, so ye'll no have to preach just to the bare walls and the laird's family.'

I have now to speak of the coming of Mrs Malcolm. She was the widow of a Clyde shipmaster, that was lost at sea with his vessel. She was a genty[5] body, calm and methodical. From morning to night she sat at her wheel, spinning the finest lint,[6] which suited well with her pale hands. She never changed her widow's weeds, and she was aye as if she had just been ta'en out of a bandbox. The tear was often in her e'e when the bairns were at the school; but when they came home, her spirit was lighted up with gladness, although, poor woman, she had many a time very little to give them. They were, however, wonderful well-bred things, and took with thankfulness whatever she set before them, for they knew that their father, the breadwinner, was away, and that she had to work sore for their bit and drap.[1] I dare say, the only vexation that ever she had from any of them, on their own account, was when Charlie, the eldest laddie, had won fourpence at pitch and toss at the school, which he brought home with a proud heart to his mother. I happened to be daunrin' bye[2] at the time, and just looked in at the door to say gude night: It was a sad sight. There was she sitting with the silent tear on her cheek, and Charlie greeting[3] as if he had done a great fault, and the other four looking on with sorrowful faces. Never, I am sure, did Charlie Malcolm gamble after that night.

I often wondered what brought Mrs Malcolm to our clachan,[4] instead of going to a populous town, where she might have taken up a huxtry-shop,[5] as she was but of a silly[6] constitution, the which would have been better for her than spinning from morning to far in the night, as if she was in verity drawing the thread of life. But it was, no doubt, from an honest pride to hide her poverty; for when her daughter Effie was ill with the measles—the poor lassie was very ill— nobody thought she could come through, and when she did get the turn,[7] she was for many a day a heavy handful;—our session being rich, and nobody on it but cripple Tammy Daidles, that was in that time known through all the country side for begging on a horse, I thought it my duty to call upon Mrs Malcolm, in a sympathizing way, and offer her some assistance, but she refused it.

'No, sir,' said she, 'I canna take help from the poor's-box, although it's very true that I am in great need; for it might hereafter be cast up[8] to my bairns, whom it may please God to restore to better circumstances when I am no to see't; but I would fain borrow five pounds, and if, sir, you will write to Mr Maitland, that is now the Lord Provost of Glasgow, and tell him that Marion Shaw would be obliged to him for the lend of that soom,[1] I think he will not fail to send it.'

I wrote the letter that night to Provost Maitland, and, by the retour of the post, I got an answer, with twenty pounds for Mrs Malcolm, saying, 'that it was with sorrow he heard so small a trifle could be serviceable.' When I took the letter and the money, which was in a bank-bill, she said, 'this is just like himsel'.' She then told me, that Mr Maitland had been a gentleman's son of the east country, but driven out of his father's house, when a laddie, by his step-mother; and that he had served as a servant lad with her father, who was the Laird of Yillcogie,[2] but ran through his estate, and left her, his only daughter, in little better than beggary with her auntie, the mother of Captain Malcolm, her husband that was. Provost Maitland in his servitude had ta'en a notion of[3] her, and when he recovered his patrimony, and had become a great Glasgow merchant, on hearing how she was left by her father, he offered to marry her, but she had promised herself to her cousin the Captain, whose widow she was. He then married a rich lady, and in time grew, as he was, Lord Provost of the city; but his letter with the twenty pounds to me, shewed that he had not forgotten his first love. It was a short, but a well-written letter, in a fair hand of write, containing much of the true gentleman; and Mrs Malcolm said, 'Who knows but out of the regard he once had for their mother, he may do something for my five helpless orphans.'

Thirdly, upon the subject of taking my cousin, Miss Betty Lanshaw, for my first wife, I have little to say. It was more out of a compassionate habitual affection, than the passion of love. We were brought up by our grandmother in the same house, and it was a thing spoken of from the beginning, that Betty and me were to be married. So when she heard that the Laird of Breadland had given me the presentation of Dalmailing, she began to prepare for the wedding. And as soon as the placing was well over, and the manse in order, I gaed to Ayr, where she was, and we were quietly married, and came home in a chaise, bringing with us her little brother Andrew, that died in the East Indies, and he lived and was brought up by us.

Now, this is all, I think, that happened in that year, worthy of being mentioned, except that at the sacrament, when old Mr Kilfuddie was preaching in the tent,[1] it came on such a thunder-plump, that there was not a single soul stayed in the kirk-yard to hear him; for the which he was greatly mortified, and never after came to our preachings.

CHAPTER II · YEAR 1761[1]

*The great increase of smuggling · Mr Balwhidder
disperses a tea-drinking party of gossips · He records
the virtues of Nanse Banks, the school-mistress ·
The servant of a military man, who had been
prisoner in France, comes into the parish, and
opens a dancing-school*

─────────

IT was in this year that the great smuggling trade corrupted
all the west coast, especially the Laigh Lands about the Troon
and the Loans.[2] The tea was going like the chaff, the brandy
like well-water, and the wastrie[3] of all things was terrible.
There was nothing minded but the riding of cadgers[4] by day,
and excisemen by night—and battles between the smugglers
and the King's men, both by sea and land. There was a continual drunkenness and debauchery; and our Session, that
was but on the lip of this whirlpool of iniquity, had an awful
time o't. I did all that was in the power of nature to keep my
people from the contagion; I preached sixteen times from the
text, Render to Cæsar the things that are Cæsar's. I visited
and I exhorted; I warned and I prophesied; I told them, that,
although the money came in like sclate stones,[5] it would go
like the snow off the dyke. But for all I could do, the evil got
in among us, and we had no less than three contested bastard
bairns upon our hands at one time, which was a thing never
heard of in a parish of the shire of Ayr, since the Reformation.
Two of the bairns, after no small sifting and searching, we
got fathered at last; but the third, that was by Meg Glaiks,
and given to one Rab Rickerton, was utterly refused, though
the fact was not denied; but he was a termagant fellow, and

snappit his fingers at the elders. The next day he listed in the Scotch Greys, who were then quartered at Ayr, and we never heard more of him, but thought he had been slain in battle, till one of the parish, about three years since, went up to London to lift a legacy from a cousin, that died among the Hindoos; when he was walking about, seeing the curiosities, and among others Chelsea Hospital,[1] he happened to speak to some of the invalids, who found out from his tongue that he was a Scotchman; and speaking to the invalids, one of them, a very old man, with a grey head, and a leg of timber, inquired what part of Scotland he was come from; and when he mentioned my parish, the invalid gave a great shout, and said he was from the same place himself; and who should this old man be, but the very identical Rab Rickerton, that was art and part in[2] Meg Glaiks' disowned bairn. Then they had a long converse together, and he had come through many hardships, but had turned out a good soldier; and so, in his old days, was an in-door pensioner, and very comfortable; and he said that he had, to be sure, spent his youth in the devil's service, and his manhood in the king's, but his old age was given to that of his Maker, which I was blithe and thankful to hear; and he inquired about many a one in the parish, the blooming and the green of his time, but they were all dead and buried; and he had a contrite and penitent spirit, and read his Bible every day, delighting most in the Book of Joshua, the Chronicles, and the Kings.

Before this year, the drinking of tea[3] was little known in the parish, saving among a few of the heritors'[4] houses on a Sabbath evening, but now it became very rife, yet the commoner sort did not like to let it be known that they were taking to the new luxury, especially the elderly women, who, for that reason, had their ploys[5] in out-houses and bye-places,[6] just as the witches lang syne[7] had their sinful possets[8] and galravitchings;[9] and they made their tea for common in the pint-stoup,[10] and drank it out of caps and luggies,[11] for there were but few among them that had cups and saucers. Well do I remember one night in harvest, in this very year, as I was taking my twilight dawner[1] aneath the hedge along the back side of Thomas Thorl's yard, meditating on the goodness of Providence, and looking at the sheafs of victual on the field, that I heard his wife, and two three other carlins,[2] with their bohea[3] in the inside of the hedge, and no doubt but it had a lacing of the conek,*[4] for they were all cracking like pen-guns.[5] But I gave them a sign by a loud host,[6] that Providence sees all, and it skailed the bike;[7] for I heard them, like guilty creatures, whispering and gathering up their truck-pots[8] and trenchers, and cowering away home.

It was in this year that Patrick Dilworth, (he had been schoolmaster of the parish from the time, as his wife said, of Anna Regina, and before the Rexes came to the crown,) was disabled by a paralytic, and the heritors, grudging the cost of another schoolmaster as long as he lived, would not allow the Session to get his place supplied, which was a wrong thing, I must say of them; for the children of the parishioners were obliged, therefore, to go to the neighbouring towns for their schooling, and the custom was to take a piece of bread and cheese in their pockets for dinner, and to return in the evening always voracious for more, the long walk helping the natural crave of their young appetites. In this way Mrs Malcolm's two eldest laddies, Charlie and Robert, were wont to go to Irville, and it was soon seen that they kept themselves aloof from the other callans[9] in the clachan,[10] and had a genteeler turn than the grulshy[11] bairns of the cotters.[12] Her bit lassies, Kate and Effie, were better off; for, some years before, Nanse Banks had taken up a teaching in a garret-room of a house, at the corner where John Bayne has biggit[13] the sclate-house[14] for his grocery-shop. Nanse learnt them reading and working stockings, and how to sew the semplar, for twal-pennies

* Cogniac.

a-week. She was a patient creature, well cut out for her calling, with bleer eyn,[1] a pale face, and a long neck, but meek and contented withall, tholing the dule[2] of this world with a Christian submission of the spirit; and her garret-room was a cordial of cleanliness, for she made the scholars set the house in order, time and time about, every morning; and it was a common remark for many a day, that the lassies, who had been at Nanse Banks's school, were always well spoken of, both for their civility, and the trigness[3] of their houses, when they were afterwards married. In short, I do not know, that in all the long epoch of my ministry, any individual body did more to improve the ways of the parishioners, in their domestic concerns, than did that worthy and innocent creature, Nanse Banks, the schoolmistress; and she was a great loss when she was removed, as it is to be hoped, to a better world; but anent[4] this I shall have to speak more at large hereafter.

It was in this year that my patron, the Laird of Breadland, departed this life, and I preached his funeral-sermon; but he was none beloved in the parish, for my people never forgave him for putting me upon them, although they began to be more on a familiar footing with myself. This was partly owing to my first wife, Betty Lanshaw, who was an active through-going woman, and wonderfu' useful to many of the cotters' wives at their lying-in; and when a death happened among them, her helping hand, and any thing we had at the Manse, was never wanting; and I went about myself to the bed-sides of the frail, leaving no stone unturned to win the affections of my people, which, by the blessing of the Lord, in process of time, was brought to a bearing.[5]

But a thing happened in this year, which deserves to be recorded, as manifesting what effect the smuggling was beginning to take in the morals of the country side. One Mr Macskipnish, of Highland parentage, who had been a valet-de-chambre with a Major in the campaigns, and taken a prisoner with him by the French, he having come home in a cartel,[1] took up a dancing-school at Irville,[2] the which art he had learnt in the genteelest fashion, in the mode of Paris, at the French court. Such a thing as a dancing-school had never, in the memory of man, been known in our country side; and there was such a sound about the steps and cottillions of Mr Macskipnish, that every lad and lass, that could spare time and siller,[3] went to him, to the great neglect of their work. The very bairns on the loan,[4] instead of their wonted play, gaed linking and louping[5] in the steps of Mr Macskipnish, who was, to be sure, a great curiosity, with long spindle legs, his breast shot out like a duck's, and his head powdered and frizzled up like a tappit-hen.[6] He was, indeed, the proudest peacock that could be seen, and he had a ring on his finger, and when he came to drink his tea at the Breadland, he brought no hat on his head, but a droll cockit thing[7] under his arm, which, he said, was after the manner of the courtiers at the petty suppers[8] of one Madam Pompadour,[9] who was, at that time, the concubine of the French king.

I do not recollect any other remarkable thing that happened in this year. The harvest was very abundant, and the meal so cheap, that it caused a great defect in my stipend, so that I was obligated to postpone the purchase of a mahogany scrutoire[10] for my study, as I had intended. But I had not the heart to complain of this; on the contrary, I rejoiced thereat, for what made me want my scrutoire till another year, had carried blitheness into the hearth of the cotter, and made the widow's heart sing with joy; and I would have been an unnatural creature, had I not joined in the universal gladness, because plenty did abound.

CHAPTER III · YEAR 1762

*Havoc produced by the small-pox · Charles Malcolm
is sent off a cabin-boy, on a voyage to Virginia ·
Mizy Spaewell dies on Halloween · Tea begins to be
admitted at the Manse, but the Minister continues to
exert his authority against smuggling*

─────────

THE third year of my ministry was long held in remembrance
for several very memorable things. William Byres of the
Loanhead had a cow that calved two calves at one calving;
Mrs Byres, the same year, had twins, male and female; and
there was such a crop on his fields, testifying that the Lord
never sends a mouth into the world without providing meat
for it. But what was thought a very daunting sign of something,
happened on the Sacrament Sabbath at the conclusion of the
action sermon,[1] when I had made a very suitable discourse.
The day was tempestuous, and the wind blew with such a pith
and birr,[2] that I thought it would have twirled the trees in the
kirk-yard out by the roots, and, blowing in this manner, it
tirled the thack from the rigging[3] of the Manse stable; and
the same blast that did that, took down the lead that was on the
kirk-roof, which hurled off, as I was saying, at the conclusion
of the action sermon, with such a dreadful sound, as the like
was never heard, and all the congregation thought that it
betokened a mutation to me. However, nothing particular
happened to me; but the small-pox came in among the weans
of the parish, and the smashing[4] that it made of the poor bits
o' bairns was indeed woeful.

One Sabbath, when the pestilence was raging, I preached
a sermon about Rachel weeping for her children, which

Thomas Thorl, who was surely a great judge of good preaching, said 'was a monument of divinity whilk searched the heart of many a parent that day;' a thing I was well pleased to hear, for Thomas, as I have related at length, was the most zealous champion against my getting the parish; but, from this time, I set him down in my mind for the next vacancy among the elders. Worthy man! it was not permitted him to arrive at that honour. In the fall of that year he took an income[1] in his legs, and could no go about, and was laid up for the remainder of his days, a perfect Lazarus, by the fireside. But he was well supported in his affliction. In due season, when it pleased HIM that alone can give and take, to pluck him from this life, as the fruit ripened and ready for the gathering, his death, to all that knew him, was a gentle dispensation, for truly he had been in sore trouble.

It was in this year that Charlie Malcolm, Mrs Malcolm's eldest son, was sent to be a cabin-boy in the Tobacco trader,[2] a three masted ship, that sailed between Port-Glasgow and Virginia in America. She was commanded by Captain Dickie, an Irville man; for at that time the Clyde was supplied with the best sailors from our coast, the coal-trade with Ireland[3] being a better trade for bringing up good mariners than the long voyages in the open sea; which was the reason, as I often heard said, why the Clyde shipping got so many of their men from our country-side. The going to sea of Charlie Malcolm was, on divers accounts, a very remarkable thing to us all, for he was the first that ever went from our parish, in the memory of man, to be a sailor, and every body was concerned at it, and some thought it was a great venture of his mother to let him, his father having been lost at sea. But what could the forlorn widow do? She had five weans[4] and little to give them; and, as she herself said, he was aye in the hand of his Maker, go where he might, and the will of God would be done in spite of all earthly wiles and devices to the contrary.

On the Monday morning, when Charlie was to go away to

meet the Irville carrier on the road, we were all up, and I
walked by myself from the Manse into the clachan to bid him
farewell, and I met him just coming from his mother's door,
as blithe as a bee, in his sailor's dress, with a stick, and a bundle
tied in a Barcelona silk handkerchief hanging o'er his shoulder,
and his two little brothers were with him, and his sisters, Kate
and Effie, looking out from the door all begreeten;[1] but his
mother was in the house, praying to the Lord to protect her
orphan, as she afterwards told me. All the weans of the
clachan were gathered at the kirk-yard yett[2] to see him pass,
and they gave him three great shouts as he was going bye;
and every body was at their doors, and said something en-
couraging to him; but there was a great laugh when auld Mizy
Spaewell came hirpling[3] with her bachle[4] in her hand, and
flung it after him for gude luck. Mizy had a wonderful faith
in freats,[5] and was just an oracle of sagacity at expounding
dreams, and bodes of every sort and description—besides,
she was reckoned one of the best howdies[6] in her day; but by
this time she was grown frail and feckless, and she died the
same year on Hallowe'en, which made every body wonder,
that it should have so fallen out for her to die on Hallowe'en.

Shortly after the departure of Charlie Malcolm, the Lady of
Breadland, with her three daughters, removed to Edinburgh,
where the young laird, that had been my pupil, was learning
to be an advocate, and the Breadland house was set[7] to Major
Gilchrist, a nabob[8] from India; but he was a narrow[9] ailing
man, and his maiden-sister, Miss Girzie, was the scrimpetest[10]
creature that could be; so that, in their hands, all the pretty
policy[11] of the Breadlands, that had cost a power of money
to the old laird, that was my patron, fell into decay and disorder; and the bonny yew trees, that were cut into the shape
of peacocks, soon grew out of all shape, and are now doleful
monuments of the Major's tack,[12] and that of Lady Skim-milk,
as Miss Girzie Gilchrist, his sister, was nicknamed by every
ane that kent[13] her.

But it was not so much on account of the neglect of the Breadland, that the incoming of Major Gilchrist was to be deplored. The old men, that had a light labour in keeping the policy in order, were thrown out of bread, and could do little; and the poor women, that whiles got a bit and a drap[1] from the kitchen of the family, soon felt the change, so that, by little and little, we were obligated to give help from the Session; insomuch, that before the end of the year, I was necessitated to preach a discourse on almsgiving, specially for the benefit of our own poor, a thing never before known in the parish.

But one good thing came from the Gilchrists to Mrs Malcolm. Miss Girzie, whom they called Lady Skim-milk, had been in a very penurious way as a seamstress, in the Gorbals of Glasgow, while her brother was making the fortune in India, and she was a clever needle-woman—none better, as it was said; and she having some things to make, took Kate Malcolm to help her in the coarse work; and Kate, being a nimble and birky[2] thing, was so useful to the lady, and the complaining man the Major, that they invited her to stay with them at the Breadland for the winter, where, although she was holden to her seam from morning to night, her food lightened the hand of her mother, who, for the first time since her coming into the parish, found the penny for the day's dark[3] more than was needed for the meal-basin; and the tea-drinking was beginning to spread more openly, insomuch, that by the advice of the first Mrs Balwhidder, Mrs Malcolm took in tea to sell, and in this way was enabled to eke something to the small profits of her wheel. Thus the tide, that had been so long ebbing to her, began to turn; and here I am bound in truth to say, that although I never could abide the smuggling, both on its own account, and the evils that grew therefrom to the country-side, I lost some of my dislike to the tea, after Mrs Malcolm began to traffic in it, and we then had it for our breakfast in the morning at the Manse, as well as in the afternoon. But what I thought most of it for, was, that it did no harm to the head of the drinkers, which was not always the case with the possets[1] that were in fashion before. There is no meeting now in the summer evenings, as I remember often happened in my younger days, with decent ladies coming home with red faces, tozy and cosh[2] from a posset masking;[3] so, both for its temperance, and on account of Mrs Malcolm's sale, I refrained from the November in this year to preach against tea; but I never lifted the weight of my displeasure from off the smuggling trade, until it was utterly put down by the strong hand of government.

There was no other thing of note in this year, saving only that I planted in the garden the big pear-tree, which had the two great branches that we call the Adam and Eve. I got the plant, then a sapling, from Mr Graft, that was Lord Eglesham's head-gardener; and he said it was, as indeed all the parish now knows well, a most juicy sweet pear, such as was not known in Scotland till my lord brought down the father plant from the King's garden in London, in the forty-five, when he went up to testify his loyalty to the House of Hanover.

CHAPTER IV · YEAR 1763

*Charles Malcolm's return from sea · Kate Malcolm
is taken to live with Lady Macadam · Death of the
first Mrs Balwhidder*

———

THE An. Dom. 1763, was, in many a respect, a memorable
year, both in public and in private. The King granted peace
to the French, and Charlie Malcolm, that went to sea in the
Tobacco trader, came home to see his mother. The ship, after
being at America, had gone down to Jamaica, an island in the
West Indies, with a cargo of live lumber, as Charlie told me
himself, and had come home with more than a hundred and
fifty hoggits[1] of sugar, and sixty-three puncheons[2] full of rum;
for she was, by all accounts, a stately galley, and almost two
hundred tons in the burden, being the largest vessel then
sailing from the creditable[3] town of Port-Glasgow. Charlie
was not expected; and his coming was a great thing to us all,
so I will mention the whole particulars.

One evening, towards the gloaming, as I was taking my walk
of meditation, I saw a brisk sailor laddie coming towards me.
He had a pretty green parrot, sitting on a bundle, tied in
a Barcelona silk handkerchief, which he carried with a stick
over his shoulder, and in this bundle was a wonderful big nut,
such as no one in our parish had ever seen. It was called
a cocker-nut.[4] This blithe callant[5] was Charlie Malcolm, who
had come all the way that day his leaful lane,[6] on his own legs
from Greenock, where the Tobacco trader was then 'livering
her cargo. I told him how his mother, and his brothers, and his
sisters were all in good health, and went to convoy him home;
and as we were going along he told me many curious things,

and he gave me six beautiful yellow limes, that he had brought in his pouch all the way across the seas, for me to make a bowl of punch with, and I thought more of them than if they had been golden guineas, it was so mindful of the laddie.[1]

When we got to the door of his mother's house, she was sitting at the fire-side, with her three other bairns at their bread and milk, Kate being then with Lady Skim-milk at the Breadland sewing. It was between the day and dark, when the shuttle stands still till the lamp is lighted. But such a shout of joy and thankfulness as rose from that hearth, when Charlie went in! The very parrot, ye would have thought, was a participator, for the beast gied a skraik[2] that made my whole head dirl;[3] and the neighbours came flying and flocking to see what was the matter, for it was the first parrot ever seen within the bounds of the parish, and some thought it was but a foreign hawk, with a yellow head and green feathers.

In the midst of all this, Effie Malcolm had run off to the Breadland for her sister Kate, and the two lassies came flying breathless, with Miss Girzie Gilchrist, the Lady Skim-milk, pursuing them like desperation, or a griffon, down the avenue; for Kate, in her hurry, had flung down her seam, a new printed gown, that she was helping to make, and it had fallen into a boyne[4] of milk that was ready for the creaming, by which ensued a double misfortune to Miss Girzie, the gown being not only ruined, but licking up the cream. For this, poor Kate was not allowed ever to set her face in the Breadland again.

When Charlie Malcolm had staid about a week with his mother, he returned to his birth[5] in the Tobacco trader, and shortly after his brother Robert was likewise sent to serve his time to the sea, with an owner that was master of his own bark, in the coal trade at Irville. Kate, who was really a surprising lassie for her years, was taken off her mother's hands by the old Lady Macadam, that lived in her jointure house,[6] which is now the Cross Keys Inns.[7] Her ladyship was a woman of high-breeding, her husband having been a great general, and knighted by the King for his exploits; but she was lame, and could not move about in her dining-room without help, so hearing from the first Mrs Balwhidder how Kate had done such an unatonable deed to Miss Girzie Gilchrist, she sent for Kate, and finding her sharp and apt, she took her to live with her as a companion. This was a vast advantage, for the lady was versed in all manner of accomplishments, and could read and speak French with more ease than any professor at that time in the College of Glasgow; and she had learnt to sew flowers on satin, either in a nunnery abroad, or in a boarding-school in England, and took pleasure in teaching Kate all she knew, and how to behave herself like a lady.

In the summer of this year, old Mr Patrick Dilworth, that had so long been doited[1] with the paralytics, died, and it was a great relief to my people, for the heritors could no longer refuse to get a proper schoolmaster; so we took on trial Mr Loremore, who has ever since the year after, with so much credit to himself, and usefulness to the parish, been school-master, session-clerk, and precentor[2]—a man of great mildness, and extraordinary particularity. He was then a very young man, and some objection was made on account of his youth, to his being session-clerk, especially as the smuggling immorality still gave us much trouble in the making up of irregular marriages; but his discretion was greater than could have been hoped for from his years; and after a twelvemonth's probation in the capacity of schoolmaster, he was installed in all the offices that had belonged to his predecessor, old Mr Patrick Dilworth that was.

But the most memorable thing that befell among my people this year, was the burning of the lint-mill[3] on the Lugton Water, which happened, of all the days of the year, on the very self-same day that Miss Girzie Gilchrist, better known as Lady Skim-milk, hired the chaise from Mrs Watts of the New Inns of Irville, to go with her brother the Major, to consult the faculty in Edinburgh, concerning his complaints. For, as the chaise was coming by the mill, William Huckle, the miller that was, came flying out of the mill like a demented man, crying fire!—and it was the driver that brought the melancholy tidings to the clachan—and melancholy they were; for the mill was utterly destroyed, and in it not a little of all that year's crop of lint in our parish. The first Mrs Balwhidder lost upwards of twelve stone, which we had raised on the glebe with no small pains, watering it in the drouth, as it was intended for sarking[1] to ourselves, and sheets and napery. A great loss indeed it was, and the vexation thereof had a visible effect on Mrs Balwhidder's health, which from the spring had been in a dwining[2] way. But for it, I think she might have wrestled through the winter; however, it was ordered otherwise, and she was removed from mine to Abraham's bosom on Christmas day, and buried on Hogmanae,[3] for it was thought uncanny[4] to have a dead corpse in the house on the new-year's day. She was a worthy woman, studying with all her capacity to win the hearts of my people towards me—in the which good work she prospered greatly; so that when she died, there was not a single soul in the parish that was not contented with both my walk and conversation. Nothing could be more peaceable than the way we lived together. Her brother Andrew, a fine lad, I had sent to the College at Glasgow, at my own cost, and when he came out to the burial, he staid with me a month, for the Manse after her decease was very dull, and it was during this visit that he gave me an inkling of his wish to go out to India as a cadet, but the transactions anent[5] that fall within the scope of another year—as well as what relates to her headstone, and the epitaph in metre, which I indicted myself thereon; John Truel the mason carving the same, as may be seen in the kirk-yard, where it wants a little reparation and setting upright, having settled the wrong way when the second Mrs Balwhidder was laid by her side.—But I must not here enter upon an anticipation.

CHAPTER V · YEAR 1764

He gets a marble headstone for Mrs Balwhidder,
and writes an Epitaph for it · He is afflicted with
melancholy, and thinks of writing a book · Nichol
Snipe the gamekeeper's device when reproved in
church

THIS year well deserved the name of the monumental year
in our parish; for the young Laird of the Breadland, that had
been my pupil, being learning to be an advocate among the
faculty in Edinburgh, with his lady mother, who had removed
thither with the young ladies her daughters, for the benefit of
education, sent out to be put up in the kirk, under the loft
over the family vault, an elegant marble headstone, with an
epitaph engraven thereon, in fair Latin, setting forth many
excellent qualities which the old laird, my patron that was,
the inditer thereof, said he possessed. I say the inditer, because
it could no have been the young laird himself, although he
got the credit o't on the stone, for he was nae daub in my
aught[1] at the Latin or any other language. However, he
might improve himself at Edinburgh, where a' manner of
genteel things were then to be got at an easy rate, and doubtless, the young laird got a probationer at the College to write
the epitaph; but I have often wondered sin' syne,[2] how he
came to make it in Latin, for assuredly his dead parent, if he
could have seen it, could not have read a single word o't,
notwithstanding it was so vaunty[3] about his virtues, and other
civil and hospitable qualifications.

The coming of the laird's monumental stone had a great
effect on me, then in a state of deep despondency, for the loss of

the first Mrs Balwhidder; and I thought I could not do a better thing, just by way of diversion in my heavy sorrow, than to get a well-shapen headstone made for her—which, as I have hinted at in the record of the last year, was done and set up. But a headstone without an epitaph, is no better than a body without the breath of life in't; and so it behoved me to make a posey[1] for the monument, the which I conned and pondered upon for many days. I thought as Mrs Balwhidder, worthy woman as she was, did not understand the Latin tongue, it would not do to put on what I had to say, in that language, as the laird had doné—nor indeed would it have been easy, as I found upon the experimenting, to tell what I had to tell in Latin, which is naturally a crabbed language, and very difficult to write properly. I therefore, after mentioning her age and the dates of her birth and departure, composed in sedate poetry, the following epitaph, which may yet be seen on the tomb-stone.

EPITAPH[2]

A lovely Christian, spouse, and friend,
Pleasant in life, and at her end.—
A pale consumption dealt the blow
That laid her here, with dust below.
Sore was the cough that shook her frame;
That cough her patience did proclaim—
And as she drew her latest breath,
She said, 'The Lord is sweet in death.'
O pious reader, standing by,
Learn like this gentle one to die.
The grass doth grow and fade away,
And time runs out by night and day;
The King of Terrors has command
To strike us with his dart in hand.
Go where we will by flood or field,
He will pursue and make us yield.
But though to him we must resign
The vesture of our part divine,

There is a jewel in our trust,
That will not perish in the dust,
A pearl of price, a precious gem,
Ordain'd for Jesus' diadem;
Therefore, be holy while you can,
And think upon the doom of man.
Repent in time and sin no more,
That when the strife of life is o'er,
On wings of love your soul may rise,
To dwell with angels in the skies,
Where psalms are sung eternally,
And martyrs ne'er again shall die;
But with the saints still bask in bliss,
And drink the cup of blessedness.

This was greatly thought of at the time, and Mr Loremore, who had a nerve[1] for poesy himself in his younger years, was of opinion, that it was so much to the purpose and suitable withal, that he made his scholars write it out for their examination copies, at the reading whereof before the heritors, when the examination of the school came round, the tear came into my eye, and every one present sympathised with me in my great affliction for the loss of the first Mrs Balwhidder.

Andrew Lanshaw, as I have recorded, having come from the Glasgow College to the burial of his sister, my wife that was, staid with me a month to keep me company; and staying with me, he was a great cordial, for the weather was wet and sleety, and the nights were stormy, so that I could go little out, and few of the elders came in, they being at that time old men in a feckless condition, not at all qualified to warsle[2] with the blasts of winter. But when Andrew left me to go back to his classes, I was eirie[3] and lonesome, and but for the getting of the monument ready, which was a blessed entertainment to me in these dreary nights, with consulting anent the shape of it with John Truel, and meditating on the verse for the epitaph, I might have gone altogether demented. However, it pleased HIM, who is the surety of the sinner, to help me through the Slough of Despond,[1] and to get my feet on a fair land, establishing my way thereon.

But the work of the monument, and the epitaph, could not endure for a constancy,[2] and after it was done, I was again in great danger of sinking into the hypochonderies[3] a second time. However, I was enabled to fight with my affliction, and by and by, as the spring began to open her green lattice, and to set out her flower-pots to the sunshine, and the time of the singing of birds was come, I became more composed, and like myself, so I often walked in the fields, and held communion with nature, and wondered at the mysteries thereof.

On one of these occasions, as I was sauntering along the edge of Eglesham-wood, looking at the industrious bee going from flower to flower, and the idle butterfly, that layeth up no store,[4] but perisheth ere it is winter, I felt as it were a spirit from on high descending upon me, a throb at my heart, and a thrill in my brain, and I was transported out of myself, and seized with the notion of writing a book—but what it should be about, I could not settle to my satisfaction: Sometimes I thought of an orthodox poem, like Paradise Lost, by John Milton, wherein I proposed to treat more at large of Original Sin, and the great mystery of Redemption; at others, I fancied that a connect[5] treatise on the efficacy of Free Grace, would be more taking; but although I made divers beginnings in both subjects, some new thought ever came into my head, and the whole summer passed away, and nothing was done. I therefore postponed my design of writing a book till the winter, when I would have the benefit of the long nights. Before that, however, I had other things of more importance to think about: My servant lasses, having no eye of a mistress over them, wastered[6] every thing at such a rate, and made such a galravitching[7] in the house, that, long before the end of the year, the year's stipend was all spent, and I did not know what to do. At lang and length I mustered courage to send for Mr Auld, who was then living, and an elder. He was a douce[1] and discreet man, fair and well-doing in the world, and had a better handful of strong common sense than many even of the heritors. So I told him how I was situate, and conferred with him, and he advised me, for my own sake, to look out for another wife, as soon as decency would allow, which, he thought, might very properly be after the turn of the year, by which time the first Mrs Balwhidder would be dead more than twelve months; and when I mentioned my design to write a book, he said, (and he was a man of good discretion,) that the doing of the book was a thing that would keep, but wasterful servants were a growing evil; so, upon his counselling, I resolved not to meddle with the book till I was married again, but employ the interim, between then and the turn of the year, in looking out for a prudent woman to be my second wife, strictly intending, as I did perform, not to mint[2] a word about my choice, if I made one, till the whole twelve months and a day, from the date of the first Mrs Balwhidder's interment, had run out.

In this the hand of Providence was very visible, and lucky for me it was that I had sent for Mr Auld when I did send, as the very week following, a sound began to spread in the parish, that one of my lassies had got herself with bairn, which was an awful thing to think had happened in the house of her master, and that master a minister of the Gospel. Some there were, for backbiting appertaineth to all conditions, that jealoused[3] and wondered if I had not a finger in the pye; which, when Mr Auld heard, he bestirred himself in such a manful and godly way in my defence, as silenced the clash,[4] telling that I was utterly incapable of any such thing, being a man of a guileless heart, and a spiritual simplicity, that would be ornamental in a child. We then had the latheron[5] summoned before the Session, and was not long of making her confess, that the father was Nichol Snipe, Lord Glencairn's game-keeper; and both her and Nichol were obligated to stand in the kirk,[6] but Nichol was a graceless reprobate, for he came with two coats, one buttoned behind him, and another buttoned before him, and two wigs of my lord's, lent him by the valet-de-chamer; the one over his face, and the other in the right way; and he stood with his face to the church-wall. When I saw him from the pu'-pit, I said to him—'Nichol, you must turn your face towards me!' At the which, he turned round to be sure, but there he presented the same show as his back. I was confounded, and did not know what to say, but cried out, with a voice of anger—'Nichol, Nichol! if ye had been a' back, ye would nae hae been there this day;' which had such an effect on the whole congregation, that the poor fellow suffered afterwards more derision, than if I had rebuked him in the manner prescribed by the Session.

This affair, with the previous advice of Mr Auld, was, however, a warning to me, that no pastor of his parish should be long without a helpmate. Accordingly, as soon as the year was out, I set myself earnestly about the search for one, but as the particulars fall properly within the scope and chronicle of the next year, I must reserve them for it; and I do not recollect that any thing more particular befell in this, excepting that William Mutchkins, the father of Mr Mutchkins, the great spirit-dealer in Glasgow, set up a change-house[1] in the clachan, which was the first in the parish, and which, if I could have helped it, would have been the last; for it was opening a howf[2] to all manner of wickedness, and was an immediate get and offspring of the smuggling trade, against which I had so set my countenance. But William Mutchkins himself was a respectable man, and no house could be better ordered than his change. At a stated hour he made family worship, for he brought up his children in the fear of God and the Christian religion; and although the house was full, he would go into the customers, and ask them if they would want any thing for half an hour, for that he was going to make exercise with his family; and many a wayfaring traveller has joined in the prayer. There is no such thing, I fear, now-a-days, of publicans entertaining travellers in this manner.

CHAPTER VI · YEAR 1765

Establishment of a whisky distillery · He is again
married to Miss Lizy Kibbock · Her industry in the
dairy · Her example diffuses a spirit of industry
through the parish

———

As there was little in the last year that concerned the parish, but only myself, so in this the like fortune continued; and saving a rise in the price of barley, occasioned, as was thought, by the establishment of a house for brewing whisky in a neighbouring parish, it could not be said that my people were exposed to the mutations and influences of the stars, which ruled in the seasons of Ann. Dom. 1765. In the winter there was a dearth of fuel, such as has not been since; for when the spring loosened the bonds of the ice, three new coal-heughs were shanked[1] in the Douray moor, and ever since there has been a great plenty of that necessary article. Truly, it is very wonderful to see how things come round; when the talk was about the shanking of thir[2] heughs, and a paper to get folk to take shares in them, was carried through the circumjacent parishes, it was thought a gowk's[3] errand; but no sooner were the coal reached, but up sprung such a traffic, that it was a Godsend to the parish, and the opening of a trade and commerce, that has, to use an old bye-word, brought gold in gowpins[4] amang us. From that time my stipend has been on the regular increase, and therefore I think that the incoming[5] of the heritors must have been in like manner augmented.

Soon after this, the time was drawing near for my second marriage. I had placed my affections, with due consideration, on Miss Lizy Kibbock,[6] the well-brought up daughter of

Mr Joseph Kibbock, of the Gorbyholm, who was the first that made a speculation in the farming way in Ayrshire, and whose cheese were of such an excellent quality, that they have, under the name of Delap-cheese, spread far and wide over the civilized world. Miss Lizy and me, we were married on the 29th day of April, with some inconvenience to both sides, on account of the dread that we had of being married in May, for it is said,

> 'Of the marriages in May,
> The bairns die of a decay.'

However, married we were, and we hired the Irville stage, and with Miss Jenny her sister, and Becky Cairns her niece, who sat on a portmanty at our feet, we went on a pleasure jaunt to Glasgow, where we bought a miracle of useful things for the Manse, that neither the first Mrs Balwhidder nor me ever thought of; but the second Mrs Balwhidder that was, had a geni[1] for management, and it was extraordinary what she could go through. Well may I speak of her with commendations, for she was the bee that made my honey, although at first things did not go so clear with us. For she found the Manse rookit and herrit,[2] and there was such a supply of plenishing of all sort wanted, that I thought myself ruined and undone by her care and industry. There was such a buying of wool to make blankets, with a booming of the meikle wheel[3] to spin the same, and such birring[4] of the little wheel for sheets and napery, that the Manse was for many a day like an organ kist.[5] Then we had milk cows, and the calves to bring up, and a kirning[6] of butter, and a making of cheese; in short, I was almost by myself with the jangle and din, which prevented me from writing a book as I had proposed, and I for a time thought of the peaceful and kindly nature of the first Mrs Balwhidder with a sigh; but the out-coming was soon manifest. The second Mrs Balwhidder sent her butter on the market-days to Irville, and her cheese from time to time to Glasgow, to

Mrs Firlot, that kept the huxtry[1] in the Saltmarket, and they were both so well made, that our dairy was just a coining of money, insomuch, that after the first year, we had the whole tot[2] of my stipend to put untouched into the bank.

But I must say, that although we were thus making siller like sclate stones,[3] I was not satisfied in my own mind, that I had got the Manse merely to be a factory of butter and cheese, and to breed up veal calves for the slaughter; so I spoke to the second Mrs Balwhidder, and pointed out to her what I thought the error of our way; but she had been so ingrained with the profitable management of cows and grumphies[4] in her father's house, that she could not desist, at the which I was greatly grieved. By and by, however, I began to discern that there was something as good in her example, as the giving of alms to the poor folk. For all the wives of the parish were stirred up by it into a wonderful thrift, and nothing was heard of in every house, but of quiltings and wabs[5] to weave; insomuch, that before many years came round, there was not a better stocked parish, with blankets and napery, than mine was, within the bounds of Scotland.

It was about the Michaelmas of this year that Mrs Malcolm opened her shop, which she did chiefly on the advice of Mrs Balwhidder, who said it was far better to allow a little profit on the different haberdasheries that might be wanted, than to send to the neighbouring towns an end's errand[6] on purpose for them, none of the lasses that were so sent ever thinking of making less than a day's play on every such occasion. In a word, it is not to be told how the second Mrs Balwhidder, my wife, shewed the value of flying time, even to the concerns of this world, and was the mean of giving a life and energy to the housewifery of the parish, that has made many a one beak[7] his shins in comfort, that would otherwise have had but a cold coal to blow at. Indeed, Mr Kibbock, her father, was a man beyond the common, and had an insight of things, by which he was enabled to draw profit and advantage, where others could only see risk and detriment. He planted mounts of fir-trees on the bleak and barren tops of the hills of his farm, the which every body, and I among the rest, considered as a thrashing of the water, and raising of bells.[1] But as his tack ran[2] his trees grew, and the plantations supplied him with stabs[3] to make *stake and rice*[4] between his fields, which soon gave them a trig[5] and orderly appearance, such as had never before been seen in the west country; and his example has, in this matter, been so followed, that I have heard travellers say, who have been in foreign countries, that the shire of Ayr, for its bonny round green plantings on the tops of the hills, is above comparison either with Italy or Switzerland, where the hills are, as it were, in a state of nature.

Upon the whole, this was a busy year in the parish, and the seeds of many great improvements were laid. The king's road, which then ran through the Vennel,[6] was mended; but it was not till some years after, as I shall record by and by, that the trust-road, as it was called, was made, the which had the effect of turning the town inside out.

Before I conclude, it is proper to mention, that the kirk-bell, which had to this time, from time immemorial, hung on an ash-tree, was one stormy night cast down by the breaking of the branch, which was the cause of the heritors agreeing to build the steeple. The clock was a mortification[7] to the parish from the Lady Breadland, when she died some years after.

CHAPTER VII · YEAR 1766

*The burning of the Breadland · a new bell, and also
a steeple · Nanse Birrel found drowned in a well ·
The parish troubled with wild Irishmen*

IT was in this An. Dom. that the great calamity happened,
the which took place on a Sabbath evening in the month of
February. Mrs Balwhidder had just infused or masket[1] the
tea, and we were set round the fire-side, to spend the night in
an orderly and religious manner, along with Mr and Mrs
Petticrew, who were on a friendly visitation to the Manse, the
mistress being full cousin to Mrs Balwhidder—Sitting, as
I was saying at our tea, one of the servant lasses came into the
room with a sort of a panic laugh, and said, 'What are ye all
doing there when the Breadland's in a low?'[2] 'The Breadland
in a low!' cried I.—'O, aye,' cried she; 'bleezing at the
windows and the rigging,[3] and out at the lum,[4] like a killogie.'[5]
Upon the which we all went to the door, and there, to be sure,
we did see that the Breadland was burning, the flames crackling high out o'er the trees, and the sparks flying like a comet's
tail in the firmament.

Seeing this sight, I said to Mr Petticrew that, in the strength
of the Lord, I would go and see what could be done, for it was
as plain as the sun in the heavens, that the ancient place of the
Breadlands would be destroyed; whereupon he accorded to
go with me, and we walked at a lively course[6] to the spot, and
the people from all quarters were pouring in, and it was an
awsome scene. But the burning of the house, and the droves
of the multitude, were nothing to what we saw when we got
forenent[7] the place. There was the rafters crackling, the flames

raging, the servants running, some with bedding, some with looking-glasses, and others with chamber utensils, as little likely to be fuel to the fire, but all testifications to the confusion and alarm. Then there was a shout, 'Whar's Miss Girzie? whar's the Major?' The Major, poor man, soon cast up,[1] lying upon a feather-bed, ill with his complaints, in the garden; but Lady Skim-milk was nowhere to be found. At last, a figure was seen in the upper-flat, pursued by the flames, and that was Miss Grizy. O! it was a terrible sight to look at her in that jeopardy at the window, with her gold watch in the one hand and the silver tea-pot in the other, skreighing[2] like desperation for a ladder and help. But, before a ladder or help could be found, the floor sunk down, and the roof fell in, and poor Miss Grizy, with her idols, perished in the burning. It was a dreadful business; I think to this hour, how I saw her at the window, how the fire came in behind her, and claught[3] her like a fiery Belzebub, and bore her into perdition before our eyes. The next morning the atomy[4] of the body was found among the rubbish, with a piece of metal in what had been each of its hands, no doubt the gold watch and the silver tea-pot. Such was the end of Miss Grizy, and the Breadland, which the young laird, my pupil that was, by growing a resident at Edinburgh, never rebuilt. It was burnt to the very ground, nothing was spared but what the servants in the first flaught[5] gathered up in a hurry and ran with, but no one could tell how the Major, who was then, as it was thought by the faculty, past the power of nature to recover, got out of the house, and was laid on the feather-bed in the garden. However, he never got the better of that night, and before Whitsunday he was dead too, and buried beside his sister's bones at the south side of the kirk-yard dyke, where his cousin's son, that was his heir, erected the handsome monument, with the three urns and weeping cherubims, bearing witness to the great valour of the Major among the Hindoos, as well as other commendable virtues, for which, as the epitaph says, he was universally esteemed and beloved by all who knew him, in his public and private capacity.

But although the burning of the Breadland-House was justly called the great calamity, on account of what happened to Miss Girzy with her gold watch and silver teapot, yet, as Providence never fails to bring good out of evil, it turned out a catastrophe that proved advantageous to the parish; for the laird, instead of thinking to build it up, was advised to let the policy out as a farm, and the tack[1] was taken by Mr Coulter,[2] than whom there had been no such man in the agriculturing line among us before, not even excepting Mr Kibbock of the Gorbyholm, my father-in-law that was. Of the stabling, Mr Coulter made a comfortable dwelling-house, and having rugget[3] out the evergreens and other unprofitable plants, saving the twa ancient yew-trees which the near-begun[4] Major and his sister had left to go to ruin about the mansion-house, he turned all to production, and it was wonderful what an increase he made the land bring forth. He was from far beyond Edinburgh, and had got his insight among the Lothian farmers, so that he knew what crop should follow another, and nothing could surpass the regularity of his rigs[5] and furrows.—Well do I remember the admiration that I had, when, in a fine sunny morning of the first spring after he took the Breadland, I saw his braird[6] on what had been the cows' grass, as even and pretty as if it had been worked and stripped in the loom with a shuttle. Truly, when I look back at the example he set, and when I think on the method and dexterity of his management, I must say, that his coming to the parish was a great God's-send, and tended to do far more for the benefit of my people, than if the young laird had rebuilded the Breadland-house in a fashionable style, as was at one time spoken of.

But the year of the great calamity was memorable for another thing: In the December foregoing, the wind blew, as I have recorded in the chronicle of the last year, and broke down the bough of the tree, whereon the kirk-bell had hung from the time, as was supposed, of the Persecution, before the bringing over of King William. Mr Kibbock, my father-in-law then that was, being a man of a discerning spirit, when he heard of the unfortunate fall of the bell, advised me to get the heritors to big[1] a steeple, but which, when I thought of the expence, I was afraid to do. He, however, having a great skill in the heart of man, gave me no rest on the subject, but told me, that if I allowed the time to go by, till the heritors were used to come to the kirk without a bell, I would get no steeple at all. I often wondered what made Mr Kibbock so fond of a steeple, which is a thing that I never could see a good reason for, saving that it is an ecclesiastical adjunct, like the gown and bands. However, he set me on to get a steeple proposed, and after no little argol-bargling[2] with the heritors, it was agreed to. This was chiefly owing to the instrumentality of Lady Moneyplack, who, in that winter, was much subjected to the rheumatics, she having, one cold and raw Sunday morning, there being no bell to announce the time, come half an hour too soon to the kirk, made her bestir herself to get an interest awakened among the heritors in behalf of a steeple.

But when the steeple was built, a new contention arose. It was thought that the bell, which had been used in the ash-tree, would not do in a stone and lime fabric, so, after great agitation among the heritors, it was resolved to sell the old bell to a foundry in Glasgow, and buy a new bell suitable to the steeple, which was a very comely fabric. The buying of the new bell led to other considerations, and the old Lady Bread-land, being at the time in a decaying condition, and making her will, she left a mortification to the parish, as I have intimated, to get a clock, so that, by the time the steeple was finished, and the bell put up, the Lady Breadland's legacy came to be implemented, according to the ordination of the testatrix.

Of the casualties that happened in this year, I should not forget to put down, as a thing for remembrance, that an aged woman, one Nanse Birrel, a distillator of herbs, and well

skilled in the healing of sores, who had a great repute among
the quarriers and coalliers,—she having gone to the physic
well in the sandy hills, to draw water, was found with her
feet uppermost in the well, by some of the bairns of Mr Loremore's school; and there was a great debate whether Nanse
had fallen in by accident head foremost, or, in a temptation,
thrown herself in that position, with her feet sticking up to
the evil one; for Nanse was a curious discontented blear-
eyed woman, and it was only with great ado that I could get
the people keepit[1] from calling her a witchwife.

I should, likewise, place on record, that the first ass, that
had ever been seen in this part of the country, came in the
course of this year with a gang of tinklers,[2] that made horn-
spoons, and mended bellows. Where they came from never
was well made out, but being a blackaviced[3] crew, they were
generally thought to be Egyptians. They tarried about a week
among us, living in tents, with their little ones squattling[4]
among the litter; and one of the older men of them set and
tempered to me two razors, that were as good as nothing,
but which he made better than when they were new.

Shortly after, but I am not quite sure whether it was
in the end of this year, or the beginning of the next, although
I have a notion that it was in this, there came over from Ireland a troop of wild Irish, seeking for work as they said,
but they made free quarters, for they herrit[5] the roosts of the
clachan, and cutted the throat of a sow of ours, the carcase
of which they no doubt intended to steal, but something
came over them, and it was found lying at the back-side of
the Manse, to the great vexation of Mrs Balwhidder, for she
had set her mind on a clecking[6] of pigs, and only waited for
the China boar, that had been brought down from London
by Lord Eglesham, to mend the breed of pork—a profitable
commodity, that her father, Mr Kibbock, cultivated for the
Glasgow market. The destruction of our sow, under such
circumstances, was therefore held to be a great crime and

cruelty, and it had the effect to raise up such a spirit in the clachan, that the Irish were obligated to decamp; and they set out for Glasgow, where one of them was afterwards hanged for a fact, but the truth concerning how he did it, I either never heard, or it has passed from my mind, like many other things I should have carefully treasured.

CHAPTER VIII · YEAR 1767

*Lord Eglesham meets with an accident, which is the
means of getting the parish a new road · I preach for
the benefit of Nanse Banks, the schoolmistress,
reduced to poverty*

———

ALL things in our parish were now beginning to shoot up
into a great prosperity. The spirit of farming began to get
the upper hand of the spirit of smuggling, and the coal-heughs
that had been opened in the Douray,[1] now brought a pour
of money among us. In the Manse, the thrift and frugality
of the second Mrs Balwhidder throve exceedingly, so that
we could save the whole stipend for the bank.

The king's highway,[2] as I have related in the foregoing,
ran through the Vennel, which was a narrow and a crooked
street, with many big stones here and there, and every now
and then, both in the spring and the fall, a gathering of
middens[3] for the fields, insomuch that the coal carts from the
Dowray-moor were often reested[4] in the middle of the causeway, and on more than one occasion some of them laired[5]
altogether in the middens, and others of them broke down.
Great complaint was made by the carters anent these difficul-
ties, and there was, for many a day, a talk and sound of an
alteration and amendment, but nothing was fulfilled in the
matter till the month of March in this year, when the Lord
Eglesham was coming from London to see the new lands
that he had bought in our parish. His lordship was a man
of genteel spirit, and very fond of his horses, which were the
most beautiful creatures of their kind that had been seen in all
the country side. Coming, as I was noting, to see his new lands,

he was obliged to pass through the clachan one day, when all the middens were gathered out reeking and sappy[1] in the middle of the causeway. Just as his lordship was driving in with his prancing steeds like a Jehu at the one end of the Vennel, a long string of loaded coal carts came in at the other, and there was hardly room for my lord to pass them. What was to be done? his lordship could not turn back, and the coal carts were in no less perplexity. Every body was out of doors to see and to help, when, in trying to get his lordship's carriage over the top of a midden, the horses gave a sudden loup,[2] and couped[3] the coach, and threw my lord, head foremost, into the very scent-bottle of the whole commodity, which made him go perfect mad, and he swore like a trooper, that he would get an act of parliament to put down the nuisance— the which now ripened in the course of this year into the undertaking of the trust road.

His lordship being in a woeful plight, left the carriage and came to the Manse, till his servant went to the Castle for a change for him; but he could not wait nor abide himself, so he got the lend of my best suit of clothes, and was wonderful jocose both with Mrs Balwhidder and me, for he was a portly man, and I but a thin body, and it was really a droll curiosity to see his lordship clad in my garments.

Out of this accident grew a sort of a neighbourliness between that Lord Eglesham and me, so that when Andrew Lanshaw, the brother that was of the first Mrs Balwhidder, came to think of going to India, I wrote to my lord for his behoof, and his lordship got him sent out as a cadet, and was extraordinary discreet[4] to Andrew when he went up to London to take his passage, speaking to him of me as if I had been a very saint, which the Searcher of Hearts knows I am far from thinking myself.

But to return to the making of the trust-road, which, as I have said, turned the town inside out. It was agreed among the heritors, that it should run along the back-side of the south houses; and that there should be steadings[1] fewed off[2] on each side, according to a plan that was laid down, and this being gone into, the town gradually, in the course of years, grew up into that orderlyness which makes it now a pattern to the country-side—all which was mainly owing to the accident that befel the Lord Eglesham, which is a clear proof how improvements came about, as it were, by the immediate instigation of Providence, which should make the heart of man humble, and change his eyes of pride and haughtiness into a lowly demeanour.

But, although this making of the trust-road was surely a great thing for the parish, and of an advantage to my people, we met, in this year, with a loss not to be compensated,—that was the death of Nanse Banks, the schoolmistress. She had been long in a weak and frail state, but, being a methodical creature, still kept on the school, laying the foundation for many a worthy wife and mother. However, about the decline of the year her complaints increased, and she sent for me to consult about her giving up the school; and I went to see her on a Saturday afternoon, when the bit lassies, her scholars, had put the house in order, and gone home till the Monday.

She was sitting in the window-nook, reading THE WORD to herself, when I entered, but she closed the book, and put her spectacles in for a mark when she saw me; and, as it was expected I would come, her easy chair, with a clean cover, had been set out for me by the scholars, by which I discerned that there was something more than common to happen, and so it appeared when I had taken my seat.

'Sir,' said she, 'I hae sent for you on a thing troubles me sairly.[3] I have warsled with poortith[4] in this shed,[5] which it has pleased the Lord to allow me to possess, but my strength is worn out, and I fear I maun[6] yield in the strife;' and she wiped her eye with her apron. I told her, however, to be of good cheer; and then she said, 'that she could no longer thole[7] the din of the school, and that she was weary, and ready to lay herself down to die whenever the Lord was pleased to permit. But,' continued she, 'what can I do without the school; and, alas! I can neither work nor want; and I am wae to go on the Session,[1] for I am come of a decent family.' I comforted her, and told her, that I thought she had done so much good in the parish, that the Session was deep in her debt, and that what they might give her was but a just payment for her service. 'I would rather, however, sir,' said she, 'try first what some of my auld scholars will do, and it was for that I wanted to speak with you. If some of them would but just, from time to time, look in upon me, that I may not die alane;[2] and the little pick and drap[3] that I require would not be hard upon them—I am more sure that in this way their gratitude would be no discredit, than I am of having any claim on the Session.'

As I had always a great respect for an honest pride, I assured her that I would do what she wanted, and accordingly, the very morning after, being Sabbath, I preached a sermon on the helplessness of them that have no help of man, meaning aged single women, living in garret-rooms, whose forlorn state, in the gloaming[4] of life, I made manifest to the hearts and understandings of the congregation, in such a manner that many shed tears, and went away sorrowful.

Having thus roused the feelings of my people, I went round the houses on the Monday morning, and mentioned what I had to say more particularly about poor old Nanse Banks the schoolmistress, and truly I was rejoiced at the condition of the hearts of my people. There was a universal sympathy among them; and it was soon ordered that, what with one and another, her decay should be provided for. But it was not ordained that she should be long heavy on their good will. On the Monday the school was given up, and there was nothing but wailing among the bit lassies, the scholars, for getting the vacance,[5] as the poor things said, because the mistress was going to lie down to dee. And, indeed, so it came to pass, for she took to her bed the same afternoon, and, in the course of the week, dwindled away, and slippet out of this howling wilderness into the kingdom of heaven, on the Sabbath following, as quietly as a blessed saint could do. And here I should mention, that the Lady Macadam, when I told her of Nanse Banks's case, inquired if she was a snuffer, and, being answered by me that she was, her ladyship sent her a pretty French enamel box full of Macabaw,[1] a fine snuff that she had in a bottle; and, among the Macabaw, was found a guinea, at the bottom of the box, after Nanse Banks had departed this life, which was a kind thing of Lady Macadam to do.

About the close of this year there was a great sough[2] of old prophecies, foretelling mutations and adversities, chiefly on account of the canal that was spoken of to join the rivers of the Clyde and the Forth, it being thought an impossible thing to be done; and the Adam and Eve pear-tree, in our garden, budded out in an awful manner, and had divers flourishes on it at Yule, which was thought an ominous thing, especially as the second Mrs Balwhidder was at the down-lying[3] with my eldest son Gilbert, that is the merchant in Glasgow, but nothing came o't, and the howdie[4] said she had an easy time when the child came into the world, which was on the very last day of the year, to the great satisfaction of me, and of my people, who were wonderful lifted up because their minister had a man-child born unto him.

CHAPTER IX · YEAR 1768

*Lord Eglesham uses his interest in favour of Charles
Malcolm · The finding of a new Schoolmistress ·
Miss Sabrina Hooky gets the place · Change of
fashions in the parish*

━━━━━

IT'S a surprising thing how time flieth away, carrying off our
youth and strength, and leaving us nothing but wrinkles and
the ails of old age. Gilbert, my son, that is now a corpulent
man, and a Glasgow merchant, when I take up my pen to
record the memorables of this An. Dom., seems to me yet
but a suckling in swaddling clothes, mewing and peevish in
the arms of his mother, that has been long laid in the cold
kirk-yard, beside her predecessor, in Abraham's bosom. It is
not, however, my design to speak much anent my own affairs,
which would be a very improper and uncomely thing, but
only of what happened in the parish, this book being for a
witness and testimony of my ministry. Therefore, setting out
of view both me and mine, I will now resuscitate the concerns
of Mrs Malcolm and her children; for, as I think, never was
there such a visible preordination seen in the lives of any
persons, as was seen in that of this worthy decent woman, and
her well-doing offspring. Her morning was raw, and a sore
blight fell upon her fortunes, but the sun looked out on her
mid-day, and her evening closed loun[1] and warm, and the stars
of the firmament, that are the eyes of Heaven, beamed, as
it were, with gladness, when she lay down to sleep the sleep
of rest.

Her son Charles was by this time grown up into a stout
buirdly[2] lad, and it was expected that before the return of the

Tobacco trader, he would have been out of his time,[1] and a man afore the mast, which was a great step of preferment, as I heard say by persons skilled in sea-faring concerns. But this was not ordered to happen; for, when the Tobacco trader was lying in the harbour of Virginia in the North Americas, a press-gang, that was in need of men for a man of war, came on board, and pressed poor Charles and sailed away with him on a cruize, nobody, for many a day, could tell where, till I thought of the Lord Eglesham's kindness. His lordship having something to say with the King's government, I wrote to him, telling him who I was, and how jocose he had been when buttoned in my clothes, that he might recollect me, thanking him, at the same time, for his condescension and patronage to Andrew Lanshaw, in his way to the East Indies. I then slipped in, at the end of the letter, a bit nota bene[2] concerning the case of Charles Malcolm, begging his lordship, on account of the poor lad's widow mother, to inquire at the government if they could tell us any thing about Charles. In the due course of time, I got a most civil reply from his lordship, stating all about the name of the man of war, and where she was; and at the conclusion his lordship said, that I was lucky in having the brother of a Lord of the Admiralty on this occasion for my agent, as otherwise, from the vagueness of my statement, the information might not have been procured; which remark of his lordship was long a great riddle to me, for I could not think what he meant about an agent, till, in the course of the year, we heard that his own brother was concerned in the Admiralty; so that all his lordship meant was only to crack a joke with me, and that he was ever ready and free to do, as shall be related in the sequel, for he was an excellent man.

There being a vacancy for a school-mistress, it was proposed to Mrs Malcolm, that, under her superintendance, her daughter Kate, that had been learning great artifices in needle-work so long with Lady Macadam, should take up the school, and the Session undertook to make good to Kate the sum of five pounds sterling per annum, over and above what the scholars were to pay. But Mrs Malcolm said she had not strength herself to warsle[1] with so many unruly brats, and that Kate, though a fine lassie, was a tempestuous spirit, and might lame some of the bairns in her passion; and that self-same night, Lady Macadam wrote me a very complaining letter, for trying to wile away her companion; but her ladyship was a canary-headed[2] woman, and given to flights and tantrums, having in her youth been a great toast among the quality. It would, however, have saved her from a sore heart, had she never thought of keeping Kate Malcolm. For this year her only son, who was learning the art of war at an academy in France, came to pay her, his lady mother, a visit. He was a brisk and light-hearted stripling, and Kate Malcolm was budding into a very rose of beauty; so between them a hankering began, which, for a season, was productive of great heaviness of heart to the poor old cripple lady; indeed, she assured me herself, that all her rheumatics were nothing to the heart-ache which she suffered in the progress of this business. But that will be more treated of hereafter; suffice it to say for the present, that we have thus recorded how the plan for making Kate Malcolm our school-mistress came to nought. It pleased however Him, from whom cometh every good and perfect gift, to send at this time among us a Miss Sabrina Hookie, the daughter of old Mr Hookie, who had been schoolmaster in a neighbouring parish. She had gone, after his death, to live with an auntie in Glasgow, that kept a shop in the Gallowgate. It was thought that the old woman would have left her heir to all her gatherings,[3] and so she said she would, but alas! our life is but within our lip.[4] Before her testament was made, she was carried suddenly off by an apoplectick, an awful monument of the uncertainty of time, and the nearness of eternity, in her own shop, as she was in the very act of weighing out an ounce of snuff to a Professor of the College, as Miss Sabrina herself told me. Being thus destitute, it happened that Miss Sabrina heard of the vacancy in our parish, as it were, just by the cry of a passing bird, for she could not tell how; although I judge myself that William Keckle the elder had a hand in it, as he was at the time in Glasgow; and she wrote me a wonderful well-penned letter, bespeaking the situation, which letter came to hand on the morn following Lady Macadam's stramash[1] to me about Kate Malcolm, and I laid it before the Session the same day; so that by the time her auntie's concern was taken off her hands, she had a home and a howff[2] among us to come to, in the which she lived upwards of thirty years in credit and respect, although some thought she had not the art of her predecessor, and was more uppish in her carriage than befitted the decorum of her vocation. Her's, however, was but a harmless vanity; and, poor woman, she needed all manner of graces to set her out, for she was made up of odds and ends, and had but one good eye, the other being blind, and just like a blue bead; at first she plainly set her cap for Mr Loremore, but after ogling and gogling[3] at him every Sunday in the kirk for a whole half year and more, Miss Sabrina desisted in despair.

But the most remarkable thing about her coming into the parish, was the change that took place in Christian names among us. Old Mr Hookie, her father, had, from the time he read his Virgil, maintained a sort of intromission with the Nine Muses, by which he was led to baptize her Sabrina,[4] after a name mentioned by John Milton in one of his works. Miss Sabrina began by calling our Jennies, Jessies, and our Nannies, Nancies; alas! I have lived to see even these likewise grow old-fashioned. She had also a taste in the mantua-making[5] line, which she had learnt in Glasgow, and I could date from the very Sabbath of her first appearance in the kirk, a change growing in the garb of the younger lassies, who from that day began to lay aside the silken plaidie[6] over the head, the which had been the pride and bravery[7] of their grandmothers, and instead of the snood,[1] that was so snod[2] and simple, they hided their heads in round-eared bees-cap[3] mutches,[4] made of gauze and catgut, and other curious contrivances of French millendery; all which brought a deal of custom to Miss Sabrina, over and above the incomings[5] and Candlemas offerings[6] of the school; insomuch, that she saved money, and in the course of three years had ten pounds to put in the bank.

At the time, these alterations and revolutions in the parish were thought a great advantage; but now when I look back upon them, as a traveller on the hill over the road he has passed, I have my doubts. For with wealth come wants, like a troop of clamorous beggars at the heels of a generous man, and it's hard to tell wherein the benefit of improvement in a country parish consists, especially to those who live by the sweat of their brow. But it is not for me to make reflections, my task and duty is to note the changes of time and habitudes.

CHAPTER X · YEAR 1769

*A toad found in the heart of a stone · Robert
Malcolm, who had been at sea, returns from a
northern voyage · Kate Malcolm's clandestine
correspondence with Lady Macadam's son*

I HAVE my doubts whether it was in the beginning of this
year, or in the end of the last, that a very extraordinar thing
came to light in the parish; but howsoever that may be, there
is nothing more certain than the fact, which it is my duty to
record. I have mentioned already how it was that the toll, or
trust-road,[1] was set a-going, on account of the Lord Eglesham's tumbling on the midden in the vennel. Well, it happened to one of the labouring men, in breaking the stones to
make metal for the new road, that he broke a stone that was
both large and remarkable, and in the heart of it, which was
boss,[2] there was found a living creature, that jumped out the
moment it saw the light of heaven, to the great terrification
of the man, who could think it was nothing but an evil spirit
that had been imprisoned therein for a time. The man came
to me like a demented creature, and the whole clachan
gathered out, young and old, and I went at their head, to
see what the miracle could be, for the man said it was a fiery
dragon, spuing smoke and flames. But when we came to the
spot, it was just a yird[3] toad, and the laddie weans nevelled[4] it
to death with stones, before I could persuade them to give
over. Since then I have read of such things coming to light
in the Scots Magazine,[5] a very valuable book.

Soon after the affair of 'the wee deil[6] in the stane,' as it was
called, a sough[7] reached us that the Americas were seized with

the rebellious spirit of the ten tribes, and were snapping their fingers[1] in the face of the King's government. The news came on a Saturday night, for we had no newspapers in those days, and was brought by Robin Modewort,[2] that fetched the letters from the Irville post. Thomas Fullarton (he has been dead many a day) kept the grocery-shop in Irville, and he had been in at Glasgow, as was his yearly custom, to settle his accounts, and to buy a hogshead of tobacco, with sugar and other spiceries; and being in Glasgow, Thomas was told by the merchant of a great rise in tobacco, that had happened by reason of the contumacity of the plantations, and it was thought that blood would be spilt before things were ended, for that the King and Parliament were in a great passion with them. But as Charles Malcolm, in the King's ship, was the only one belonging to the parish that was likely to be art or part[3] in the business, we were in a manner little troubled at the time with this first gasp of the monster of war, who, for our sins, was ordained to swallow up, and devour so many of our fellow-subjects, before he was bound again in the chains of mercy and peace.

I had, in the mean time, written a letter to the Lord Eglesham, to get Charles Malcolm out of the clutches of the pressgang in the man of war; and about a month after, his lordship sent me an answer, wherein was inclosed a letter from the captain of the ship, saying, that Charles Malcolm was so good a man, that he was reluctant to part with him, and that Charles himself was well contented to remain aboard. Anent which, his lordship said to me, that he had written back to the captain to make a midshipman of Charles, and that he would take him under his own protection, which was great joy on two accounts to us all, especially to his mother; first, to hear that Charles was a good man, although in years still but a youth; and, secondly, that my lord had, of his own free will, taken him under the wing of his patronage.

But the sweet of this world is never to be enjoyed without

some of the sour. The coal bark between Irville and Belfast, in which Robert Malcolm, the second son of his mother, was serving his time to be a sailor, got a charter, as it was called, to go with to Norway for deals,[1] which grieved Mrs Malcolm to the very heart, for there was then no short cut by the canal, as now is, between the rivers of the Forth and Clyde,[2] but every ship was obligated to go far away round by the Orkneys, which, although a voyage in the summer not overly[3] dangerous, there being long days and short nights then, yet in the winter it was far otherwise, many vessels being frozen up in the Baltic till the spring; and there was a story told at the time, of an Irville bark coming home in the dead of the year, that lost her way altogether, and was supposed to have sailed north into utter darkness, for she was never more heard of; and many an awful thing was said of what the auld mariners about the shore thought concerning the crew of that misfortunate vessel. However, Mrs Malcolm was a woman of great faith, and having placed her reliance on Him who is the orphan's stay and widow's trust, she resigned her bairn into His hands, with a religious submission to His pleasure, though the mother's tear of weak human nature was on her cheek and in her e'e. And her faith was well rewarded, for the vessel brought him safe home, and he had seen such a world of things, that it was just to read a story-book to hear him tell of Elsineur and Gottenburgh, and other fine and great places that we had never heard of till that time; and he brought me a bottle of Riga balsam, which for healing cuts was just miraculous, besides a clear bottle of Rososolus for his mother, a spirit which for cordiality could not be told; for though since that time we have had many a sort of Dantzick cordial, I have never tasted any to compare with Robin Malcolm's Rososolus. The Lady Macadam, who had a knowledge of such things, declared it was the best of the best sort; for Mrs Malcolm sent her ladyship some of it in a doctor's bottle, as well as to Mrs Balwhidder, who was then at the down-lying[4] with our daughter Janet—a woman now in the married state, that makes a most excellent wife, having been brought up with great pains, and well educated, as I shall have to record by and by.

About the Christmas of this year, Lady Macadam's son having been perfected in the art of war at a school in France, had, with the help of his mother's friends, and his father's fame, got a stand[1] of colours in the Royal Scots regiment; he came to shew himself in his regimentals to his lady mother, like a dutiful son, as he certainly was. It happened that he was in the kirk in his scarlets and gold, on the same Sunday that Robert Malcolm came home from the long voyage to Norway for deals; and I thought when I saw the soldier and the sailor from the pulpit, that it was an omen of war, among our harmless country folks, like swords and cannon amidst ploughs and sickles, coming upon us, and I became laden in spirit, and had a most weighty prayer upon the occasion, which was long after remembered, many thinking, when the American war broke out, that I had been gifted with a glimmering of prophecy on that day.

It was during this visit to his lady mother, that young Laird Macadam settled the correspondence with Kate Malcolm, which, in the process of time, caused us all so much trouble; for it was a clandestine concern, but the time is not yet ripe for me to speak of it more at large. I should however mention, before concluding this annal, that Mrs Malcolm herself was this winter brought to death's door by a terrible host[2] that came on her in the kirk, by taking a kittling[3] in her throat. It was a terrification to hear her sometimes; but she got the better of it in the spring, and was more herself thereafter than she had been for years before; and her daughter Effie, or Euphemia, as she was called by Miss Sabrina, the schoolmistress, was growing up to be a gleg and clever quean;[4] she was, indeed, such a spirit in her way, that the folks called her Spunkie;[5] while her son William, that was the youngest of the five, was making a wonderful proficiency with Mr Loremore.

He was indeed a douce,[1] well-doing laddie, of a composed
nature; insomuch, that the master said he was surely chosen
for the ministry. In short, the more I think on what befell this
family, and of the great meekness and Christian worth of the
parent, I verily believe there never could have been in any
parish such a manifestation of the truth, that they who put
their trust in the Lord,[2] are sure of having a friend that will
never forsake them.

CHAPTER XI · YEAR 1770

*This year a happy and tranquil one · Lord Eglesham
establishes a fair in the village · The show of Punch
appears for the first time in the parish*

———

THIS blessed An. Dom. was one of the Sabbaths of my
ministry; when I look back upon it, all is quiet and good
order; the darkest cloud of the smuggling had passed over,
at least from my people, and the rumours of rebellion in
America, were but like the distant sound of the bars[1] of Ayr.
We sat, as it were, in a lown[2] and pleasant place, beholding our
prosperity, like the apple-tree adorned with her garlands of
flourishes, in the first fair mornings of the spring, when the
birds are returning thanks to their Maker for the coming
again of the seed-time, and the busy bee goeth forth from her
cell, to gather honey from the flowers of the field, and the
broom of the hill, and the blue-bells and gowans,[3] which
Nature, with a gracious and a gentle hand, scatters in the
valley, as she walketh forth in her beauty, to testify to the
goodness of the Father of all mercies.

Both at the spring and the harvest sacraments, the weather
was as that which is in Paradise; there was a glad composure
in all hearts, and the minds of men were softened towards
each other. The number of communicants was greater than
had been known for many years, and the tables were filled by
the pious from many a neighbouring parish, those of my
hearers who had opposed my placing, declaring openly for a
testimony of satisfaction and holy thankfulness, that the tent,[4]
so surrounded as it was on both occasions, was a sight they
never had expected to see. I was, to be sure, assisted by some of

the best divines then in the land, but I had not been a sluggard myself in the vineyard.

Often, when I think on this year, so fruitful in pleasant intimacies, has the thought come into my mind, that as the Lord blesses the earth from time to time with a harvest of more than the usual increase, so, in like manner, he is sometimes for a season pleased to pour into the breasts of mankind a larger portion of good will and charity, disposing them to love one another, to be kindly to all creatures, and filled with the delight of thankfulness to himself, which is the greatest of blessings.

It was in this year that the Earl of Eglesham ordered the fair[1] to be established in the village; and it was a day of wonderful festivity to all the bairns, and lads and lassies, for miles round. I think, indeed, that there has never been such a fair as the first since; for although we have more mountebanks and Merry Andrews[2] now, and richer cargoes of groceries and packman's stands, yet there has been a falling off in the light-hearted daffing,[3] while the hobble-shows[4] in the change-houses[5] have been awfully augmented. It was on this occasion that Punch's opera[6] was first seen in our country side, and surely never was there such a funny curiosity; for although Mr Punch himself was but a timber idol, he was as droll as a true living thing, and napped[7] with his head so comical; but O he was a sorrowful contumacious captain, and it was just a sport to see how he rampaged, and triumphed, and sang. For months after, the laddie weans did nothing but squeak and sing like Punch. In short, a blithe spirit was among us throughout this year, and the briefness of the chronicle bears witness to the innocency of the time.

CHAPTER XII · YEAR 1771

The nature of Lady Macadam's amusements · She intercepts letters from her Son to Kate Malcolm

———

IT was in this year that my troubles with Lady Macadam's affair began. She was a woman, as I have by a hint here and there intimated, of a prelatic disposition, seeking all things her own way, and not overly scrupulous about the means, which I take to be the true humour of prelacy. She was come of a high episcopal race in the east country, where sound doctrine had been long but little heard, and she considered the comely humility of a presbyter as the wickedness of hypocrisy; so that, saving in the way of neighbourly visitation, there was no sincere communion between us. Nevertheless, with all her vagaries, she had the element of a kindly spirit, that would sometimes kythe[1] in actions of charity, that showed symptoms of a true Christian grace, had it been properly cultivated; but her morals had been greatly neglected in her youth, and she would waste her precious time in the long winter nights, playing at the cards with her visitors; in the which thriftless and sinful pastime,[2] she was at great pains to instruct Kate Malcolm, which I was grieved to understand. What, however, I most misliked in her ladyship, was a lightness and juvenility of behaviour, altogether unbecoming her years, for she was far past three score, having been long married without children. Her son, the soldier officer, came so late, that it was thought she would have been taken up as an evidence in the Douglas cause.[3] She was, to be sure, crippled with the rheumatics, and no doubt the time hung heavy on her hands; but the best friends of recreation and

sport must allow, that an old woman, sitting whole hours
jingling with that paralytic chattel a spinnet, was not a natural
object! What then could be said for her singing Italian songs,[1]
and getting all the newest from Vauxhall[2] in London, a boxful
at a time, with new novel-books, and trinkum-trankum[3]
flowers and feathers, and sweet-meats, sent to her by a lady
of the blood royal of Paris? As for the music, she was at great
pains to instruct Kate, which, and the other things she taught,
were sufficient, as my lady said herself, to qualify poor Kate
for a duchess or a governess, in either of which capacities, her
ladyship assured Mrs Malcolm, she would do honour to her
instructor, meaning her own self; but I must come to the point
anent the affair.

One evening, early in the month of January, as I was sitting
by myself in my closet studying the Scots Magazine, which
I well remember the new number had come but that very
night, Mrs Balwhidder being at the time busy with the lasses
in the kitchen, and superintending, as her custom was, for
she was a clever woman, a great wool-spinning we then had,
both little wheel and meickle wheel, for stockings and blankets
—sitting, as I was saying, in the study, with the fire well
gathered up, for a night's reflection, a prodigious knocking
came to the door, by which the book was almost startled out
of my hand, and all the wheels in the house were silenced at
once. This was her ladyship's flunkey, to beg me to go to her,
whom he described as in a state of desperation. Christianity
required that I should obey the summons; so, with what haste
I could, thinking that perhaps, as she had been low-spirited
for some time about the young laird's going to the Indies, she
might have got a cast of grace, and been wakened in despair
to the state of darkness in which she had so long lived, I made
as few steps of the road between the Manse and her house
as it was in my ability to do.

On reaching the door, I found a great light in the house—
candles burning up stairs and down stairs, and a sough[4] of

something extraordinar going on. I went into the dining-room, where her ladyship was wont to sit; but she was not there—only Kate Malcolm all alone, busily picking bits of paper from the carpet. When she looked up, I saw that her eyes were red with weeping, and I was alarmed, and said, 'Katy, my dear, I hope there is no danger?' Upon which the poor lassie rose, and flinging herself in a chair, covered her face with her hands, and wept bitterly.

'What is the old fool doing with the wench?' cried a sharp angry voice from the drawing-room—'why does not he come to me?' It was the voice of Lady Macadam herself, and she meant me. So I went to her; but, O, she was in a far different state from what I had hoped. The pride of this world had got the upper-hand of her, and was playing dreadful antics with her understanding. There was she, painted like a Jezebel, with gum-flowers[1] on her head, as was her custom every afternoon, sitting on a settee, for she was lame, and in her hand she held a letter. 'Sir,' said she, as I came into the room, 'I want you to go instantly to that young fellow, your clerk, (meaning Mr Loremore, the schoolmaster, who was likewise session-clerk and precentor,) and tell him I will give him a couple of hundred pounds to marry Miss Malcolm without delay, and undertake to procure him a living from some of my friends.'

'Softly, my lady, you must first tell me the meaning of all this haste of kindness,' said I, in my calm methodical manner. At the which she began to cry and sob, like a petted bairn, and to bewail her ruin, and the dishonour of her family. I was surprised, and beginning to be confounded, at length out it came. The flunkie had that night brought two London letters from the Irville post, and Kate Malcolm being out of the way when he came home, he took them both in to her ladyship on the silver server, as was his custom; and her ladyship, not jealousing that Kate could have a correspondence with London, thought both the letters were for herself, for they were

franked, so, as it happened, she opened the one that was for
Kate, and this, too, from the young laird, her own son. She
could not believe her eyes when she saw the first words in
his hand of write, and she read, and she better read, till she
read all the letter, by which she came to know that Kate and
her darling were trysted,[1] and that this was not the first love-
letter which had passed between them. She, therefore, tore
it in pieces, and sent for me, and screamed for Kate; in short,
went, as it were, off at the head, and was neither to bind nor
to hold[2] on account of this intrigue, as she, in her wrath,
stigmatized the innocent gallanting of poor Kate and the
young laird.

I listened in patience to all she had to say anent the dis-
covery, and offered her the very best advice; but she derided
my judgment, and because I would not speak outright to
Mr Loremore, and get him to marry Kate off hand, she bade
me good night with an air, and sent for him herself. He, however, was on the brink of marriage with his present worthy
helpmate, and declined her ladyship's proposals, which
angered her still more. But although there was surely a great
lack of discretion in all this, and her ladyship was entirely
overcome with her passion, she would not part with Kate, nor
allow her to quit the house with me, but made her sup with
her as usual that night, calling her sometimes a perfidious
baggage, and at other times, forgetting her delirium, speaking
to her as kindly as ever. At night, Kate as usual helped her
ladyship into her bed, (this she told me with tears in her eyes
next morning) and when Lady Macadam, as was her wont,
bent to kiss her for good night, she suddenly recollected 'the
intrigue,' and gave Kate such a slap on the side of the head, as
quite dislocated for a time the intellects of the poor young
lassie. Next morning, Kate was solemnly advised never to
write again to the laird, while the lady wrote him a letter,
which, she said, would be as good as a birch to the breech of
the boy. Nothing, therefore, for some time, indeed throughout

the year, came of this matter, but her ladyship, when Mrs Balwhidder soon after called on her, said that I was a nose of wax,[1]
and that she never would speak to me again, which surely was
not a polite thing to say to Mrs Balwhidder, my second wife.

This stramash[2] was the first time that I had interposed in
the family concerns of my people, for it was against my nature
to make or meddle with private actions, saving only such as,
in course of nature, came before the Session; but I was not
satisfied with the principles of Lady Macadam, and I began
to be weary about Kate Malcolm's situation with her ladyship,
whose ways of thinking I saw were not to be depended on,
especially in those things wherein her pride and vanity were
concerned. But the time ran on—the butterflies and the blossoms were succeeded by the leaves and the fruit, and nothing
of a particular nature farther molested the general tranquillity
of this year; about the end of which, there came on a sudden
frost, after a tack[3] of wet weather. The roads were just a sheet
of ice, like a frozen river; insomuch, that the coal-carts could
not work; and one of our cows, (Mrs Balwhidder said after
the accident it was our best, but it was not so much thought
of before,) fell in coming from the glebe to the byre, and broke
its two hinder legs, which obligated us to kill it, in order to put
the beast out of pain. As this happened after we had salted our
mart,[4] it occasioned us to have a double crop of puddings, and
such a show of hams in the kitchen, as was a marvel to our
visitors to see.

CHAPTER XIII · YEAR 1772

*The detection of Mr Heckletext's guilt · He
threatens to prosecute the Elders for defamation ·
The Muscovy duck gets an operation performed on it*

―――――――

ON New-Year's night, this year, a thing happened, which, in
its own nature, was a trifle, but it turned out as a mustard-seed
that grows into a great tree.[1] One of the elders, who has long
been dead and gone, came to the Manse about a fact[2] that was
found out in the clachan, and after we had discoursed on it
some time, he rose to take his departure. I went with him to the
door with the candle in my hand—it was a clear frosty night,
with a sharp wind, and the moment I opened the door, the
blast blew out the candle, so that I heedlessly, with the candlestick in my hand, walked with him to the yett without my hat,
by which I took a sore cold in my head, that brought on a
dreadful tooth-ache; insomuch, that I was obliged to go into
Irville to get the tooth drawn, and this caused my face to
swell to such a fright, that, on the Sabbath-day, I could not
preach to my people. There was, however, at that time, a
young man, one Mr Heckletext, tutor in Sir Hugh Montgomerie's family,[3] and who had shortly before been licenced.
Finding that I would not be able to preach myself, I sent to
him, and begged he would officiate for me, which he very
pleasantly consented to do, being like all the young clergy,
thirsting to shew his light to the world. 'Twixt the fore and
afternoon's worship, he took his check[4] of dinner at the Manse,
and I could not but say, that he seemed both discreet and
sincere. Judge, however, what was brewing, when the same
night Mr Loremore came and told me, that Mr Heckletext

was the suspected person anent the fact, that had been instrumental in the hand of a chastising Providence, to afflict me
with the tooth-ache, in order, as it afterwards came to pass, to
bring the hidden hypocrisy of the ungodly preacher to light.
It seems that the donsie[1] lassie, who was in fault,[2] had gone
to the kirk in the afternoon, and seeing who was in the pulpit,
where she expected to see me, was seized with the hystericks,
and taken with her crying[3] on the spot, the which being un-
timely, proved the death of both mother and bairn, before
the thing was properly laid to the father's charge.

This caused a great uproar in the parish. I was sorely
blamed to let such a man as Mr Heckletext go up into my
pulpit, although I was as ignorant of his offences as the
innocent child that perished; and, in an unguarded hour, to
pacify some of the elders, who were just distracted about the
disgrace, I consented to have him called before the Session.
He obeyed the call, and in a manner that I will never forget,
for he was a sorrow of sin and audacity, and demanded to know
why and for what reason he was summoned. I told him the
whole affair in my calm and moderate way, but it was oil cast
upon a burning coal.[4] He flamed up in a terrible passion,
threapit[5] at the elders that they had no proof whatever of his
having had any trafficking in the business, which was the case,
for it was only a notion, the poor deceased lassie never having
made a disclosure; called them libellous conspirators against
his character, which was his only fortune, and concluded by
threatening to punish them, though he exempted me from the
injury which their slanderous insinuations had done to his
prospects in life. We were all terrified, and allowed him to go
away without uttering a word; and sure enough he did bring
a plea in the courts of Edinburgh against Mr Loremore and
the elders for damages, laid at a great sum.

What might have been the consequence, no one can tell;
but soon after he married Sir Hugh's house-keeper, and went
with her into Edinburgh, where he took up a school, and,

before the trial came on, that is to say, within three months of the day that I myself married them, Mrs Heckletext was delivered of a thriving lad bairn, which would have been a witness for the elders, had the worst come to the worst. This was, indeed, we all thought, a joyous deliverance to the parish, and it was a lesson to me never to allow any preacher to mount my pulpit, unless I knew something of his moral character.

In other respects, this year passed very peaceably in the parish; there was a visible increase of worldly circumstances, and the hedges which had been planted along the toll-road, began to put forth their branches, and to give new notions of orderlyness and beauty to the farmers. Mrs Malcolm heard from time to time from her son Charles, on board the man of war the Avenger, where he was midshipman, and he had found a friend in the captain, that was just a father to him. Her second son Robert, being out of his time at Irville, went to the Clyde to look for a birth, and was hired to go to Jamaica, in a ship called the Trooper. He was a lad of greater sobriety of nature than Charles; douce,[1] honest, and faithful; and when he came home, though he brought no limes to me to make punch, like his brother, he brought a Muscovy duck[2] to Lady Macadam, who had, as I have related, in a manner educated his sister Kate. That duck was the first of the kind we had ever seen, and many thought it was of the goose species, only with short bowly[3] legs. It was however, a tractable and homely beast, and after some confabulation, as my lady herself told Mrs Balwhidder, it was received into fellowship by her other ducks and poultry. It is not, however, so much on account of the rarity of the creature, that I have introduced it here, as for the purpose of relating a wonderful operation that was performed on it by Miss Sabrina, the schoolmistress.

There happened to be a sack of beans in our stable, and Lady Macadam's hens and fowls, which were not overly fed at home, through the inattention of her servants, being great stravaggers[1] for their meat, in passing the door, went in to pick, and the Muscovy seeing a hole in the bean-sack, dabbled out a crap[2] full before she was disturbed. The beans swelled on the poor bird's stomach, and her crap bellied out like the kyte[3] of a Glasgow magistrate, until it was just a sight to be seen with its head back on its shoulders. The bairns of the clachan followed it up and down, crying, the lady's muckle jock[4]'s ay growing bigger, till every heart was wae for the creature. Some thought it was afflicted with a tympathy,[5] and others, that it was the natural way for such like ducks to cleck[6] their young. In short, we were all concerned, and my lady having a great opinion of Miss Sabrina's skill, had a consultation with her on the case, at which Miss Sabrina advised, that what she called the Cæsarian operation should be tried, which she herself performed accordingly, by opening the creature's crap, and taking out as many beans as filled a mutchkin stoup,[7] after which she sewed it up, and the Muscovy went its way to the water-side, and began to swim, and was as jocund as ever; insomuch, that in three days after it was quite cured of all the consequences of its surfeit.

I had at one time a notion to send an account of this to the Scots Magazine, but something always came in the way to prevent me; so that it has been reserved for a place in this chronicle, being, after Mr Heckletext's affair, the most memorable thing in our history of this year.

CHAPTER XIV · YEAR 1773

*The new school-house · Lord Eglesham comes down
to the Castle · I refuse to go and dine there on Sunday,
but go on Monday, and meet with an English dean*

———

IN this Ann. Dom. there was something like a plea getting to
a head,[1] between the Session and some of the heritors, about
a new school-house; the thatch having been torn from the
rigging of the old one by a blast of wind, on the first Monday of
February, by which a great snow storm got admission, and the
school was rendered utterly uninhabitable. The smaller sort
of lairds were very willing to come into the plan with an extra
contribution, because they respected the master, and their
bairns were at the school; but the gentlemen, who had tutors
in their own houses, were not so manageable, and some of
them even went so far as to say, that the kirk being only wanted
on Sunday, would do very well for a school all the rest of the
week, which was a very profane way of speaking, and I was
resolved to set myself against any such thing, and to labour
according to the power and efficacy of my station, to get a new
school built.

Many a meeting the Session had on the subject, and the
heritors debated and discussed, and revised their proceedings,
and still no money for the needful work was forthcoming.
Whereupon it happened one morning, as I was rummaging in
my scrutoire, that I laid my hand on the Lord Eglesham's letter
anent Charles Malcolm, and it was put into my head at that
moment, that if I was to write his lordship, who was the
greatest heritor, and owned now the major part of the parish,
that by his help and influence, I might be an instrument to the

building of a comfortable new school; accordingly I sat down and wrote my lord all about the accident, and the state of the school-house, and the divisions and seditions among the heritors, and sent the letter to him at London by the post the same day, without saying a word to any living soul on the subject.

This in me was an advised[1] thought, for, by the return of post, his lordship, with his own hand, in a most kind manner, authorized me to say that he would build a new school at his own cost, and bade me go over and consult about it with his steward, at the Castle, to whom he had written by the same post the necessary instructions. Nothing could exceed the gladness which the news gave to the whole parish, and none said more in behalf of his lordship's bounty and liberality, than the heritors; especially those gentry who grudged the undertaking, when it was thought that it would have to come out of their own pock-nook.[2]

In the course of the summer, just as the roof was closing in of the school-house, my lord came to the castle with a great company, and was not there a day till he sent for me to come over on the next Sunday, to dine with him; but I sent him word that I could not do so, for it would be a transgression of the Sabbath, which made him send his own gentleman, to make his apology for having taken so great a liberty with me, and to beg me to come on the Monday, which I accordingly did, and nothing could be better than the discretion[3] with which I was used. There was a vast company of English ladies and gentlemen, and his lordship, in a most jocose manner, told them all how he had fallen on the midden, and how I had clad him in my clothes, and there was a wonder of laughing and diversion; but the most particular thing in the company, was a large, round-faced man, with a wig, that was a dignitary in some great Episcopalian church in London, who was extraordinary condescending towards me, drinking wine with me at the table, and saying weighty sentences[4] in a fine style of language, about the becoming grace of simplicity and innocence of heart, in the clergy of all denominations of Christians, which I was pleased to hear; for really he had a proud red countenance, and I could not have thought he was so mortified to humility within, had I not heard with what sincerity he delivered himself, and seen how much reverence and attention was paid to him by all present, particularly by my lord's chaplain, who was a pious and pleasant young divine, though educated at Oxford for the Episcopalian persuasion.

One day soon after, as I was sitting in my closet conning a sermon for the next Sunday, I was surprised by a visit from the dean, as the dignitary was called. He had come, he said, to wait on me as rector of the parish, for so it seems they call a pastor in England, and to say, that, if it was agreeable, he would take a family dinner with us before he left the castle. I could make no objection to this kindness, but said I hoped my lord would come with him, and that we would do our best to entertain them with all suitable hospitality. About an hour or so after he had returned to the castle, one of the flunkies brought a letter from his lordship to say, that not only he would come with the dean, but that they would bring his other guests with them, and that, as they could only drink London wine, the butler would send me a hamper in the morning, assured, as he was pleased to say, that Mrs Balwhidder would otherwise provide good cheer.

This notification, however, was a great trouble to my wife, who was only used to manufacture the produce of our glebe and yard to a profitable purpose, and not used to the treatment of deans and lords, and other persons of quality. However, she was determined to stretch a point on this occasion, and we had, as all present declared, a charming dinner; for fortunately one of the sows had a litter of pigs a few days before, and, in addition to a goose, that is but a boss[1] bird, we had a roasted pig, with an apple in its mouth, which was just a curiosity to see; and my lord called it a tythe pig, but I told him it was one of Mrs Balwhidder's own clecking,[1] which saying of mine made no little sport when expounded to the dean.

But, och how! this was the last happy summer that we had for many a year in the parish; and an omen of the dule[2] that ensued, was in a sacrilegious theft that a daft woman, Jenny Gaffaw, and her idiot daughter,[3] did in the kirk, by tearing off and stealing the green serge lining of my lord's pew, to make, as they said, a hap[4] for their shoulders in the cold weather— saving, however, the sin, we paid no attention at the time to the mischief and tribulation that so unheard of a trespass boded to us all. It took place about Yule, when the weather was cold and frosty, and poor Jenny was not very able to go about seeking her meat as usual. The deed, however, was mainly done by her daughter, who, when brought before me, said, 'her poor mother's back had mair need of claes[5] than the kirk-boards,' which was so true a thing, that I could not punish her, but wrote anent it to my lord, who not only overlooked the offence, but sent orders to the servants at the castle to be kind to the poor woman, and the natural, her daughter.

CHAPTER XV · YEAR 1774

The murder of Jean Glaikit · The young Laird
Macadam comes down and marries Kate Malcolm ·
The ceremony performed by me, and I am
commissioned to break the matter to Lady
Macadam · Her behaviour

WHEN I look back on this year, and compare what happened
therein with the things that had gone before, I am grieved to
the heart, and pressed down with an afflicted spirit. We had,
as may be read, trials and tribulations in the days that were
past, and in the rank and boisterous times of the smuggling
there was much sin and blemish among us, but nothing so
dark and awful as what fell out in the course of this unhappy
year. The evil omen of daft Jenny Gaffaw, and her daughter's
sacrilege, had soon a bloody verification.

About the beginning of the month of March in this year,
the war in America was kindling so fast, that the government
was obligated to send soldiers over the sea, in the hope to quell
the rebellious temper of the plantations, and a party of a
regiment that was quartered at Ayr was ordered to march to
Greenock, to be there shipped off. The men were wild and
wicked profligates, without the fear of the Lord before their
eyes, and some of them had drawn up with light women in
Ayr, who followed them on their march. This the soldiers did
not like, not wishing to be troubled with such gear[1] in America;
so the women, when they got the length of Kilmarnock, were
ordered to retreat, and go home, which they all did, but one
Jean Glaikit,[2] who persisted in her intent to follow her jo,[3]
Patrick O'Neil, a catholic Irish corporal. The man did, as he

said, all in his capacity to persuade her to return, but she was a contumacious limmer,[1] and would not listen to reason, so that, in passing along our toll-road, from less to more,[2] the miserable wretches fell out, and fought, and the soldier put an end to her, with a hasty knock on the head with his firelock,[3] and marched on after his comrades.

The body of the woman was, about half an hour after, found by the scholars of Mr Loremore's school, who had got the play[4] to see the marching, and to hear the drums of the soldiers. Dreadful was the shout and the cry throughout the parish at this foul work. Some of the farmer lads followed the soldiers on horseback, and others ran to Sir Hugh, who was a justice of the peace, for his advice.—Such a day as that was!

However, the murderer was taken, and, with his arms tied behind him with a cord, he was brought back to the parish, where he confessed before Sir Hugh the deed, and how it happened. He was then put in a cart, and being well guarded by six of the lads, was taken to Ayr jail.

It was not long after this that the murderer was brought to trial, and, being found guilty on his own confession, he was sentenced to be executed, and his body to be hung in chains near the spot where the deed was done. I thought that all in the parish would have run to desperation with horror when the news of this came, and I wrote immediately to the Lord Eglesham to get this done away by the merciful power of the government, which he did, to our great solace and relief.

In the autumn, the young Laird Macadam, being ordered with his regiment for the Americas, got leave from the king to come and see his lady-mother, before his departure. But it was not to see her only, as will presently appear.

Knowing how much her ladyship was averse to the notion he had of Kate Malcolm, he did not write of his coming, lest she would send Kate out of the way, but came in upon them at a late hour, as they were wasting their precious time, as was the nightly wont of my lady, with a pack of cards; and so far was she from being pleased to see him, that no sooner did she behold his face, but like a tap of tow,[1] she kindled upon both him and Kate, and ordered them out of her sight and house. The young folk had discretion: Kate went home to her mother, and the laird came to the Manse, and begged us to take him in. He then told me what had happened, and that having bought a Captain's commission, he was resolved to marry Kate, and hoped I would perform the ceremony, if her mother would consent. 'As for mine,' said he, 'she will never agree'; but, when the thing is done, her pardon will not be difficult to get, for, with all her whims and caprice, she is generous and affectionate.' In short, he so wiled and beguiled me, that I consented to marry them, if Mrs Malcolm was agreeable. 'I will not disobey my mother,' said he, 'by asking her consent, which I know she will refuse; and, therefore, the sooner it is done the better.' So we then stepped over to Mrs Malcolm's house, where we found that saintly woman, with Kate, and Effie, and Willie, sitting peacefully at their fire-side, preparing to read their bibles for the night. When we went in, and when I saw Kate, that was so lady-like there, with the decent humility of her parent's dwelling, I could not but think she was destined for a better station; and when I looked at the Captain, a handsome youth, I thought surely their marriage is made in Heaven; and so I said to Mrs Malcolm, who after a time consented, and likewise agreed that her daughter should go with the Captain to America, for her faith and trust in the goodness of Providence was great and boundless, striving, as it were, to be even with its tender mercies. Accordingly, the Captain's man was sent to bid the chaise wait that had taken him to the lady's, and the marriage was sanctified by me before we left Mrs Malcolm's. No doubt, they ought to have been proclaimed three several Sabbaths, but I satisfied the Session, at our first meeting, on account of the necessity of the case. The young couple went in the chaise travelling to Glasgow, authorising me to break the matter to Lady Macadam, which was a sore task, but I was spared from the performance. For her ladyship had come to herself, and thinking on her own rashness in sending away Kate and the Captain in the way she had done, she was like one by herself; all the servants were scattered out and abroad in quest of the lovers, and some of them, seeing the chaise drive from Mrs Malcolm's door, with them in it, and me coming out, jealoused[1] what had been done, and told their mistress outright of the marriage, which was to her like a clap of thunder; insomuch, that she flung herself back in her settee, and was beating and drumming with her heels on the floor, like a mad woman in Bedlam, when I entered the room. For some time she took no notice of me, but continued her din; but, by and by, she began to turn her eyes in fiery glances upon me, till I was terrified lest she would fly at me with her claws in her fury. At last she stopped all at once, and in a calm voice, said, 'But it cannot now be helped, where are the vagabonds?'—'They are gone,' replied I.—'Gone?' cried she, 'gone where?'—'To America, I suppose,' was my answer; upon which she again threw herself back in the settee, and began again to drum and beat with her feet as before. But not to dwell on small particularities, let it suffice to say, that she sent her coachman on one of her coach horses, which being old and stiff, did not overtake the fugitives till they were in their bed at Kilmarnock, where they stopped that night; but when they came back to the lady's in the morning, she was as cagey and meikle taken up[2] with them, as if they had gotten her full consent and privilege to marry from the first. Thus was the first of Mrs Malcolm's children well and creditably settled. I have only now to conclude with observing, that my son Gilbert was seized with the small-pox, about the beginning of December, and was blinded by them for seventeen days; for the inoculation[3] was not in practice yet among us, saving only in the genteel families, that went into Edinburgh for the education of their children, where it was performed by the faculty[4] there.

CHAPTER XVI · YEAR 1775

*Captain Macadam provides a house and an annuity
for old Mrs Malcolm · Miss Betty Wudrife brings
from Edinburgh a new-fashioned silk mantle, but
refuses to give the pattern to old Lady Macadam ·
Her revenge*

━━━━━━

THE regular course of nature is calm and orderly, and tempests
and troubles are but lapses from the accustomed sobriety with
which Providence works out the destined end of all things.
From Yule till Pace[1]-Monday there had been a gradual
subsidence of our personal and parochial tribulations, and the
spring, though late, set in bright and beautiful, and was
accompanied with the spirit of contentment, so that, excepting
the great concern that we all began to take in the American
rebellion, especially on account of Charles Malcolm that was
in the man of war, and of Captain Macadam that had married
Kate, we had throughout the better half of the year but little
molestation of any sort. I should, however, note the upshot of
the marriage.

By some cause that I do not recollect, if I ever heard it
properly told, the regiment wherein the Captain had bought
his commission was not sent to the plantations, but only over
to Ireland, by which the Captain and his lady were allowed to
prolong their stay in the parish with his mother, and he,
coming of age, while he was among us, in making a settlement
on his wife, bought the house at the braehead, which was then
just built by Thomas Shivers the mason, and he gave that
house, with a judicious income, to Mrs Malcolm, telling her
that it was not becoming, he having it in his power to do the

contrary, that she should any longer be dependent on her own industry. For this the young man got a name like a sweet odour in all the country-side; but that whimsical and prelatic[1] lady his mother, just went out of all bounds, and played such pranks, for an old woman, that cannot be told. To her daughter-in-law, however, she was wonderful kind; and in fitting her out for going with the Captain to Dublin, it was extraordinary to hear what a parapharnalia she provided her with. But who could have thought that in this kindness a sore trial was brewing for me!

It happened that Miss Betty Wudrife, the daughter of an heritor, had been on a visit to some of her friends in Edinburgh; and, being in at Edinburgh, she came out with a fine mantle, decked and adorned with many a ribbon-knot, such as had never been seen in the parish. The Lady Macadam, hearing of this grand mantle, sent to beg Miss Betty to lend it to her, to make a copy for young Mrs Macadam. But Miss Betty was so vogie[2] with her gay mantle, that she sent back word, it would be making it o'er common; which so nettled the old courtly lady, that she vowed revenge, and said the mantle would not be long seen on Miss Betty. Nobody knew the meaning of her words; but she sent privately for Miss Sabrina, the schoolmistress, who was ay proud of being invited to my lady's, where she went on the Sabbath night to drink tea, and read Thomson's Seasons and Harvey's Meditations for her ladyship's recreation. Between the two, a secret plot was laid against Miss Betty and her Edinburgh mantle; and Miss Sabrina, in a very treacherous manner, for the which I afterwards chided her severely, went to Miss Betty, and got a sight of the mantle, and how it was made, and all about it, until she was in a capacity to make another like it; by which my lady and her, from old silk and satin negligées which her ladyship had worn at the French court, made up two mantles of the self-same fashion as Miss Betty's, and, if possible, more sumptuously garnished, but in a flagrant[3] fool way. On the

Sunday morning after, her ladyship sent for Jenny Gaffaw, and her daft daughter Meg, and shewed them the mantles, and said she would give them half-a-crown if they would go with them to the kirk, and take their place in the bench beside the elders, and, after worship, walk home before Miss Betty Wudrife. The two poor natural things were just transported with the sight of such bravery,[1] and needed no other bribe; so, over their bits of ragged duds,[2] they put on the pageantry, and walked away to the kirk like peacocks, and took their place on the bench, to the great diversion of the whole congregation.

I had no suspicion of this, and had prepared an affecting discourse about the horrors of war, in which I touched, with a tender hand, on the troubles that threatened families and kindred in America; but all the time I was preaching, doing my best, and expatiating till the tears came into my eyes, I could not divine what was the cause of the inattention of my people. But the two vain haverels[3] were on the bench under me, and I could not see them; where they sat, spreading their feathers and picking their wings, stroking down and setting right their finery, with such an air as no living soul could see and withstand; while every eye in the kirk was now on them, and now at Miss Betty Wudrife, who was in a worse situation than if she had been on the stool of repentance.[4]

Greatly grieved with the little heed that was paid to my discourse, I left the pulpit with a heavy heart; but when I came out into the kirk-yard, and saw the two antics linking[5] like ladies, and aye keeping in the way before Miss Betty, and looking back and around in their pride and admiration, with high heads and a wonderful pomp, I was really overcome, and could not keep my gravity, but laughed loud out among the graves, and in the face of all my people, who, seeing how I was vanquished in that unguarded moment by the enemy, made a universal and most unreverent breach of all decorum, at which Miss Betty, who had been the cause of all, ran into the first open door, and almost fainted away with mortification.

This affair was regarded by the elders as a sinful trespass on the orderlyness that was needful in the Lord's house, and they called on me at the Manse that night, and said it would be a guilty connivance, if I did not rebuke and admonish Lady Macadam of the evil of her way; for they had questioned daft Jenny, and had got at the bottom of the whole plot and mischief. But I, who knew her ladyship's light way, would fain have had the elders to overlook it, rather than expose myself to her tantrums; but they considered the thing as a great scandal, so I was obligated to conform to their wishes. I might, however, have as well stayed at home, for her ladyship was in one of her jocose humours when I went to speak to her on the subject; and it was so far from my power to make a proper impression on her of the enormity that had been committed, that she made me laugh, in spite of my reason, at the fantastical drollery of her malicious prank on Miss Betty Wudrife.

It, however, did not end here; for the Session, knowing that it was profitless to speak to the daft mother and daughter, who had been the instruments, gave orders to Willy Howking, the betheral,[1] not to let them again so far into the kirk, and Willy having scarcely more sense than them both, thought proper to keep them out next Sunday altogether. They twa[2] said nothing at the time, but the adversary[3] was busy with them; for, on the Wednesday following, there being a meeting of the Synod[4] at Ayr, to my utter amazement, the mother and daughter made their appearance there in all their finery, and raised a complaint against me and the Session, for debarring them from church privileges. No stage play could have produced such an effect; I was perfectly dumb-foundered, and every member of the Synod might have been tied with a straw, they were so overcome with this new device of that endless[5] woman, when bent on provocation—the Lady Macadam; in whom the saying was verified, that old folk are twice bairns, for in such plays, pranks, and projects, she was as playrife[1] as a very lassie at her sampler, and this is but a swatch[2] to what lengths she would go. The complaint was dismissed, by which the Session and me were assoilzied;[3] but I'll never forget till the day of my death, what I suffered on that occasion, to be so put to the wall[4] by two born idiots.

CHAPTER XVII · YEAR 1776

*A recruiting party comes to Irville · Thomas Wilson
and some others enlist · Charles Malcolm's return*

━━━━━━━━

IT belongs to the chroniclers of the realm, to describe the damage and detriment which fell on the power and prosperity of the kingdom, by reason of the rebellion that was fired into open war[1] against the name and authority of the king in the plantations of America; for my task is to describe what happened within the narrow bound of the pasturage of the Lord's flock, of which, in his bounty and mercy, he made me the humble, willing, but, alas! the weak and ineffectual shepherd.

About the month of February, a recruiting party came to our neighbour town of Irville, to beat up for men to be soldiers against the rebels; and thus the battle was brought, as it were, to our gates, for the very first man that took on with them was one Thomas Wilson, a cotter in our clachan, who, up to that time, had been a decent and creditable character. He was at first a farmer lad, but had foregathered with a doited tawpy,[2] whom he married, and had offspring three or four. For some time it was noticed, that he had a down and thoughtful look, that his cleeding[3] was growing bare, and that his wife kept an untrig house, which, it was feared by many, was the cause of Thomas going o'er often to the change-house;[4] he was, in short, during the greater part of the winter, evidently a man foregone in the pleasures of this world, which made all that knew him compassionate his situation.

No doubt, it was his household ills that burdened him past bearing, and made him go into Irville, when he heard of the recruiting, and take on to be a soldier. Such a wally wallying[5]

as the news of this caused at every door; for the red-coats,—
from the persecuting days, when the black-cuffs[1] rampaged
through the country,—soldiers that fought for hire, were held
in dread and as a horror among us, and terrible were the stories
that were told of their cruelty and sinfulness; indeed, there
had not been wanting in our own time a sample of what they
were, as witness the murder of Jean Glaikit by Patrick O'Neal,
the Irish corporal, anent which I have treated at large in the
memorables of the year 1774.

A meeting of the Session was forthwith held; for here was
Thomas Wilson's wife and all his weans,[2] an awful cess,[3]
thrown upon the parish; and it was settled outright among us,
that Mr Docken, who was then an elder, but is since dead,
a worthy man, with a soft tongue and a pleasing manner,
should go to Irville, and get Thomas, if possible, released
from the recruiters. But it was all in vain, the serjeant would
not listen to him, for Thomas was a strapping lad; nor would
the poor infatuated man himself agree to go back, but cursed
like a cadger,[4] and swore that if he staid any longer among his
plagues,[5] he would commit some rash act; so we were saddled
with his family, which was the first taste and preeing[6] of what
war is when it comes into our hearths, and among the bread-
winners.

The evil, however, did not stop here. Thomas, when he was
dressed out in the King's clothes, came over to see his bairns,
and take a farewell of his friends, and he looked so gallant,
that the very next market-day, another lad of the parish listed
with him; but he was a ramplor,[7] roving sort of a creature,
and, upon the whole, it was thought he did well for the parish
when he went to serve the King.

The listing was a catching distemper. Before the summer
was over, other three of the farming lads went off with the
drum, and there was a wailing in the parish, which made me
preach a touching discourse. I likened the parish to a widow
woman with a small family, sitting in their cottage by the

fire-side, herself spinning with an eydent[1] wheel, ettling[2] her best to get them a bit and a brat,[3] and the poor weans all canty[4] about the hearth-stane—the little ones at their playocks,[5] and the elder at their tasks—the callans[6] working with hooks and lines to catch them a meal of fish in the morning—and the lassies working stockings to sell at the next Marymas[7] fair.— And then I likened war to a calamity coming among them— the callans drowned at their fishing—the lassies led to a mis- doing—and the feckless wee bairns laid on the bed of sickness, and their poor forlorn mother sitting by herself at the embers of a cauldrife[8] fire; her tow[9] done, and no a bodle[10] to buy more; dropping a silent and salt tear for her babies, and think- ing of days that war gone, and, like Rachel weeping for her children,[11] she would not be comforted. With this I concluded, for my own heart filled full with the thought, and there was a deep sob in the church, verily, it was Rachel weeping for her children.

In the latter end of the year, the man of war, with Charles Malcolm in her, came to the tail of the Bank at Greenock, to press men as it was thought, and Charles got leave from his captain to come and see his mother; and he brought with him Mr Howard, another midshipman, the son of a great Parlia- ment man in London, which, as we had tasted the sorrow, gave us some insight into the pomp of war. Charles was now grown up into a fine young man, rattling,[12] light-hearted, and just a cordial of gladness, and his companion was every bit like him. They were dressed in their fine gold-laced garbs, and nobody knew Charles when he came to the clachan, but all wondered, for they were on horseback, and rode to the house where his mother lived when he went away, but which was then occupied by Miss Sabrina and her school. Miss Sabrina had never seen Charles, but she had heard of him, and when he inquired for his mother, she guessed who he was, and shewed him the way to the new house that the Captain had bought for her.

Miss Sabrina, who was a little overly perjinct[1] at times, behaved herself on this occasion with a true spirit, and gave her lassies the play[2] immediately, so that the news of Charles's return was spread by them like wild-fire, and there was a wonderful joy in the whole town. When Charles had seen his mother, and his sister Effie, with that douce and well-mannered lad William, his brother, for of their meeting I cannot speak, not being present, he then came with his friend to see me at the Manse, and was most jocose with me, and in a way of great pleasance, got Mrs Balwhidder to ask his friend to sleep at the Manse. In short, we had just a ploy[3] the whole two days they staid with us, and I got leave from Lord Eglesham's steward to let them shoot on my lord's land, and I believe every laddie wean in the parish attended them to the field. As for old Lady Macadam, Charles being, as she said, a near relation, and she having likewise some knowledge of his comrade's family, she was just in her element with them, though they were but youths, for she was a woman naturally of a fantastical,[4] and, as I have narrated, given to comical devices and pranks to a degree. She made for them a ball, to which she invited all the bonniest lassies, far and near, in the parish, and was out of the body[5] with mirth, and had a fiddler from Irville; and it was thought by those that were there, that had she not been crippled with the rheumatics, she would have danced herself. But I was concerned to hear both Charles and his friend, like hungry hawks, rejoicing at the prospect of the war, hoping thereby, as soon as their midship term was out, to be made lieutenants; saving this, there was no allay in the happiness they brought with them to the parish, and it was a delight to see how auld and young of all degrees made of Charles, for we were proud of him, and none more than myself, though he began to take liberties with me, calling me old governor; it was, however, in a warm-hearted manner, only I did not like it when any of the elders heard. As for his mother, she deported herself like a saint on the occasion.

There was a temperance in the pleasure of her heart, and in her thankfulness, that is past the compass of words to describe. Even Lady Macadam, who never could think a serious thought all her days, said, in her wild way, that the gods had bestowed more care in the making of Mrs Malcolm's temper, than on the bodies and souls of all the saints in the calendar. On the Sunday the strangers attended divine worship, and I preached a sermon purposely for them, and enlarged at great length and fullness on how David overcame Goliah; and they both told me that they had never heard such a good discourse, but I do not think they were great judges of preachings. How, indeed, could Mr Howard know any thing of sound doctrine, being educated, as he told me, at Eton school, a prelatic establishment. Nevertheless, he was a fine lad, and though a little given to frolic and diversion, he had a principle of integrity, that afterwards kithed[1] into much virtue; for, during this visit, he took a notion of Effie Malcolm, and the lassie of him, then a sprightly and blooming creature, fair to look upon, and blithe to see; and he kept up a correspondence with her till the war was over, when, being a captain of a frigate, he came down among us, and they were married by me, as shall be related in its proper place.

CHAPTER XVIII · YEAR 1777

Old Widow Mirkland · Bloody accounts of the war ·
He gets a newspaper · Great flood

THIS may well be called the year of the heavy heart, for we had sad tidings of the lads that went away as soldiers to America. First, there was a boding in the minds of all their friends that they were never to see them more, and their sadness, like a mist spreading from the waters and covering the fields, darkened the spirit of the neighbours. Secondly, a sound[1] was bruited[2] about, that the King's forces would have a hot and a sore struggle before the rebels were put down, if they were ever put down. Then came the cruel truth of all the poor lads' friends had feared; but it is fit and proper that I should relate at length, under their several heads, the sorrows and afflictions as they came to pass.

One evening, as I was taking my walk alone, meditating my discourse for the next Sabbath—it was shortly after Candlemas—it was a fine clear frosty evening, just as the sun was setting. Taking my walk alone, and thinking of the dreadfulness of Almighty Power, and how that if it was not tempered and restrained by infinite goodness, and wisdom, and mercy, the miserable sinner man, and all things that live, would be in a woeful state, I drew near the beild[3] where old widow Mirkland lived by herself, who was grandmother to Jock Hempy, the ramplor[4] lad that was the second who took on for a soldier. I did not mind of this at the time, but passing the house, I heard the croon,[5] as it were, of a laden soul, busy with the Lord, and, not to disturb the holy workings of grace, I paused, and listened. It was old Mizy Mirkland herself, sitting at the gable of the house, looking at the sun setting in all his glory behind the Arran hills; but she was not praying—only moaning to herself,—an oozing out, as it might be called, of the spirit from her heart, then grievously oppressed with sorrow, and heavy bodements of grey-hairs and poverty.—'Yonder it slips awa',' she was saying, 'and my poor bairn, that's o'er the seas in America, is maybe looking on its bright face, thinking of his hame, and aiblins[1] of me, that did my best to breed him up in the fear of the Lord; but I couldna warsle[2] wi' what was ordained. Ay, Jock! as ye look at the sun gaun down, as many a time, when ye were a wee innocent laddie at my knee here, I hae bade ye look at him as a type of your Maker, you will hae a sore heart; for ye hae left me in my need, when ye should hae been near at hand to help me, for the hard labour and industry with which I brought you up. But it's the Lord's will,—blessed be the name of the Lord, that makes us to thole[3] the tribulations of this world, and will reward us, through the mediation of Jesus, hereafter.' She wept bitterly as she said this, for her heart was tried, but the blessing of a religious contentment was shed upon her; and I stepped up to her, and asked about her concerns, for, saving as a parishioner, and a decent old woman, I knew little of her. Brief was her story, but if was one of misfortune.—'But I will not complain,' she said, 'of the measure that has been meted unto me. I was left myself an orphan; when I grew up, and was married to my gudeman, I had known but scant and want. Our days of felicity were few, and he was ta'en awa' from me shortly after my Mary was born—a wailing baby, and a widow's heart, was a' he left me. I nursed her with my salt tears, and bred her in straits, but the favour of God was with us, and she grew up to womanhood, as lovely as the rose, and as blameless as the lilly. In her time she was married to a farming lad; there never was a brawer pair in the kirk, than on that day when they gaed there first as man and wife. My heart was proud, and it pleased the Lord to chastize my pride—to nip my happiness even in the bud. The very next day he got his arm crushed. It never got well again, and he fell into a decay, and died in the winter, leaving my Mary far on in the road to be a mother.

'When her time drew near, we both happened to be working in the yard. She was delving to plant potatoes, and I told her it would do her hurt, but she was eager to provide something, as she said, for what might happen. O, it was an ill-omened word. The same night her trouble came on, and before the morning she was a cauld[1] corpse, and another wee wee fatherless baby was greeting[2] at my bosom—It was him that's noo awa' in America. He grew up to be a fine bairn, with a warm heart, but a light head, and, wanting the rein of a father's power upon him, was no sae douce[3] as I could have wished; but he was no man's foe save his own. I thought, and hoped, as he grew to years of discretion, he would have sobered, and been a consolation to my old age; but he's gone, and he'll never come back—disappointment is my portion in this world, and I have no hope; while I can do, I will seek no help, but threescore and fifteen can do little, and a small ail is a great evil to an aged woman, who has but the distaff for her breadwinner.'

I did all that I could to bid her be of good cheer, but the comfort of a hopeful spirit was dead within her; and she told me, that by many tokens she was assured, her bairn was already slain.—'Thrice,' said she, 'I have seen his wraith—The first time he was in the pride of his young manhood, the next he was pale and wan, with a bloody and a gashy wound in his side, and the third time there was a smoke, and when it cleared away, I saw him in a grave, with neither winding-sheet nor coffin.'

The tale of this pious and resigned spirit dwelt in mine ear, and when I went home, Mrs Balwhidder thought that I had met with an o'ercome,[4] and was very uneasy; so she got the tea soon ready to make me better, but scarcely had we tasted the first cup when a loud lamentation was heard in the kitchen.

This was from that tawpy[1] the wife of Thomas Wilson, with her three weans. They had been seeking their meat among the farmer houses, and, in coming home, forgathered on the road with the Glasgow carrier, who told them, that news had come in the London Gazette, of a battle, in which the regiment that Thomas had listed in was engaged, and had suffered loss both in rank and file;[2] none doubting that their head was in the number of the slain, the whole family grat[3] aloud, and came to the Manse, bewailing him as no more; and it afterwards turned out to be the case, making it plain to me that there is a far-seeing discernment in the spirit, that reaches beyond the scope of our incarnate senses.

But the weight of the war did not end with these afflictions; for, instead of the sorrow that the listing caused, and the anxiety after, and the grief of the bloody tidings, operating as wholesome admonition to our young men, the natural perversity of the human heart was more and more manifested. A wonderful interest was raised among us all to hear of what was going on in the world, insomuch, that I myself was no longer contented with the relation of the news of the month in the Scots Magazine, but joined with my father-in-law, Mr Kibbock, to get a newspaper twice a-week[4] from Edinburgh. As for Lady Macadam, who being naturally an impatient woman, she had one sent to her three times a-week from London, so that we had something fresh five times every week; and the old papers were lent out to the families who had friends in the wars. This was done on my suggestion, hoping it would make all content with their peaceable lot, but dominion for a time had been given to the power of contrariness, and it had quite an opposite effect. It begot a curiosity, egging on to enterprize, and, greatly to my sorrow, three of the brawest lads in the parish, or in any parish, all in one day took on with a party of the Scots Greys that were then lying in Ayr; and nothing would satisfy the callans[5] at Mr Loremore's school, but, instead of their innocent plays with girs[6] and shintys,[1] and sicklike,[2] they must go ranking like soldiers, and fight sham-fights in bodies. In short, things grew to a perfect hostility, for a swarm of weans came out from the schools of Irville on a Saturday afternoon, and, forgathering with ours, they had a battle with stones on the toll-road, such as was dreadful to hear of, for many a one got a mark that day he will take to the grave with him.

It was not, however, by accidents of the field only, that we were afflicted; those of the flood, too, were sent likewise against us. In the month of October, when the corn was yet in the holms,[3] and on the cold land by the river side, the water of Irville swelled to a great speat,[4] from bank to brae, sweeping all before it, and roaring, in its might, like an agent of divine displeasure, sent forth to punish the inhabitants of the earth. The loss of the victual was a thing reparable, and those that suffered did not greatly complain; for, in other respects, their harvest had been plenteous; but the river, in its fury, not content with overflowing the lands, burst through the sandy hills with a raging force, and a riving asunder of the solid ground, as when the fountains of the great deep were broken up. All in the parish was a-foot, and on the hills, some weeping and wringing their hands, not knowing what would happen, when they beheld the landmarks of the waters deserted, and the river breaking away through the country, like the war-horse set loose in his pasture, and glorying in his might.[5] By this change in the way and channel of the river, all the mills in our parish were left more than half a mile from dam or lade;[6] and the farmers, through the whole winter, till the new mills were built, had to travel through a heavy road with their victual, which was a great grievance, and added not a little to the afflictions of this unhappy year, which to me were not without a particularity, by the death of a full cousin of Mrs Balwhidder, my first wife; she was grievously burnt by looting[7] over a candle. Her mutch,[8] which was of the high structure then in vogue, took fire, and being fastened with corking pins[1] to a great toupee,[2] it could not be got off until she had sustained a deadly injury, of which, after lingering long, she was kindly eased by her removal from trouble. This sore accident was to me a matter of deep concern and cogitation; but as it happened in Tarbolton, and no in our parish, I have only alluded to it to shew, that when my people were chastised by the hand of Providence, their pastor was not spared, but had a drop from the same vial.

CHAPTER XIX · YEAR 1778

Revival of the smuggling trade · Betty and Janet
Pawkie, and Robin Bicker, an exciseman, come to
the parish · Their doings · Robin is succeeded by
Mungo Argyle · Lord Eglesham assists William
Malcolm

THIS year was as the shadow of the bygane;[1] there was less actual suffering, but what we came through cast a gloom among us, and we did not get up our spirits till the spring was far advanced; the corn was in the ear, and the sun far towards Midsummer height, before there was any regular shew of gladness in the parish.

It was clear to me that the wars were not to be soon over, for I noticed, in the course of this year, that there was a greater christening of lad bairns, than had ever been in any year during my incumbency; and grave and wise persons, observant of the signs of the times, said, that it had been long held as a sure prognostication of war, when the births of male children outnumbered that of females.

Our chief misfortune in this year, was a revival of that wicked mother of many mischiefs, the smuggling trade, which concerned me greatly; but it was not allowed to it to make any thing like a permanent stay among us, though in some of the neighbouring parishes, its ravages, both in morals and property, was very distressing, and many a mailing[2] was sold to pay for the triumphs of the cutters[3] and gaugers;[4] for the government was by this time grown more eager, and the war caused the King's ships to be out and about, which increased the trouble of the smugglers,

whose wits in their turn were thereby much sharp-
ened.

After Mrs Malcolm, by the settlement of Captain Macadam, had given up her dealing,[1] two maiden-women, that
were sisters, Betty and Janet Pawkie,[2] came in among us from
Ayr, where they had friends in league with some of the laigh[3]
land folk, that carried on the contraband with the Isle of Man,
which was the very eye of the smuggling. They took up the
tea-selling, which Mrs Malcolm had dropped, and did business on a larger scale, having a general huxtry,[4] with parliament-cakes,[5] and candles, and pincushions, as well as other
groceries, in their window. Whether they had any contraband
dealings, or were only back-bitten,[6] I cannot take it upon me
to say, but it was jealoused[7] in the parish, that the meal in the
sacks, that came to their door at night, and was sent to the
Glasgow market in the morning, was not made of corn. They
were, however, decent women, both sedate and orderly; the
eldest, Betty Pawkie, was of a manly stature, and had a long
beard, which made her have a coarse look, but she was, nevertheless, a worthy, well-doing creature, and, at her death, she
left ten pounds to the poor of the parish, as may be seen in the
mortification board, that the Session put up in the kirk as a
testification and an example.

Shortly after the revival of the smuggling, an exciseman
was put among us, and the first was Robin Bicker, a very
civil lad, that had been a flunkie with Sir Hugh Montgomerie,[8]
when he was a residenter in Edinburgh, before the old Sir
Hugh's death. He was a queer[9] fellow, and had a coothy[10]
way of getting in about folk, the which was very serviceable
to him in his vocation; nor was he overly gleg,[11] but when
a job was ill done, and he was obliged to notice it, he would
often break out on the smugglers for being so stupid, so that
for an exciseman he was wonderful well liked, and did not
object to a waught[12] of brandy at a time, when the auld
wives ca'd it well-water. It happened, however, that some

unneighbourly person sent him notice of a clecking[1] of tea
chests, or brandy kegs, at which both Jenny and Betty Pawkie
were the howdies.[2] Robin could not but therefore enter their
house; however, before going in, he just cried at the door to
somebody on the road, so as to let the twa industrious lassies
hear he was at hand. They were not slack in closing the trance-
door,[3] and putting stoups[4] and stools behind it, so as to cause
trouble, and give time before any body could get in. They
then emptied their chaff-bed,[5] and filled the tikeing[6] with tea,
and Betty went in on the top, covering herself with the blanket,
and graining[7] like a woman in labour. It was thought that
Robin Bicker himself would not have been overly particular
in searching the house, considering there was a woman
seemingly in the dead thraws;[8] but a sorner,[9] an incomer from
the east country, and that hung about the change-house as a
divor[10] hostler, that would rather gang[11] a day's journey in
the dark than turn a spade in day-light, came to him as he stood
at the door, and went in with him to see the sport. Robin, for
some reason, could not bid him go away, and both Betty and
Janet were sure he was in the plot against them; indeed, it was
always thought he was an informer, and no doubt he was something not canny,[12] for he had a down[13] look.

It was some time before the door-way was cleared of the
stoups and stools, and Janet was in great concern, and
flustered, as she said, for her poor sister, who was taken with
a heart-cholic. 'I'm sorry for her,' said Robin, 'but I'll be as
quiet as possible;' and so he searched all the house, but found
nothing, at the which his companion, the divor east-country
hostler, swore an oath that could not be misunderstood, so,
without more ado, but as all thought against the grain, Robin
went up to sympathize with Betty in the bed, whose groans
were loud and vehement. 'Let me feel your pulse,' said Robin,
and he looted[14] down as she put forth her arm from aneath the
clothes, and laying his hand on the bed, cried, 'Hey! what's
this? this is a costly filling.' Upon which Betty jumpet up quite

recovered, and Janet fell to the wailing and railing, while the hostler from the east country took the bed of tea on his back, to carry it to the change-house, till a cart was gotten to take it into the custom-house at Irville.

Betty Pawkie being thus suddenly cured, and grudging the loss of property, took a knife in her hand, and as the divor was crossing the burn at the stepping-stones, that lead to the back of the change-house, she ran after him, and ripped up the tikeing, and sent all the tea floating away on the burn, which was thought a brave action of Betty, and the story not a little helped to lighten our melancholy meditations.

Robin Bicker was soon after this affair removed to another district, and we got in his place one Mungo Argyle, who was as proud as a provost, being come of Highland parentage. Black was the hour he came among my people, for he was needy and greedy, and rode on the top of[1] his commission. Of all the manifold ills in the train of smuggling, surely the excisemen are the worst, and the setting of this rabiator[2] over us was a severe judgment for our sins. But he suffered for't, and peace be with him in the grave, where the wicked cease from troubling.[3]

Willie Malcolm, the youngest son of his mother, had by this time learnt all that Mr Loremore, the schoolmaster, could teach, and, as it was evidenced to every body, by his mild manners and saintliness of demeanour, that he was a chosen vessel,[4] his mother longed to fulfil his own wish, which was doubtless the natural working of the act of grace that had been shed upon him; but she had not the wherewithal to send him to the college of Glasgow, where he was desirous to study, and her just pride would not allow her to cess[5] his brother-in-law, the Captain Macadam, whom, I should now mention, was raised, in the end of this year, as we read in the news-papers, to be a Major. I thought her in this somewhat un-reasonable, for she would not be persuaded to let me write to the Captain; but when I reflected on the good that Willie

Malcolm might in time do as a preacher, I said nothing more
to her, but indited a letter to the Lord Eglesham, setting forth
the lad's parts, telling who he was, and all about his mother's
scruples; and, by the retour of the post from London, his
lordship sent me an order on his steward, to pay me twenty
pounds[1] towards equipping my protegée, as he called Willie,
with a promise to pay for his education, which was such a great
thing for his lordship to do off-hand[2] on my recommendation,
that it won him much affection throughout the country side;
and folk began to wonder, rehearsing the great things, as was
said, that I had gotten my lord at different times, and on
divers occasions, to do, which had a vast of influence among
my brethren of the presbytery, and they grew into a state of
greater cordiality with me, looking on me as a man having
authority; but I was none thereat lifted up, for not being
gifted with the power of a kirk-filling eloquence, I was but
little sought for at sacraments and fasts, and solemn days,
which was doubtless well ordained, for I had no motive to seek
fame in foreign[3] pulpits, but was left to walk in the paths of
simplicity within my own parish. To eschew evil myself, and
to teach others to do the same, I thought the main duties of
the pastoral office, and with a sincere heart endeavoured what
in me lay to perform them with meekness, sobriety, and a
spirit wakeful to the inroads of sin and Satan. But O the
sordidness of human nature!—The kindness of the Lord
Eglesham's own disposition, was ascribed to my influence,
and many a dry answer I was obliged to give to applicants that
would have me trouble his lordship, as if I had a claim upon
him. In the ensuing year, the notion of my cordiality with him
came to a great head, and brought about an event, that could
not have been forethought by me as a thing within the compass
of possibility to bring to pass.

CHAPTER XX · YEAR 1779

*He goes to Edinburgh to attend the General
Assembly[1] · Preaches before the Commissioner*

―――――――

I WAS named in this year for the General Assembly, and
Mrs Balwhidder, by her continual thrift, having made our
purse able to stand a shake against the wind, we resolved to
go into Edinburgh in a creditable manner. Accordingly, in
conjunct with Mrs Dalrymple, the lady of a Major of that
name, we hired the Irville chaise, and we put up in Glasgow
at the Black Boy, where we staid all night. Next morning, by
seven o'clock, we got into the fly[2] coach for the capital of
Scotland; which we reached after a heavy journey, about the
same hour in the evening, and put up at the public where it
stopped, till the next day; for really both me and Mrs Balwhidder were worn out with the undertaking, and found a cup
of tea a vast refreshment.

Betimes, in the morning, having taken our breakfast, we
got a caddy[3] to guide us and our wallise to widow M'Vicar's,
at the head of the Covenanter's Close.[4] She was a relation to my
first wife, Betty Lanshaw, my own full cousin that was, and
we had advised her, by course of post, of our coming, and
intendment to lodge with her, as uncos[5] and strangers. But
Mrs M'Vicar kept a cloth shop, and sold plaidings and flannels,
besides Yorkshire superfines, and was used to the sudden
incoming of strangers, especially visitants, both from the
West and the North Highlands, and was withal a gawsy
furthy[6] woman, taking great pleasure in hospitality, and every
sort of kindliness and discretion. She would not allow of such
a thing as our being lodgers in her house, but was so cagey[7] to

see us, and to have it in her power to be civil to a minister, as
she was pleased to say, of such repute, that nothing less would
content her, but that we must live upon her, and partake of
all the best that could be gotten for us within the walls of 'the
gude town.'

When we found ourselves so comfortable, Mrs Balwhidder
and me waited on my patron's family, that was, the young
ladies, and the laird, who had been my pupil, but was now an
advocate high in the law. They likewise were kind also. In
short, every body in Edinburgh were in a manner wearisome
kind, and we could scarcely find time to see the Castle and the
palace of Holyrood-house, and that more sanctified place,[1]
where that Maccabeus of the Kirk of Scotland, John Knox,
was wont to live.

Upon my introduction to his Grace the Commissioner,[2]
I was delighted and surprised to find the Lord Eglesham at the
levee, and his lordship was so glad on seeing me, that he made
me more kentspeckle[3] than I could have wished to have been
in his Grace's presence; for, owing to the same, I was required
to preach before his Grace, upon a jocose recommendation of
his lordship; the which gave me great concern, and daunted
me, so that in the interim I was almost bereft of all peace and
studious composure of mind. Fain would I have eschewed
the honour that was thus thrust upon me, but both my wife
and Mrs M'Vicar were just lifted out of themselves with the
thought.

When the day came, I thought all things in this world were
loosened from their hold, and that the sure and steadfast
earth[4] itself was grown coggly[5] beneath my feet, as I mounted
the pulpit. With what sincerity I prayed for help that day,
and never stood man more in need of it, for through all my
prayer the congregation was so watchful and still, doubtless
to note if my doctrine was orthodox, that the beating of my
heart might have been heard to the uttermost corners of the
kirk.

I had chosen as my text, from Second Samuel, xixth chapter, and 35th verse, these words—'Can I hear any more the voice of singing men and singing women? Wherefore, then, should thy servant be yet a burden to the King.' And hardly had I with a trembling voice read the words, when I perceived an awful stir in the congregation, for all applied the words to the state of the church, and the appointment of his Grace the Commissioner. Having paused after giving out the text, the same fearful and critical silence again ensued, and every eye was so fixed upon me, that I was for a time deprived of courage to look about; but Heaven was pleased to compassionate my infirmity, and as I proceeded, I began to warm as in my own pulpit. I described the gorgeous Babylonian harlot riding forth in her chariots of gold and silver, with trampling steeds, and a hurricane of followers, drunk with the cup of abominations, all shouting with revelry, and glorying in her triumph, treading down in their career those precious pearls, the saints and martyrs, into the mire beneath their swinish feet.[1] 'Before her you may behold Wantonness playing the tinkling cymbal, Insolence beating the drum, and Pride blowing the trumpet. Every vice is there with his emblems, and the seller of pardons, with his crucifix and triple crown, is distributing his largess of perdition. The voices of men shout to set wide the gates, to give entrance to the Queen of nations, and the gates are set wide, and they all enter. The avenging gates close on them— they are all shut up in hell.'

There was a sough[2] in the kirk as I said these words, for the vision I described seemed to be passing before me as I spoke, and I felt as if I had witnessed the everlasting destruction of Antichrist, and the worshippers of the beast. But soon recovering myself, I said, in a soft and gentle manner, 'Look at yon lovely creature in virgin-raiment, with the Bible in her hand. See how mildly she walks along, giving alms to the poor as she passes on towards the door of that lowly dwelling—Let us follow her in—She takes her seat in the chair at the bed-side of the poor old dying sinner, and as he tosses in the height of penitence and despair, she reads to him the promise of the Saviour.—'This night thou shalt be with me in Paradise;' and he embraces her with transports, and falling back on his pillow, calmly closes his eyes in peace. She is the true religion; and when I see what she can do even in the last moments of the guilty, well may we exclaim, when we think of the symbols and pageantry of the departed superstition, Can I hear any more the voice of singing men and singing women? No; let us cling to the simplicity of the Truth that is now established in our native land.'

At the conclusion of this clause of my discourse, the congregation, which had been all so still and so solemn, never coughing, as was often the case among my people, gave a great rustle, changing their positions, by which I was almost overcome; however, I took heart, and ventured on, and pointed out, that with our Bible and an orthodox priesthood, we stood in no need of the King's authority, however bound we were in temporal things to respect it, and I shewed this at some length, crying out, in the words of my text, 'Wherefore, then, should thy servant be yet a burden to the King?' in the saying of which I happened to turn my eyes towards his Grace the Commissioner, as he sat on the throne, and I thought his countenance was troubled, which made me add, that he might not think I meant him any offence, That the King of the Church was one before whom the great, and the wise, and the good,—all doomed and sentenced convicts—implore his mercy. 'It is true,' said I, 'that in the days of his tribulation he was wounded for our iniquities, and died to save us; but, at his death, his greatness was proclaimed by the quick and the dead. There was sorrow, and there was wonder, and there was rage, and there was remorse; but there was no shame there—none blushed on that day at that sight but yon glorious luminary.' The congregation rose, and looked round, as the sun that I pointed at shone in at the window. I was disconcerted by their movement, and my spirit was spent, so that I could say no more.

When I came down from the pulpit, there was a great pressing in of acquaintance and ministers, who lauded me exceedingly; but I thought it could be only in derision, therefore I slipped home to Mrs M'Vicar's as fast as I could.

Mrs M'Vicar, who was a clever, hearing-all sort of a neighbour, said my sermon was greatly thought of, and that I had surprised every body; but I was fearful there was something of jocularity at the bottom of this, for she was a flaunty[1] woman, and liked well to give a good-humoured jibe or jeer. However, his Grace the Commissioner was very thankful for the discourse, and complimented me on what he called my apostolical earnestness; but he was a courteous man, and I could not trust to him, especially as my Lord Eglesham had told me in secrecy before—it's true, it was in his gallanting way,—that, in speaking of the King's servant as I had done, I had rather gone beyond the bounds of modern moderation. Altogether, I found neither pleasure nor profit in what was thought so great an honour, but longed for the privacy of my own narrow pasture, and little flock.

It was in this visit to Edinburgh that Mrs Balwhidder bought her silver tea-pot, and other ornamental articles; but this was not done, as she assured me, in a vain spirit of bravery, which I could not have abided, but because it was well known, that tea draws better in a silver pot, and drinks pleasanter in a china cup, than out of any other kind of cup or tea-pot.

By the time I got home to the Manse, I had been three whole weeks and five days absent, which was more than all my absences together, from the time of my placing, and my people were glowing with satisfaction, when they saw us driving in a Glasgow chaise through the clachan to the Manse.

The rest of the year was merely a quiet succession of small incidents, none of which are worthy of notation, though they were all severally, no doubt, of aught[2] somewhere, as they took up both time and place in the coming to pass, and nothing comes to pass without helping onwards some great end; each particular little thing that happens in the world, being a seed sown by the hand of Providence to yield an increase, which increase is destined, in its turn, to minister to some higher purpose, until at last the issue affects the whole earth. There is nothing in all the world that doth not advance the cause of goodness; no, not even the sins of the wicked, though through the dim casement of her mortal tabernacle, the soul of man cannot discern the method thereof.

Lord George Gordon · Report of an illumination

―――――

THIS was, among ourselves, another year of few events. A sound, it is true, came among us of a design on the part of government in London, to bring back the old harlotry of papistry; but we spent our time in the lea of the hedge, and the lown[1] of the hill. Some there were that a panic seized upon, when they heard of Lord George Gordon,[2] that zealous protestant, being committed to the Tower; but for my part, I had no terror upon me, for I saw all things around me going forward improving, and I said to myself, it is not so when Providence permits scathe and sorrow to fall upon a nation. Civil troubles, and the casting down of thrones, is always forewarned by want and poverty striking the people. What I have, therefore, chiefly to record as the memorables of this year, are things of small import,—the main of which are, that some of the neighbouring lairds, taking example by Mr Kibbock, my father-in-law that was, began in this fall to plant the tops of their hills with mounts of fir-trees; and Mungo Argyle, the exciseman, just herried[3] the poor smugglers to death, and made a power of prize-money, which, however, had not the wonted effect of riches; for it brought him no honour, and he lived in the parish like a leper, or any other kind of ex-communicated person.

But I should not forget a most droll thing that took place with Jenny Gaffaw, and her daughter. They had been missed from the parish for some days, and folk began to be uneasy about what could have become of the two silly creatures; till one night, at the dead hour, a strange light was seen beaming and burning at the window of the bit hole[1] where they lived. It was first observed by Lady Macadam, who never went to bed at any Christian hour, but sat up reading her new French novels and play books with Miss Sabrina, the schoolmistress. She gave the alarm, thinking that such a great and continuous light from a lone house, where never candle had been seen before, could be nothing less than the flame of a burning. And sending Miss Sabrina and the servants to see what was the matter, they beheld daft Jenny, and her as daft daughter, with a score of candle doups,[2] (Heaven only knows where they got them!) placed in the window, and the twa fools dancing, and linking,[3] and admiring before the door. 'What's all this about, Jenny,' said Miss Sabrina.—'Awa' wi' you, awa' wi' you—ye wicked pope, ye whore of Babylon—Is na it for the glory of God, and the Protestant religion? d'ye think I will be a pope as long as light can put out darkness?'—And with that the mother and daughter began again to leap and dance as madly as before.

It seems, that poor Jenny having heard of the luminations that were lighted up through the country, on the ending of the Popish Bill, had, with Meg, travelled by themselves into Glasgow, where they had gathered or begged a stock of candles, and coming back under the cloud of night, had surprised and alarmed the whole clachan, by lighting up their window in the manner that I have described. Poor Miss Sabrina, at Jenny's uncivil salutation, went back to my lady with her heart full, and would fain have had the idiots brought to task before the Session, for what had been said to her. But I would not hear tell of such a thing, for which Miss Sabrina owed me a grudge, that was not soon given up. At the same time, I was grieved to see the testimonies of joyfulness for a holy victory, brought into such disrepute by the ill-timed demonstrations of the two irreclaimable naturals, that had not a true conception of the cause for which they were triumphing.

CHAPTER XXII · YEAR 1781

Argyle, the exciseman, grows a gentleman · Lord Eglesham's concubine · His death · The parish children afflicted with the measles

━━━━━

IF the two last years passed o'er the heads of me and my people without any manifest dolour, which is a great thing to say for so long a period in this world, we had our own trials and tribulations in the one of which I have now to make mention. Mungo Argyle, the exciseman, waxing rich, grew proud and petulant, and would have ruled the country side with a rod of iron.[1] Nothing less would serve him than a fine horse to ride on, and a world of other conveniencies and luxuries, as if he had been on an equality with gentlemen. And he bought a grand gun, which was called a fowling-piece; and he had two pointer dogs,[2] the like of which had not been seen in the parish since the planting of the Eglesham-wood on the moorland, which was four years before I got the call. Every body said the man was fay,[3] and truly, when I remarked him so gallant and gay on the Sabbath at the kirk, and noted his glowing face and his gleg[4] e'en, I thought at times there was something no canny[5] about him. It was, indeed, clear to be seen, that the man was hurried out of himself, but nobody could have thought that the death he was to dree,[6] would have been what it was.

About the end of summer, my Lord Eglesham came to the castle, bringing with him an English madam, that was his Miss.[7] Some days after he came down from London, as he was riding past the Manse, his lordship stopped to inquire for my health, and I went to the door to speak to him. I thought that he did not meet me with that blithe countenance he was wont, and in going away, he said with a blush, 'I fear I dare not ask you to come to the castle.' I had heard of his concubine, and I said, 'In saying so, my lord, you shew a spark of grace, for it would not become me to see what I have heard; and I am surprised, my lord, you will not rather take a lady of your own.' He looked kindly, but confused, saying, he did not know where to get one; so seeing his shame, and not wishing to put him out of conceit entirely with himself, I replied, 'Na, na, my lord, there's nobody will believe that, for there never was a silly Jock, but there was as silly a Jenny,' at which he laughed heartily, and rode away. But I know not what was in't, I was troubled in mind about him, and thought, as he was riding away, that I would never see him again; and sure enough it so happened,[1] for the next day, being airing in his coach with Miss Spangle, the lady he had brought, he happened to see Mungo Argyle with his dogs and his gun, and my lord being as particular about his game as the other was about boxes of tea and kegs of brandy, he jumped out of the carriage, and run to take the gun. Words passed, and the exciseman shot my lord. Never shall I forget that day; such riding, such running, the whole country side afoot; but the same night my lord breathed his last, and the mad and wild reprobate, that did the deed, was taken up and sent off to Edinburgh. This was a woeful riddance of that oppressor, for my lord was a good landlord and a kind-hearted man; and albeit, though a little thoughtless, was aye ready to make his power, when the way was pointed out, minister to good works. The whole parish mourned for him, and there was not a sorer heart in all its bounds than my own. Never was such a sight seen as his burial: the whole country side was there, and all as solemn as if they had been assembled in the valley of Jehoshaphat in the latter day.[2] The hedges where the funeral was to pass were clad with weans, like bunches of hips and haws,[3] and the kirk-yard was as if all its own dead were risen. Never, do I think, was such a multitude gathered together. Some thought there could not be less than three thousand grown men, besides women and children.

Scarcely was this great public calamity past, for it could be reckoned no less, when one Saturday afternoon, as Miss Sabrina, the schoolmistress, was dining with Lady Macadam, her ladyship was stricken with the paralytics, and her face so thrown[1] in the course of a few minutes, that Miss Sabrina came flying to the Manse for the help and advice of Mrs Balwhidder. A doctor was gotten with all speed by express, but her lady-ship was smitten beyond the reach of medicine. She lived, however, some time after; but O she was such an object, that it was a grief to see her. She could only mutter when she tried to speak, and was as helpless as a baby. Though she never liked me, nor could I say there was many things in her demeanour that pleased me, yet she was a free-handed woman to the needful, and when she died she was more missed than it was thought she could have been.

Shortly after her funeral, which was managed by a gentle-man sent from her friends in Edinburgh, that I wrote to about her condition, the Major, her son, with his lady, Kate Mal-colm, and two pretty bairns, came and stayed in her house for a time, and they were a great happiness to us all, both in the way of drinking tea, and sometimes taking a bit dinner, their only mother now, the worthy and pious Mrs Malcolm, being regularly of the company.

Before the end of the year, I should mention, that the fortune of Mrs Malcolm's family got another shove upwards, by the promotion of her second son, Robert Malcolm, who being grown an expert and careful mariner, was made Captain of a grand ship, whereof Provost Maitland of Glasgow, that was kind to his mother in her distresses, was the owner. But that douce lad Willie, her youngest son, who was at the Uni-versity of Glasgow, under the Lord Eglesham's patronage, was like to have suffered a blight; however, Major Macadam, when I spoke to him anent the young man's loss of his patron, said, with a pleasant generosity, he should not be stickit;[1] and, accordingly, he made up, as far as money could, for the loss of his lordship, but there was none that made up for the great power and influence, which, I have no doubt, the Earl would have exerted in his behalf, when he was ripened for the church. So that, although in time William came out a sound and heart-searching preacher, he was long obliged, like many another unfriended saint, to cultivate sand, and wash Ethiopians in the shape of an east-country gentleman's camstrairy[2] weans; than which, as he wrote me himself, there cannot be on earth a greater trial of temper. However, in the end, he was rewarded, and is not only now a placed minister, but a doctor of divinity.

The death of Lady Macadam was followed by another parochial misfortune, for, considering the time when it happened, we could count it as nothing less: Auld Thomas Howkings, the betherel,[3] fell sick, and died in the course of a week's illness, about the end of November, and the measles coming at that time upon the parish, there was such a smashery[4] of the poor weans, as had not been known for an age; insomuch, that James Banes, the lad who was Thomas Howking's helper, rose in open rebellion against the Session, during his superior's illness, and we were constrained to augment his pay, and to promise him the place, if Thomas did not recover, which it was then thought he could not do. On the day this happened, there were three dead children in the clachan, and a panic and consternation spread about the burial of them, when James Banes's insurrection was known, which made both me and the Session glad to hush up the affair, that the heart of the public might have no more than the sufferings of individuals to hurt it.—Thus ended a year, on many accounts, heavy to be remembered.

News of the victory over the French fleet · He has to inform Mrs Malcolm of the death of her son Charles in the engagement

————

ALTHOUGH I have not been particular in noticing it, from time to time, there had been an occasional going off, at fairs and on market-days, of the lads of the parish as soldiers, and when Captain Malcolm got the command of his ship, no less than four young men sailed with him from the clachan; so that we were deeper and deeper interested in the proceedings of the doleful war, that was raging in the plantations. By one post we heard of no less than three brave fellows belonging to us being slain in one battle, for which there was a loud and general lamentation.

Shortly after this, I got a letter from Charles Malcolm, a very pretty letter it indeed was; he had heard of my Lord Eglesham's murder, and grieved for the loss, both because his lordship was a good man, and because he had been such a friend to him and his family. 'But,' said Charles, 'the best way that I can shew my gratitude for his patronage, is to prove myself a good officer to my King and country.' Which I thought a brave sentiment, and was pleased thereat; for somehow Charles, from the time he brought me the limes to make a bowl of punch, in his pocket from Jamaica, had built a nest of affection in my heart. But, oh! the wicked wastry of life in war. In less than a month after, the news came of a victory over the French fleet,[1] and by the same post I got a letter from Mr Howard, that was the midshipman who came to see us with Charles, telling me that poor Charles had been mortally wounded in the action, and had afterwards died of his wounds. 'He was a hero in the engagement,' said Mr Howard, 'and he died as a good and a brave man should.'— These tidings gave me one of the sorest hearts I ever suffered, and it was long before I could gather fortitude to disclose the tidings to poor Charles's mother. But the callants of the school had heard of the victory, and were going shouting about, and had set the steeple bell a-ringing, by which Mrs Malcolm heard the news; and knowing that Charles's ship was with the fleet, she came over to the Manse in great anxiety, to hear the particulars, somebody telling her that there had been a foreign letter to me by the post-man.

When I saw her I could not speak, but looked at her in pity, and the tear fleeing up into my eyes, she guessed what had happened. After giving a deep and sore sigh, she inquired, 'How did he behave? I hope well, for he was aye a gallant laddie!'—and then she wept very bitterly. However, growing calmer, I read to her the letter, and when I had done, she begged me to give it to her to keep, saying, 'It's all that I have now left of my pretty boy; but it's mair precious to me than the wealth of the Indies;' and she begged me to return thanks to the Lord, for all the comforts and manifold mercies with which her lot had been blessed, since the hour she put her trust in Him alone, and that was when she was left a pennyless widow, with her five fatherless bairns.

It was just an edification of the spirit, to see the Christian resignation of this worthy woman. Mrs Balwhidder was confounded, and said, there was more sorrow in seeing the deep grief of her fortitude, than tongue could tell.

Having taken a glass of wine with her, I walked out to conduct her to her own house, but in the way we met with a severe trial. All the weans were out parading with napkins and kail-blades[1] on sticks, rejoicing and triumphing in the glad tidings of victory. But when they saw me and Mrs Malcolm coming slowly along, they guessed what had happened, and threw away their banners of joy; and, standing all up in a row, with silence and sadness, along the kirk-yard wall as we passed, shewed an instinct of compassion that penetrated to my very soul. The poor mother burst into fresh affliction, and some of the bairns into an audible weeping; and, taking one another by the hand, they followed us to her door, like mourners at a funeral. Never was such a sight seen in any town before. The neighbours came to look at it, as we walked along, and the men turned aside to hide their faces, while the mothers pressed their babies fondlier to their bosoms, and watered their innocent faces with their tears.

I prepared a suitable sermon, taking as the words of my text, 'Howl, ye ships of Tarshish, for your strength is laid waste.'[1] But when I saw around me so many of my people, clad in complimentary mourning for the gallant Charles Malcolm, and that even poor daft Jenny Gaffaw, and her daughter, had on an old black ribbon; and when I thought of him, the spirited laddie, coming home from Jamaica, with his parrot on his shoulder, and his limes for me, my heart filled full, and I was obliged to sit down in the pulpit, and drop a tear.

After a pause, and the Lord having vouchsafed to compose me, I rose up, and gave out that anthem of triumph, the 124th Psalm; the singing of which brought the congregation round to themselves; but still I felt that I could not preach as I had meant to do, therefore I only said a few words of prayer, and singing another psalm, dismissed the congregation.

Janet Gaffaw's death and burial

THIS was another Sabbath year of my ministry. It has left me nothing to record, but a silent increase of prosperity in the parish. I myself had now in the bank more than a thousand pounds,[1] and every thing was thriving around. My two bairns, Gilbert, that is now the merchant in Glasgow, was grown into a sturdy ramplor[2] laddie, and Janet, that is married upon Dr Kittleword, the minister of Swappington, was as fine a lassie for her years, as the eye of a parent could desire to see.

Shortly after the news of the peace, an event at which all gave themselves up to joy, a thing happened among us, that at the time caused much talk; but although very dreadful, was yet not so serious, some how or other, as such an awsome doing should have been. Poor Jenny Gaffaw happened to take a heavy cold, and soon thereafter died. Meg went about from house to house, begging dead-clothes, and got the body straighted[3] in a wonderful decent manner, with a plate of earth and salt[4] placed upon it—an admonitory type of mortality and eternal life, that has ill-advisedly gone out of fashion. When I heard of this, I could not but go to see how a creature that was not thought possessed of a grain of understanding, could have done so much herself. On entering the door, I beheld Meg sitting with two or three of the neighbouring kimmers,[5] and the corpse laid out on a bed. 'Come awa', sir,' said Meg, 'this is an altered house; they're gane[6] that keepit it bein;[7] but, sir, we maun a' come to this—we maun pay the debt o' nature—death is a grim creditor, and a doctor but brittle bail[8] when the hour of reckoning's at han'! What a pity it is, mother, that you're now dead, for here's the minister come to see you. O, sir, but she would have had a proud heart to see you in her dwelling, for she had a genteel turn, and would not let me, her only daughter, mess or mell we the lathron lasses[1] of the clachan. Ay, ay, she brought me up with care, and edicated me for a lady; nae coarse wark darkened my lilly-white hands. But I maun work now, I maun dree[2] the penalty of man.'

Having stopped some time, listening to the curious maunnering[3] of Meg, I rose to come away, but she laid her hand on my arm, saying, 'No, sir, ye maun taste before ye gang! My mother had aye plenty in her life, nor shall her latter day be needy.'

Accordingly, Meg, with all the due formality common on such occasions, produced a bottle of water, and a dram glass, which she filled and tasted, then presented to me, at the same time offering me a bit of bread on a slate. It was a consternation to every body how the daft creature had learnt all the ceremonies, which she performed in a manner past the power of pen to describe, making the solemnity of death, by her strange mockery, a kind of merriment, that was more painful than sorrow; but some spirits are gifted with a faculty of observation, that, by the strength of a little fancy, enables them to make a wonderful and truth-like semblance of things and events, which they never saw, and poor Meg seemed to have this gift.

The same night the Session having provided a coffin, the body was put in, and removed to Mr Mutchkin's brew-house, where the lads and lassies kept the late wake.[4]

Saving this, the year flowed in a calm, and we floated on in the stream of time towards the great ocean of eternity, like ducks and geese in the river's tide, that are carried down without being sensible of the speed of the current. Alas! we have not wings like them, to fly back to the place we set out from.

CHAPTER XXV · YEAR 1784

A Year of sunshine and pleasantness

―――――

I HAVE ever thought, that this was a bright year, truly an An. Dom., for in it many of the lads came home that had listed to be soldiers; and Mr Howard, that was the midshipman, being now a captain of a man of war, came down from England and married Effie Malcolm, and took her up with him to London, where she wrote to her mother, that she found his family people of great note, and more kind to her than she could write. By this time, also, Major Macadam was made a Colonel, and lived with his lady in Edinburgh, where they were much respected by the genteeler classes, Mrs Macadam being considered a great unco[1] among them for all manner of ladylike ornaments, she having been taught every sort of perfection in that way by the old lady, who was educated at the court of France, and was, from her birth, a person of quality. In this year, also, Captain Malcolm, her brother, married a daughter of a Glasgow merchant, so that Mrs Malcolm, in her declining years, had the prospect of a bright setting; but nothing could change the sober Christianity of her settled mind; and although she was strongly invited, both by the Macadams and the Howards, to see their felicity, she ever declined the same, saying— 'No! I have been long out of the world, or rather, I have never been in it; my ways are not as theirs; and although I ken their hearts would be glad to be kind to me, I might fash[2] their servants, or their friends might think me unlike other folk, by which, instead of causing pleasure, mortification might ensue; so I will remain in my own house, trusting that when they can spare the time, they will come and see me.'

There was a spirit of true wisdom in this resolution, for it required a forbearance, that in weaker minds would have relaxed; but though a person of a most slender and delicate frame of body, she was a Judith[1] in fortitude, and in all the fortune that seemed now smiling upon her, she never was lifted up, but bore always that pale and meek look, which gave a saintliness to her endeavours in the days of her suffering and poverty.

But when we enjoy most, we have least to tell. I look back on this year as on a sunny spot in the valley, amidst the shadows of the clouds of time; and I have nothing to record, save the remembrance of welcomings and weddings, and a meeting of bairns and parents, that the wars and the waters had long raged between. Contentment within the bosom, lent a livelier grace to the countenance of Nature, and every body said, that in this year the hedges were greener than common, the gowans[2] brighter on the brae, and the heads of the statelier trees adorned with a richer coronal of leaves and blossoms. All things were animated with the gladness of thankfulness, and testified to the goodness of their Maker.

CHAPTER XXVI · YEAR 1785

*Mr Cayenne comes to the parish · A passionate
character · His outrageous behaviour at the
Session-house*

━━━━━

WELL may we say, in the pious words of my old friend and
neighbour, the Reverend Mr Keekie of Loupinton, that the
world is such a wheel-carriage, that it might very properly
be called the WHIRL'D. This reflection was brought home to
me in a very striking manner, while I was preparing a discourse for my people, to be preached on the anniversary day
of my placing, in which I took a view of what had passed in
the parish during the five-and-twenty years that I had been, by
the grace of God, the pastor thereof. The bairns, that were
bairns when I came among my people, were ripened into
parents, and a new generation was swelling in the bud around
me. But it is what happened that I have to give an account of.

This year the Lady Macadam's jointure-house that was,
having been long without a tenant, a Mr Cayenne[1] and his
family, American loyalists, came and took it, and settled
among us for a time. His wife was a clever woman, and they
had two daughters, Miss Virginia and Miss Carolina; but
he was himself an etter-cap, a perfect spunkie[2] of passion,
as ever was known in town or country. His wife had a terrible
time o't with him, and yet the unhappy man had a great share
of common sense, and, saving the exploits of his unmanageable temper, was an honest and creditable gentleman. Of his
humour we soon had a sample, as I shall relate at length all
about it.

Shortly after he came to the parish, Mrs Balwhidder and me

waited upon the family, to pay our respects, and Mr Cayenne, in a free and hearty manner, insisted on us staying to dinner. His wife, I could see, was not satisfied with this, not being, as I discerned afterwards, prepared to give an entertainment to strangers; however, we fell into the misfortune of staying, and nothing could exceed the happiness of Mr Cayenne. I thought him one of the blithest bodies I had ever seen, and had no notion that he was such a *tap of tow*[1] as in the sequel he proved himself.

As there was something extra to prepare, the dinner was a little longer of being on the table than usual, at which he began to fash,[2] and every now and then took a turn up and down the room, with his hands behind his back, giving a short melancholious whistle. At length the dinner was served, but it was more scanty than he had expected, and this upset his good humour altogether. Scarcely had I asked the blessing when he began to storm at his blackamoor servant, who was, however, used to his way, and did his work without minding him; but by some neglect there was no mustard down, which Mr Cayenne called for in the voice of a tempest, and one of the servant lassies came in with the pot, trembling. It happened that, as it had not been used for a day or two before, the lid was clagged,[3] and, as it were, glewed in, so that Mr Cayenne could not get it out, which put him quite wud,[4] and he attempted to fling it at Sambo, the black lad's head, but it stottit against[5] the wall, and the lid flying open, the whole mustard flew in his own face, which made him a sight not to be spoken of. However it calmed him; but really, as I had never seen such a man before, I could not but consider the accident as a providential reproof, and trembled to think what greater evil might fall out in the hands of a man so left to himself in the intemperance of passion.

But the worst thing about Mr Cayenne was his meddling with matters in which he had no concern, for he had a most irksome nature, and could not be at rest, so that he was truly a thorn in our side.[1] Among other of his strange doings, was the part he took in the proceedings of the Session, with which he had as little to do, in a manner, as the man of the moon; but, having no business in his hands, he attended every sederunt,[2] and from less to more, having no self-government, he began to give his opinion in our deliberations; and often bred us trouble, by causing strife to arise.

It happened, as the time of the summer occasion[3] was drawing near, that it behoved us to make arrangements about the assistance; and upon the suggestion of the elders, to which I paid always the greatest deference, I invited Mr Keekie[4] of Loupinton, who was a sound preacher, and a great expounder of the *kittle*[5] parts of the Old Testament, being a man well versed in the Hebrew and etymologies, for which he was much reverenced by the old people that delighted to search the Scriptures. I had also written to Mr Sprose of Annock, a preacher of another sort, being a vehement and powerful thresher of the word, making the chaff and vain babbling of corrupt commentators to fly from his hand. He was not, however, so well liked, as he wanted that connect[6] method which is needful to the enforcing of doctrine. But he had never been among us, and it was thought it would be a godly treat to the parish to let the people hear him. Besides Mr Sprose, Mr Waikle of Gowanry, a quiet hewer out of the image of holiness in the heart, was likewise invited, all in addition to our old stoops[7] from the adjacent parishes.

None of these three preachers were in any estimation with Mr Cayenne, who had only heard each of them once; and he happening to be present in the Session-house at the time, inquired how we had settled. I thought this not a very orderly question, but I gave him a civil answer, saying, that Mr Keekie of Loupinton would preach on the morning of the fast-day, Mr Sprose of Annock in the afternoon, and Mr Waikle of Gowanry on the Saturday. Never shall I or the elders, while the breath of life is in our bodies, forget the reply. Mr Cayenne struck the table like the clap of thunder, and cried, 'Mr Keekie of Loupinton, and Mr Sprose of Annock, and Mr Waikle of Gowanry, and all such trash, may go to — and be ——!' and out of the house he bounced, like a hand-ball[1] stotting on[2] a stone.

The elders and me were confounded, and for some time we could not speak, but looked at each other, doubtful if our ears heard aright. At long and length I came to myself, and, in the strength of God, took my place at the table, and said, this was an outrageous impiety not to be borne, which all the elders agreed to; and we thereupon came to a resolve, which I dictated myself, wherein we debarred Mr Cayenne from ever after entering, unless summoned, the Session-house, the which resolve we directed the Session-clerk to send to him direct, and thus we vindicated the insulted privileges of the church.

Mr Cayenne had cooled before he got home, and our paper coming to him in his appeased blood, he immediately came to the Manse, and made a contrite apology for his hasty temper, which I reported, in due time and form, to the Session, and there the matter ended. But here was an example plain to be seen of the truth of the old proverb,[3] that as one door shuts another opens; for scarcely were we in quietness by the decease of that old light-headed woman, the Lady Macadam, till a full equivalent for her was given in this hot and fiery Mr Cayenne.

CHAPTER XXVII · YEAR 1786

*Repairs required for the Manse · By the sagacious
management of Mr Kibbock, the heritors are made
to give a new Manse altogether · They begin,
however, to look upon me with a grudge, which
provokes me to claim an augmentation, which I
obtain*

FROM the day of my settlement, I had resolved, in order to
win the affections of my people, and to promote unison among
the heritors, to be of as little expence to the parish as possible;
but by this time the Manse had fallen into a sore state of
decay—the doors were wormed on the hinges—the casements
of the windows chattered all the winter, like the teeth of a
person perishing with cold, so that we had no comfort in the
house; by which, at the urgent instigations of Mrs Balwhidder,
I was obligated to represent our situation to the Session. I
would rather, having so much saved money in the bank, paid
the needful repairs myself, than have done this, but she said it
would be a rank injustice to our own family; and her father,
Mr Kibbock, who was very long-headed,[1] with more than
a common man's portion of understanding, pointed out to
me, that as my life was but in my lip,[2] it would be a wrong
thing towards whomsoever was ordained to be my successor,
to use the heritors to the custom of the minister paying for the
reparations of the Manse, as it might happen he might not
be so well able to afford it as me. So in a manner, by their
persuasion, and the constraint of the justice of the case, I made
a report of the infirmities both of doors and windows, as well as
of the rotten state of the floors, which were constantly in

want of cobbling.[1] Over and above all, I told them of the sarking[2] of the roof, which was as frush[3] as a puddock[4] stool; insomuch, that in every blast, some of the pins lost their grip, and the slates came hurling off.

The heritors were accordingly convened, and, after some deliberation, they proposed that the house should be seen to, and white-washed and painted; and I thought this might do, for I saw they were terrified at the expence of a thorough repair; but when I went home and repeated to Mrs Balwhidder what had been said at the meeting, and my thankfulness at getting the heritors consent to do so much, she was excessively angry, and told me, that all the painting and white-washing in the world would avail nothing, for that the house was as a sepulchre full of rottenness;[5] and she sent for Mr Kibbock, her father, to confer with him on the way of getting the matter put to rights.

Mr Kibbock came, and hearing of what had passed, pondered for some time, and then said, 'All was very right! The minister (meaning me) has just to get tradesmen to look at the house, and write out their opinion of what it needs. There will be plaster to mend; so, before painting, he will get a plasterer. There will be a slater wanted; he has just to get a slater's estimate, and a wright's,[6] and so forth, and when all is done, he will lay them before the Session and the heritors, who, no doubt, will direct the reparations to go forward.'

This was very pawkie[7] counselling of Mr Kibbock, but I did not see through it at the time, but did as he recommended, and took all the different estimates, when they came in, to the Session. The elders commended my prudence exceedingly for so doing, before going to work; and one of them asked me what the amount of the whole would be, but I had not cast[8] it up. Some of the heritors thought that a hundred pounds would be sufficient for the outlay, but judge of our consternation, when, in counting up all the sums of the different estimates together, we found them well on towards a thousand

pounds. 'Better big[1] a new house at once, than do this!' cried
all the elders, by which I then perceived the draughtiness[2] of
Mr Kibbock's advice. Accordingly, another meeting of the
heritors was summoned, and, after a great deal of controversy,
it was agreed, that a new Manse should be erected; and,
shortly after, we contracted with Thomas Trowel, the mason,
to build one for six hundred pounds, with all the requisite
appurtenances, by which a clear gain was saved to the parish,
by the foresight of Mr Kibbock, to the amount of nearly four
hundred pounds. But the heritors did not mean to have
allowed the sort of repair that his plan comprehended. He
was, however, a far forecasting man, the like of him for natural
parts not being in our country side, and nobody could get the
whip-hand of him, either in a bargain or an improvement,
when he once was sensible of the advantage. He was, indeed,
a blessing to the shire, both by his example as a farmer, and
by his sound and discreet advice in the contentions of his
neighbours, being a man, as was a saying among the commonality, 'wiser than the law and the fifteen Lords of Edinburgh.'[3]

The building of the new Manse occasioned a heavy cess[4] on
the heritors, which made them overly ready to pick holes in
the coats of me and the elders; so that, out of my forbearance
and delicacy in time past, grew a lordliness on their part, that
was an ill return for 'the years that I had endured no little
inconveniency for their sake. It was not in my heart or principles to harm the hair of a dog; but when I discerned the
austerity with which they were disposed to treat their minister,
I bethought me, that, for the preservation of what was due to
the establishment and the upholding of the decent administration of religion, I ought to set my face against the sordid
intolerance by which they were actuated. This notion I
weighed well before divulging it to any person, but when I had
assured myself as to the rectitude thereof, I rode over one day
to Mr Kibbock's, and broke my mind to him about claiming

out of the tiends[1] an augmentation of my stipend, not because I needed it, but in case, after me, some bare and hungry gorbie[2] of the Lord should be sent upon the parish, in no such condition to plea with the heritors as I was. Mr Kibbock highly approved of my intent, and by his help, after much tribulation, I got an augmentation, both in glebe and income; and to mark my reason for what I did, I took upon me to keep and clothe the wives and orphans of the parish, who lost their bread-winners in the American war. But, for all that, the heritors spoke of me as an avaricious Jew, and made the hard won fruits of Mrs Balwhidder's great thrift and good management a matter of reproach against me. Few of them would come to the church, but stayed away, to the detriment of their own souls hereafter, in order, as they thought, to punish me; so that, in the course of this year, there was a visible decay of the sense of religion among the better orders of the parish, and, as will be seen in the sequel, their evil example infected the minds of many of the rising generation.

It was in this year that Mr Cayenne bought the mailing[3] of the Wheatrigs, but did not begin to build his house till the following spring; for being ill to please with a plan, he fell out with the builders, and on one occasion got into such a passion with Mr Trowel the mason, that he struck him a blow in the face, for which he was obligated to make atonement. It was thought the matter would have been carried before the Lords; but, by the mediation of Mr Kibbock, with my helping hand, a reconciliation was brought about, Mr Cayenne indemnifying the mason with a sum of money to say no more anent it; after which, he employed him to build his house, a thing that no man could have thought possible, who reflected on the enmity between them.

Lady Macadam's house is changed into an Inn · The making of jelly becomes common in the parish · Meg Gaffaw is present at a payment of victual · Her behaviour

THERE had been, as I have frequently observed, a visible improvement going on in the parish. From the time of the making of the toll-road, every new house that was built in the clachan was built along that road. Among other changes thereby caused, the Lady Macadam's jointure-house[1] that was, which stood in a pleasant parterre, inclosed within a stone-wall and an iron-gate, having a pillar with a pine-apple head on each side, came to be in the middle of the town. While Mr Cayenne inhabited the same, it was maintained in good order, but on his flitting[2] to his own new house on the Wheatrigs, the parterre was soon overrun with weeds, and it began to wear the look of a waste place. Robert Toddy,[3] who then kept the change-house, and who had from the lady's death rented the coach-house byre for stabling, in this juncture thought of it for an inn; so he set[4] his own house to Thomas Treddles, the weaver, whose son, William, is now the great Glasgow manufacturer, that has cotton-mills and steam-engines; and took 'the Place,' as it was called, and had a fine sign, THE CROSS KEYS, painted and put up in golden characters, by which it became one of the most noted inns any where to be seen; and the civility of Mrs Toddy was commended by all strangers. But although this transmutation from a change-house to an inn was a vast amendment, in a manner, to the parish, there was little amendment of manners thereby, for the farmer lads began to hold dancings, and other riotous proceedings there, and to bring, as it were, the evil practices of towns into the heart of the country. All sort of licence was allowed as to drink and hours, and the edifying example of Mr Mutchkins, and his pious family, was no longer held up to the imitation of the wayfaring man.

Saving the mutation of 'the Place' into an inn, nothing very remarkable happened in this year. We got into our new Manse about the middle of March, but it was rather damp, being new plastered, and it caused me to have a severe attack of the rheumatics in the fall of the year.

I should not, in my notations, forget to mark a new luxury that got in among the commonality at this time. By the opening of new roads, and the traffic thereon with carts and carriers, and by our young men that were sailors going to the Clyde, and sailing to Jamaica and the West Indies, heaps of sugar and coffee-beans were brought home, while many, among the kail-stocks[1] and cabbages in their yards, had planted grozet and berry bushes;[2] which two things happening together, the fashion to make jam and jelly, which hitherto had been only known in the kitchens and confectionaries of the gentry, came to be introduced into the clachan. All this, however, was not without a plausible pretext, for it was found that jelly was an excellent medicine for a sore throat, and jam a remedy as good as London candy for a cough, or cold, or a shortness of breath. I could not, however, say, that this gave me so much concern as the smuggling trade, only it occasioned a great fasherie[3] to Mrs Balwhidder; for, in the berry time, there was no end to the borrowing of her brass-pan, to make jelly and jam, till Mrs Toddy, of the Cross Keys, bought one, which, in its turn, came into request, and saved ours.

It was in the Martinmas quarter of this year that I got the first payment of my augmentation. Having no desire to rip up old sores, I shall say no more anent it, the worst being anticipated in my chronicle of the last year; but there was a thing happened in the payment, that occasioned a vexation at the time of a very disagreeable nature. Daft Meg Gaffaw, who, from the tragical death of her mother, was a privileged subject, used to come to the Manse on the Saturdays for a meal of meat; and it so fell out, that as, by some neglect of mine, no steps had been taken to regulate the disposal of the victual that con- stituted the means of the augmentation, some of the heritors, in an ungracious temper, sent what they called the tythe-boll[1] (the Lord knows it was not the fiftieth) to the Manse, where I had no place to put it. This fell out on a Saturday night, when I was busy with my sermon, thinking not of silver or gold, but of much better; so that I was greatly molested and disturbed thereby. Daft Meg, who sat by the kitchen chimlay- lug[2] hearing a', said nothing for a time, but when she saw how Mrs Balwhidder and me were put to, she cried out with a loud voice, like a soul under the inspiration of prophecy—'When the widow's creuse[3] had filled all the vessels in the house, the Lord stopped the increase; verily, verily, I say unto you, if your barns be filled, and your garnel-kests[4] can hold no more, seek till ye shall find the tume[5] basins of the poor, and therein pour the corn, and the oil, and the wine[6] of your abundance; so shall ye be blessed of the Lord.' The which words I took for an admonition, and directing the sacks to be brought into the dining-room, and other chambers of the Manse, I sent off the heritors' servants, that had done me this prejudice, with an unexpected thankfulness. But this, as I afterwards was informed, both them and their masters attributed to the greedy grasp of avarice, with which they considered me as misled; and having said so, nothing could exceed their mor- tification on Monday, when they heard (for they were of those who had deserted the kirk), that I had given by the precentor notice, to every widow in the parish that was in need, to come to the Manse, and she would receive her portion of the par- titioning of the augmentation. Thus, without any offence on my part, saving the strictness of justice, was a division made between me and the heritors; but the people were with me, and my own conscience was with me; and though the fronts of the lofts[1] and the pews of the heritors were but thinly filled, I trusted that a good time was coming, when the gentry would see the error of their way. So I bent the head of resignation to the Lord, and, assisted by the wisdom of Mr Kibbock, adhered to the course I had adopted; but, at the close of the year, my heart was sorrowful for the schism, and my prayer on Hogmanay[2] was one of great bitterness of soul, that such an evil had come to pass.

CHAPTER XXIX · YEAR 1788

*A cotton-mill[1] is built · The new spirit which it
introduces among the people*

———

IT had been often remarked by ingenious men, that the Brawl
burn, which ran through the parish, though a small, was
yet a rapid stream, and had a wonderful capability for dam-
ming, and to turn mills. From the time that the Irville water
deserted its channel this brook grew into repute, and several
mills and dams had been erected on its course. In this year
a proposal came from Glasgow to build a cotton-mill on its
banks, beneath the Witch-linn, which being on a corner
of the Wheatrig, the property of Mr Cayenne, he not only
consented thereto, but took a part in the profit or loss therein;
and, being a man of great activity, though we thought him,
for many a day, a serpent plague[2] sent upon the parish,
he proved thereby one of our greatest benefactors. The
cotton-mill was built, and a spacious fabric it was—nothing
like it had been seen before in our day and generation—
and, for the people that were brought to work in it, a new
town was built in the vicinity, which Mr Cayenne, the same
being founded on his land, called Cayenneville, the name
of the plantation in Virginia that had been taken from him
by the rebellious Americans. From that day Fortune was
lavish of her favours upon him; his property swelled, and
grew in the most extraordinary manner, and the whole
country-side was stirring with a new life. For, when the
mill was set a-going, he got weavers of muslin established
in Cayenneville; and shortly after, but that did not take place
till the year following, he brought women all the way from

the neighbourhood of Manchester in England, to teach the lassie bairns in our old clachan tambouring.[1]

Some of the ancient families, in their turretted houses,[2] were not pleased with this innovation, especially when they saw the handsome dwellings that were built for the weavers of the mills, and the unstinted hand that supplied the wealth required for the carrying on of the business. It sank their pride into insignificance, and many of them would almost rather have wanted the rise that took place in the value of their lands, than have seen this incoming of what they called o'er-sea speculation. But, saving the building of the cotton-mill, and the beginning of Cayenneville, nothing more memorable happened in this year, still it was nevertheless a year of a great activity. The minds of men were excited to new enterprizes; a new genius, as it were, had descended upon the earth, and there was an erect and out-looking spirit abroad that was not to be satisfied with the taciturn regularity of ancient affairs. Even Miss Sabrina Hookie, the schoolmistress, though now waned from her meridian, was touched with the enlivening rod, and set herself to learn and to teach tambouring, in such a manner as to supersede by precept and example that old time-honoured functionary, as she herself called it, the spinning-wheel, proving, as she did one night, to Mr Kibbock and me, that, if more money could be made by a woman tambouring than by spinning, it was better for her to tambour than to spin.

But, in the midst of all this commercing and manufacturing, I began to discover signs of decay in the wonted simplicity of our country ways. Among the cotton-spinners and muslin-weavers of Cayenneville, were several unsatisfied and ambitious spirits, who clubbed together, and got a London newspaper to the Cross-keys, where they were nightly in the habit of meeting and debating about the affairs of the French, which were then gathering towards a head. They were represented to me as lads by common[3] in capacity, but with unsettled notions of religion. They were, however, quiet and orderly, and some of them since, at Glasgow, Paisley, and Manchester, even, I am told, in London, have grown into a topping[1] way.

It seems they did not like my manner of preaching, and on that account absented themselves from public worship; which, when I heard, I sent for some of them, to convince them of their error, with regard to the truth of divers points of doctrine; but they confounded me with their objections, and used my arguments, which were the old and orthodox proven opinions of the Divinity Hall, as if they had been the light sayings of a vain man. So that I was troubled, fearing that some change would ensue to my people, who had hitherto lived amidst the boughs and branches of the gospel unmolested by the fowler's snare,[2] and I set myself to watch narrowly, and with a vigilant eye, what would come to pass.

There was a visible increase among us of worldly prosperity in the course of this year; insomuch, that some of the farmers who were in the custom of taking their vendibles to the neighbouring towns on the Tuesdays, the Wednesdays, and Fridays, were led to open a market on the Saturdays in our own clachan, the which proved a great convenience. But I cannot take it upon me to say, whether this can be said to have well began in the present Ann. Dom., although I know that in the summer of the ensuing year it was grown into a settled custom; which I well recollect by the Macadams coming with their bairns to see Mrs Malcolm their mother, suddenly on a Saturday afternoon; on which occasion me and Mrs Balwhidder were invited to dine with them, and Mrs Malcolm bought in the market for the dinner that day, both mutton and fowls, such as twenty years before could not have been got for love or money on such a pinch.[3] Besides, she had two bottles of red and white wine from the Cross Keys, luxuries which, saving in the Breadland house in its best days, could not have been had in the whole parish, but must have been brought from a borough town; for Eglesham Castle is not within the bounds of Dalmailing, and my observe[1] does not apply to the stock and stores of that honourable mansion, but only to the dwellings of our own heritors, who were in general straitened in their circumstances, partly with upsetting,[2] and partly by the eating rust of family pride, which hurt the edge of many a clever fellow among them, that would have done well in the way of trade, but sunk into divors[3] for the sake of their genteelity.

CHAPTER XXX · YEAR 1789

*William Malcolm comes to the parish and preaches ·
The opinions upon his sermon*

────────────

THIS I have always reflected upon as one of our blessed years.
It was not remarkable for any extraordinary occurrence, but
there was a hopefulness in the minds of men, and a planning
of new undertakings, of which, whatever may be the upshot,
the devising is ever rich in the cheerful anticipations of good.

Another new line of road was planned, for a shorter cut to
the cotton-mill, from the main road to Glasgow, and a public-
house was opened in Cayenneville; the latter, however, was
not an event that gave me much satisfaction, but it was a
convenience to the inhabitants, and the carriers that brought
the cotton-bags and took away the yarn twice a-week, needed
a place of refreshment. And there was a stage-coach set up
thrice every week from Ayr, that passed through the town,
by which it was possible to travel to Glasgow between breakfast and dinner-time, a thing that could not, when I came to
the parish, have been thought within the compass of man.[1]

This stage-coach I thought one of the greatest conveniencies
that had been established among us; and it enabled Mrs Balwhidder to send a basket of her fresh butter into the Glasgow
market, by which, in the spring and the fall of the year, she got
a great price, for the Glasgow merchants are fond of excellent
eatables, and the payment was aye ready money—Tam Whirlit
the driver paying for the one basket when he took up the other.

In this year William Malcolm, the youngest son of the
widow, having been sometime a tutor in a family in the east
country, came to see his mother, as indeed he had done every

year from the time he went to the College, but this occasion was made remarkable by his preaching in my pulpit. His old acquaintance were curious to hear him, and I myself had a sort of a wish likewise, being desirous to know how far he was orthodox; so I thought fit, on the suggestion of one of the elders, to ask him to preach one day for me, which, after some fleeching,[1] he consented to do. I think, however, there was a true modesty in his diffidence, although his reason was a weak one, being lest he might not satisfy his mother, who had as yet never heard him. Accordingly, on the Sabbath after, he did preach, and the kirk was well packed, and I was not one of the least attentive of the congregation. His sermon assuredly was well put together, and there was nothing to object to in his doctrine; but the elderly people thought his language rather too Englified,[2] which I thought likewise, for I never could abide that the plain auld Kirk of Scotland, with her sober presbyterian simplicity, should borrow, either in word or in deed, from the language of the prelatic hierarchy of England. Nevertheless, the younger part of the congregation were loud in his praise, saying, there had not been heard before such a style of language in our side of the country. As for Mrs Malcolm, his mother, when I spoke to her anent the same, she said but little, expressing only her hope that his example would be worthy of his precepts; so that, upon the whole, it was a satisfaction to us all, that he was likely to prove a stoop[3] and upholding pillar to the Kirk of Scotland. His mother, however, had the satisfaction, before she died, to see him a placed minister, and his name among the authors of his country; for he published at Edinburgh a volume of Moral Essays, of which he sent me a pretty bound copy, and they were greatly creditable to his pen, though lacking somewhat of that birr and smeddum,[4] that is the juice and flavour of books of that sort.

CHAPTER XXXI · YEAR 1790

*A bookseller's shop is set up among the houses of
the weavers at Cayenne-ville*

THE features of this Ann. Dom. partook of the character of
its predecessor. Several new houses were added to the clachan;
Cayenneville was spreading out with weavers' shops, and
growing up fast into a town. In some respects it got the start of
our's, for one day, when I was going to dine with Mr Cayenne,
at Wheatrig-house, not a little to my amazement, did I behold
a bookseller's shop opened there, with sticks of red and black
wax, pouncet-boxes,[1] pens, pocket-books, and new publications, in the window, such as the like of was only to be seen in
cities and borough towns. And it was lighted at night by a
patent lamp,[2] which shed a wonderful beam, burning oil, and
having no smoke. The man sold likewise perfumery, powder-
puffs, trinkets, and Dublin dolls, besides pen-knives, Castile
soap,[3] and walking-sticks, together with a prodigy of other
luxuries too tedious to mention.

Upon conversing with the man, for I was enchanted to go
into this phenomenon, for as no less could I regard it, he told
me that he had a correspondence with London, and could get
me down any book published there within the same month
in which it came out, and he shewed me divers of the newest
come out, of which I did not read even in the Scots Magazine,
till more than three months after, although I had till then
always considered that work as most interesting for its early
intelligence. But what I was most surprised to hear, was that
he took in a daily London newspaper for the spinners and
weavers, who paid him a penny a-week a piece for the same;

they being all greatly taken up with what, at the time, was going on in France.

This bookseller in the end, however, proved a whawp[1] in our nest, for he was in league with some of the English reformers, and when the story took wind three years after, concerning the plots and treasons of the Corresponding Societies[2] and democrats, he was fain to make a moonlight flitting, leaving his wife for a time to manage his affairs. I could not, however, think any ill of the man notwithstanding; for he had very correct notions of right and justice, in a political sense, and when he came into the parish, he was as orderly and well-behaved as any other body; and conduct is a test that I have always found as good for a man's principles, as professions. Nor, at the time of which I am speaking, was there any of that dread or fear of reforming the government, that has since been occasioned by the wild and wasteful hand which the French employed in their Revolution.

But, among other improvements, I should mention, that a Doctor Marigold came and settled in Cayenneville, a small, round, happy-tempered man, whose funny stories were far better liked than his drugs. There was a doubt among some of the weavers, if he was a skilful Esculapian,[3] and this doubt led to their holding out an inducement to another medical man, Dr Tanzey, to settle there likewise, by which it grew into a saying, that at Cayenneville there was a doctor for health as well as sickness. For Dr Marigold was one of the best hands in the country at a pleasant punch-bowl, while Dr Tanzey had all the requisite knowledge of the faculty for the bed-side.

It was in this year, that the hour-plate and hand on the kirk steeple were renewed, as indeed may yet be seen by the date, though it be again greatly in want of fresh gilding; for it was by my advice that the figures of the Ann. Dom. were placed one in each corner. In this year, likewise, the bridge over the Brawl burn was built, a great convenience, in the winter time, to the parishioners that lived on the north side; for when there happened to be a speat[1] on the Sunday, it kept them from the kirk, but I did not find that the bridge mended the matter, till after the conclusion of the war against the democrats, and the beginning of that which we are now waging with Boney,[2] their child and champion. It is, indeed, wonderful to think of the occultation of grace that was taking place about this time, throughout the whole bound of Christendom; for I could mark a visible darkness of infidelity spreading in the corner of the vineyard committed to my keeping, and a falling away of the vincs from their wonted props and confidence in the truths of Revelation. But I said nothing. I knew that the faith could not be lost, and that it would be found purer and purer the more it was tried;[3] and this I have lived to see, many now being zealous members of the church, that were abundantly luke-warm at the period of which I am now speaking.

CHAPTER XXXII · YEAR 1791

*I place my son Gilbert in a counting-house at
Glasgow · My observations on Glasgow · On my
return I preach against the vanity of riches, and
begin to be taken for a Black-neb*

━━━━━━━

IN the spring of this year, I took my son Gilbert into Glasgow,
to place him in a counting-house, as he had no inclination
for any of the learned professions; and not having been there
from the time when I was sent to the General Assembly,
I cannot express my astonishment at the great improvements,
surpassing far all that was done in our part of the country,
which I thought was not to be paralleled. When I came afterwards to reflect on my simplicity in this, it was clear to me that
we should not judge of the rest of the world by what we see
going on around ourselves, but walk abroad into other parts,
and thereby enlarge our sphere of observation, as well as
ripen our judgment of things.

But although there was no doubt a great and visible increase
of the city,[1] loftier buildings on all sides, and streets that
spread their arms far into the embraces of the country,
I thought the looks of the population were impaired, and that
there was a greater proportion of long white faces in the
Trongate, than when I attended the Divinity class. These,
I was told, were the weavers and others concerned in the cotton
trade, which I could well believe, for they were very like in
their looks to the men of Cayenneville; but from living in
a crowded town, and not breathing a wholesome country air
between their tasks, they had a stronger cast of unhealthy
melancholy. I was, therefore, very glad, that Providence had

placed in my hand the pastoral staff of a country parish, for it cut me to the heart to see so many young men, in the rising prime of life, already in the arms of a pale consumption. 'If, therefore,' said I to Mrs Balwhidder, when I returned home to the Manse, 'we live, as it were, within the narrow circle of ignorance, we are spared from the pain of knowing many an evil; and, surely, in much knowledge, there is sadness of heart.'

But the main effect of this was to make me do all in my power to keep my people contented with their lowly estate; for in that same spirit of improvement, which was so busy every where, I could discern something like a shadow, that shewed it was not altogether of that pure advantage, which avarice led all so eagerly to believe. Accordingly, I began a series of sermons on the evil and vanity of riches, and, for the most part of the year, pointed out in what manner they led the possessor to indulge in sinful luxuries, and how indulgence begat desire, and desire betrayed integrity and corrupted the heart, making it evident, that the rich man was liable to forget his unmerited obligations to God, and to oppress the laborious and the needful when he required their services.

Little did I imagine, in thus striving to keep aloof the ravenous wolf Ambition from my guileless flock, that I was giving cause for many to think me an enemy to the king and government, and a perverter of Christianity, to suit levelling[1] doctrines. But so it was. Many of the heritors considered me a black-neb,[2] though I knew it not, but went on in the course of my duty, thinking only how best to preserve peace on earth, and good will towards men. I saw, however, an altered manner in the deportment of several, with whom I had long lived in friendly terms. It was not marked enough to make me inquire the cause, but sufficiently plain to affect my ease of mind. Accordingly, about the end of this year, I fell into a dull way: My spirit was subdued, and at times I was aweary of the day, and longed for the night, when I might close my eyes in peaceful slumbers. I missed my son Gilbert, who had been a companion to me in the long nights, while his mother was busy with the lasses, and their ceaseless wheels and cardings, in the kitchen. Often could I have found it in my heart to have banned that never-ceasing industry, and to tell Mrs Balwhidder, that the married state was made for something else than to make napery, and bittle[1] blankets; but it was her happiness to keep all at work, and she had no pleasure in any other way of life, so I sat many a night by the fire-side with resignation; sometimes in the study, and sometimes in the parlour, and, as I was doing nothing, Mrs Balwhidder said it was needless to light the candle. Our daughter Janet was in this time at a boarding-school in Ayr, so that I was really a most solitary married man.

Troubled with low spirits · Accidental meeting with
Mr Cayenne, who endeavours to remove the
prejudices entertained against me

―――――

WHEN the spring in this year began to brighten on the brae,
the cloud of dulness, that had darkened and oppressed me all
the winter, somewhat melted away, and I could now and then
joke again at the never-ending toil and trouble of that busiest
of all bees, the second Mrs Balwhidder. But still I was far
from being right, a small matter affected me, and I was overly
given to walking by myself, and musing on things that I could
tell nothing about—my thoughts were just the rack of a dream
without form, and driving witlessly as the smoke that mounteth
up,[1] and is lost in the airy heights of the sky.

Heeding little of what was going on in the clachan, and
taking no interest in the concerns of any body, I would have
been contented to die, but I had no ail about me. An accident,
however, fell out, that, by calling on me for an effort, had
the blessed influence of clearing my vapours almost entirely
away.

One morning, as I was walking on the sunny side of the
road, where the foot-path was in the next year made to the
cotton-mill, I fell in with Mr Cayenne, who was seemingly
much fashed[2]—a small matter could do that at any time; and
he came up to me with a red face and an angry eye. It was not
my intent to speak to him, for I was grown loth to enter into
conversation with any body, so I bowed and passed on. 'What,'
cried Mr Cayenne, 'and will you not speak to me?' I turned
round, and said meekly, 'Mr Cayenne, I have no objections

to speak to you; but having nothing particular to say, it did not seem necessary just now.'

He looked at me like a gled,[1] and in a minute exclaimed, 'Mad, by Jupiter! as mad as a March hare!' He then entered into conversation with me, and said, that he had noticed me an altered man, and was just so far on his way to the Manse, to inquire what had befallen me. So, from less to more, we entered into the marrow of my case; and I told him how I had observed the estranged countenances of some of the heritors; at which he swore an oath, that they were a parcel of the damn'dest boobies in the country, and told me how they had taken it into their heads that I was a leveller. 'But I know you better,' said Mr Cayenne, 'and have stood up for you as an honest conscientious man, though I don't much like your humdrum preaching. However, let that pass; I insist upon your dining with me to-day, when some of these arrant fools are to be with us, and the devil's in't, if I don't make you friends with them.' I did not think Mr Cayenne, however, very well qualified for a peace-maker, but, nevertheless, I consented to go; and having thus got an inkling of the cause of that cold back-turning which had distressed me so much, I made such an effort to remove the error that was entertained against me, that some of the heritors, before we separated, shook me by the hands with the cordiality of renewed friendship; and, as if to make amends for past neglect, there was no end to their invitations to dinner, which had the effect of putting me again on my mettle, and removing the thick and muddy melancholious humour out of my blood.

But what confirmed my cure, was the coming home of my daughter Janet from the Ayr boarding-school, where she had learnt to play on the spinet, and was become a conversible lassie, with a competent knowledge, for a woman, of geography and history; so that when her mother was busy with the wearyful booming wheel, she entertained me sometimes with a tune, and sometimes with her tongue, which made the winter nights fly cantily[1] by.

Whether it was owing to the malady of my imagination, throughout the greatest part of this year, or that really nothing particular did happen to interest me, I cannot say, but it is very remarkable that I have nothing remarkable to record— farther, than that I was at the expence myself of getting the Manse rough cast, and the window cheeks[2] painted, with roans[3] put up, rather than apply to the heritors; for they were always sorely fashed when called upon for outlay.

CHAPTER XXXIV · YEAR 1793

*I dream a remarkable dream, and preach a Sermon
in consequence, applying to the events of the times ·
Two democratical weaver lads brought before
Mr Cayenne, as justice of peace*

———

ON the first night of this year, I dreamt a very remarkable
dream, which, when I now recal to mind, at this distance of
time, I cannot but think that there was a cast of prophecy in it.
I thought that I stood on the tower of an old popish kirk,
looking out at the window upon the kirk-yard, where I beheld
ancient tombs, with effigies and coats of arms on the wall
thereof, and a great gate at the one side, and a door that led
into a dark and dismal vault, at the other. I thought all the
dead, that were lying in the common graves, rose out of their
coffins; at the same time, from the old and grand monuments,
with the effigies and coats of arms, came the great men, and
the kings of the earth with crowns on their heads, and globes
and sceptres in their hands.

I stood wondering what was to ensue, when presently
I heard the noise of drums and trumpets, and anon I beheld
an army with banners entering in at the gate; upon which the
kings and the great men came also forth in their power and
array, and a dreadful battle was foughten; but the multitude,
that had risen from the common graves, stood afar off, and
were but lookers on.

The kings and their host were utterly discomfited. They
were driven within the doors of their monuments, their coats
of arms were broken off, and their effigies cast down, and the
victors triumphed over them with the flourishes of trumpets

and the waving of banners. But while I looked, the vision was changed, and I then beheld a wide and a dreary waste, and afar off the steeples of a great city, and a tower in the midst, like the tower of Babel, and on it I could discern written in characters of fire, 'Public Opinion'. While I was pondering at the same, I heard a great shout, and presently the conquerors made their appearance, coming over the desolate moor. They were going in great pride and might towards the city, but an awful burning rose, afar as it were in the darkness, and the flames stood like a tower of fire that reached unto the Heavens. And I saw a dreadful hand and an arm stretched from out of the cloud, and in its hold was a besom made of the hail and the storm, and it swept the fugitives like dust; and in their place I saw the church-yard, as it were, cleared and spread around, the graves closed, and the ancient tombs, with their coats of arms and their effigies of stone, all as they were in the beginning. I then awoke, and behold it was a dream.

This vision perplexed me for many days, and when the news came that the King of France was beheaded by the hands of his people,[1] I received, as it were, a token in confirmation of the vision that had been disclosed to me in my sleep, and I preached a discourse on the same, and against the French Revolution, that was thought one of the greatest and soundest sermons that I had ever delivered in my pulpit.

On the Monday following, Mr Cayenne, who had been some time before appointed a justice of the peace, came over from Wheatrig-house to the Cross Keys, where he sent for me and divers other respectable inhabitants of the clachan, and told us that he was to have a sad business, for a warrant was out to bring before him two democratic weaver lads, on a suspicion of high treason. Scarcely were the words uttered, when they were brought in, and he began to ask them how they dared to think of dividing, with their liberty and equality principles, his and every other man's property in the country. The men answered him in a calm manner, and told him they sought no man's property, but only their own natural rights; upon which he called them traitors and reformers. They denied they were traitors, but confessed they were reformers, and said they knew not how that should be imputed to them as a fault, for that the greatest men of all times had been reformers.—'Was not,' they said, 'our Lord Jesus Christ a reformer?'—'And what the devil did he make of it?' cried Mr Cayenne, bursting with passion; 'Was he not crucified?'

I thought, when I heard these words, that the pillars of the earth sunk beneath me, and that the roof of the house was carried away in a whirlwind. The drums of my ears crackit, blue starns[1] danced before my sight, and I was fain to leave the house and hie me home to the Manse, where I sat down in my study, like a stupified creature awaiting what would betide. Nothing, however, was found against the weaver lads; but I never, from that day, could look on Mr Cayenne as a Christian, though surely he was a true government-man.

Soon after this affair, there was a pleasant re-edification of a gospel-spirit among the heritors, especially when they heard how I had handled the regicides of France; and on the following Sunday, I had the comfortable satisfaction to see many a gentleman in their pews, that had not been for years within a kirk-door. The democrats, who took a world of trouble to misrepresent the actions of the gentry, insinuated that all this was not from any new sense of grace, but in fear of their being reported as suspected persons to the King's government. But I could not think so, and considered their renewal of communion with the church as a swearing of allegiance to the King of Kings, against that host of French atheists, who had torn the mort-cloth from the coffin, and made it a banner, with which they were gone forth to war against the Lamb. The whole year was, however, spent in great uneasiness, and the proclamation of the war was followed by an appalling stop in trade. We heard of nothing but failures on all hands, and among others that grieved me, was that of Mr Maitland of

Glasgow who had befriended Mrs Malcolm in the days of her affliction, and gave her son Robert his fine ship. It was a sore thing to hear of so many breakings, especially of old respected merchants like him, who had been a Lord Provost, and was far declined into the afternoon of life. He did not, however, long survive the mutation of his fortune, but bending his aged head in sorrow, sunk down beneath the stroke, to rise no more.

CHAPTER XXXV · YEAR 1794

*The condition of the parish, as divided into
Government-men and Jacobins · I endeavour to
prevent Christian charity from being forgotten in
the phraseology of utility and philanthropy*

━━━━━━

THIS year had opened into all the leafiness of midsummer
before any thing memorable happened in the parish, farther
than that the sad division of my people into government-men
and jacobins[1] was perfected. This calamity, for I never could
consider such heart-burning among neighbours as any thing
less than a very heavy calamity, was assuredly occasioned by
faults on both sides, but it must be confessed that the gentry did
nothing to win the commonality from the errors of their way.
A little more condescension on their part would not have made
things worse, and might have made them better; but pride
interposed, and caused them to think that any show of
affability from them would be construed by the democrats
into a terror of their power. While the democrats were no less
to blame; for hearing how their compeers were thriving in
France and demolishing every obstacle to their ascendency,
they were crouse[2] and really insolent, evidencing none of that
temperance in prosperity that proves the possessors worthy
of their good fortune.

As for me, my duty in these circumstances was one plain
and simple. The Christian religion was attempted to be
brought into disrepute; the rising generation were taught to
jibe at its holiest ordinances; and the kirk was more frequented
as a place to while away the time on a rainy Sunday, than for
any insight of the admonitions and revelations in the sacred

book. Knowing this, I perceived that it would be of no effect
to handle much the mysteries of the faith; but as there was at
the time a bruit and a sound about universal benevolence,
philanthropy, utility, and all the other disguises with which an
infidel philosophy appropriated to itself the charity, brotherly
love, and well-doing inculcated by our holy religion, I set
myself to task upon these heads, and thought it no robbery
to use a little of the stratagem employed against Christ's
Kingdom, to promote the interests thereof in the hearts and
understandings of those whose ears would have been sealed
against me, had I attempted to expound higher things.
Accordingly, on one day it was my practice to shew what the
nature of Christian charity was, comparing it to the light and
warmth of the sun that shines impartially on the just and the
unjust[1]—shewing that man, without the sense of it as a duty,
was as the beasts that perish,[2] and that every feeling of his
nature was intimately selfish, but that, when actuated by this
divine impulse, he rose out of himself and became as a god,
zealous to abate the sufferings of all things that live.—And,
on the next day, I demonstrated that the new benevolence
which had come so much into vogue, was but another version
of this Christian virtue.—In like manner I dealt with brotherly
love, bringing it home to the business and bosoms of my
hearers, that the Christianity of it was neither enlarged nor
bettered by being baptized with the Greek name of philanthropy. With well-doing, however, I went more roundly to
work. I told my people that I thought they had more sense
than to secede from Christianity to become Utilitarians,[3] for
that it would be a confession of ignorance of the faith they
deserted, seeing that it was the main duty inculcated by our
religion to do all in morals and manners, to which the new-
fangled doctrine of utility pretended.

These discourses, which I continued for some time, had
no great effect on the men; but being prepared in a familiar
household manner, they took the fancies of the young women,

which was to me an assurance that the seed I had planted would in time shoot forth; for I reasoned with myself, that if the gudemen of the immediate generation should continue free-thinkers, their wives will take care that those of the next shall not lack that spunk[1] of grace; so I was cheered under that obscurity which fell upon Christianity at this time, with a vista beyond, in which I saw, as it were, the children unborn, walking in the bright green, and in the unclouded splendour of the faith.

But, what with the decay of trade, and the temptation of the King's bounty, and, over all, the witlessness that was in the spirit of man at this time, the number that enlisted in the course of the year from the parish was prodigious. In one week no less than three weavers and two cotton-spinners went over to Ayr, and took the bounty[2] for the Royal Artillery. But I could not help remarking to myself, that the people were grown so used to changes and extraordinary adventures, that the single enlistment of Thomas Wilson, at the beginning of the American war, occasioned a far greater grief and work among us, than all the swarms that went off week after week in the months of November and December of this year.

CHAPTER XXXVI · YEAR 1795

A recruiting party visits the town · After them,
players · then preaching quakers · the progress of
philosophy among the weavers

————

THE present Ann. Dom. was ushered in with an event that
I had never dreaded to see in my day, in our once sober and
religious country parish. The number of lads that had gone
over to Ayr to be soldiers from among the spinners and
weavers of Cayenneville had been so great, that the government got note of it, and sent a recruiting party to be quartered
in the town; for the term clachan was beginning by this time
to wear out of fashion; indeed the place itself was outgrowing
the fitness of that title. Never shall I forget the dunt[1] that the
first tap of the drum gied[2] to my heart, as I was sitting, on
Hansel Monday,[3] by myself, at the parlour fireside, Mrs Balwhidder being throng[4] with the lasses looking out a washing,
and my daughter at Ayr, spending a few days with her old
comrades of the boarding-school. I thought it was the enemy,
and then anon the sound of the fife came shrill to the ear;
for the night was lown[5] and peaceful. My wife and all the
lasses came flying in upon me, crying all, in the name of
Heaven, what could it be? by which I was obligated to put on
my big-coat, and, with my hat and staff, go out to inquire.
The whole town was aloof,[6] the aged at the doors in clusters,
and the bairns following the tattoo, as it was called, and at
every doubling beat of the drum, shouting as if they had been
in the face of their foemen.

Mr Archibald Dozendale, one of my elders, was saying to
several persons around him, just as I came up, 'Hech, sirs! but

the battle draws near our gates,' upon which there was a heavy sigh from all that heard him; and then they told me of the serjeant's business, and we had a serious communing together anent the same. But, while we were thus standing discoursing on the causeway, Mrs Balwhidder and the servant lasses could thole[1] no longer, but in a troop came in quest of me, to hear what was doing. In short, it was a night both of sorrow and anxiety. Mr Dozendale walked back to the Manse with us, and we had a sober tumbler of toddy[2] together, marvelling exceedingly where these fearful portents and changes would stop, both of us being of opinion, that the end of the world was drawing nearer and nearer.

Whether it was, however, that the lads belonging to the place did not like to shew themselves with the enlistment cockades among their acquaintance, or that there was any other reason, I cannot take it upon me to say, but certain it is, the recruiting party came no speed,[3] and in consequence were removed about the end of March.

Another thing happened in this year, too remarkable for me to neglect to put on record, as it strangely and strikingly marked the rapid revolutions that were going on. In the month of August, at the time of the fair, a gang of play-actors came, and hired Thomas Thacklan's barn for their enactments. They were the first of that clanjamfrey[4] who had ever been in the parish, and there was a wonderful excitement caused by the rumours concerning them. Their first performance was Douglas Tragedy, and the Gentle Shepherd;[5] and the general opinion was, that the lad who played Norval in the play, and Patie in the farce, was an English lord's son, who had run away from his parents, rather than marry an old cracket[6] lady, with a great portion.[7] But, whatever truth there might be in this notion, certain it is, the whole pack was in a state of perfect beggary; and yet, for all that, they not only in their parts, as I was told, laughed most heartily, but made others do the same; for I was constrained to let my daughter

go to see them, with some of her acquaintance, and she gave
me such an account of what they did, that I thought I would
have liked to have gotten a keek at them myself. At the same
time, I must own this was a sinful curiosity,[1] and I stifled it to
the best of my ability. Among other plays that they did, was
one called Macbeth and the Witches, which the Miss Cayennes
had seen performed in London, when they were there in the
winter time, with their father, for three months, seeing the
world, after coming from the boarding-school. But it was no
more like the true play of Shakespeare the poet, according to
their account, than a duddy betherel,[2] set up to fright the
sparrows from the pease, is like a living gentleman. The
hungry players, instead of behaving like guests at the royal
banquet, were voracious on the needful feast of bread, and
the strong ale, that served for wine in decanters; but the
greatest sport of all, was about a kail-pot,[3] that acted the
part of a cauldron, and which should have sunk with thunder
and lightning into the earth; however, it did quite as well,
for it made its exit, as Miss Virginia said, by walking quietly
off, being pulled by a string fastened to one of its feet. No
scene of the play was so much applauded as this one; and
the actor who did the part of King Macbeth, made a most
polite bow of thankfulness to the audience, for the approbation with which they had received the performance of
the pot.

We had likewise, shortly after the 'omnes exeunt' of the
players, an exhibition of a different sort in the same barn.
This was by two English quakers, and a quaker lady, tanners
from Kendal, who had been at Ayr on some leather[4] business,
where they preached, but made no proselytes. The travellers
were all three in a whisky,[5] drawn by one of the best ordered
horses, as the hostler at the Cross-keys told me, ever seen.
They came to the inns to their dinner, and meaning to stay
all night, sent round, to let it be known that they would hold
a meeting in friend Thacklan's barn; but Thomas denied

they were either kith or kin to him; this, however, was their way of speaking.

In the evening, owing to the notice, a great congregation was assembled in the barn, and I myself, along with Mr Archibald Dozendale, went there likewise, to keep the people in awe; for we feared the strangers might be jeered and insulted. The three were seated aloft, on a high stage, prepared on purpose, with two mares and scaffold-deals,[1] borrowed from Mr Trowel the mason. They sat long, and silent; but at last the spirit moved the woman, and she rose, and delivered a very sensible exposition of Christianity. I was really surprised to hear such sound doctrine; and Mr Dozendale said, justly, that it was more to the purpose than some that my younger brethren from Edinburgh endeavoured to teach. So, that those who went to laugh at the sincere simplicity of the pious quakers, were rebuked by a very edifying discourse on the moral duties of a Christian's life.

Upon the whole, however, this, to the best of my recollection, was another unsatisfactory year. In this we were, doubtless, brought more into the world, but we had a greater variety of temptation set before us, and there was still jealousy and estrangement in the dispositions of the gentry, and the lower orders, particularly the manufacturers. I cannot say, indeed, that there was any increase of corruption among the usual portion of my people; for their vocation calling them to work apart, in the purity of the free air of Heaven, they were kept uncontaminated by that seditious infection which fevered the minds of the sedentary weavers, and working like flatulence in the stomachs of the cotton-spinners, sent up into their heads a vain and diseased fume of infidel philosophy.

CHAPTER XXXVII · YEAR 1796

*Death of second Mrs Balwhidder · I look out for
a third, and fix upon Mrs Nugent, a widow ·
Particulars of the courtship*

———

THE prosperity of fortune is like the blossoms of spring, or
the golden hue of the evening cloud. It delighteth the spirit,
and passeth away.

In the month of February my second wife was gathered to
the Lord. She had been very ill for some time with an income[1]
in her side, which no medicine could remove. I had the best
doctors in the country-side to her, but their skill was of no
avail, their opinions being, that her ail was caused by an
internal abscess, for which physic has provided no cure. Her
death was to me a great sorrow, for she was a most excellent
wife, industrious to a degree, and managed every thing with so
brisk a hand, that nothing went wrong that she put it to. With
her I had grown richer than any other minister in the presbytery; but above all, she was the mother of my bairns, which
gave her a double claim upon me.

I laid her by the side of my first love, Betty Lanshaw, my
own cousin that was, and I inscribed her name upon the same
headstone; but time had drained my poetical vein, and I have
not yet been able to indite an epitaph on her merits and
virtues, for she had an eminent share of both. Her greatest
fault—the best have their faults—was an over-earnestness to
gather geer;[2] in the doing of which I thought she sometimes
sacrificed the comforts of a pleasant fire-side, for she was
never in her element but when she was keeping the servants
eydent[3] at their work. But, if by this she substracted something

from the quietude that was most consonant to my nature, she has left cause, both in bank and bond,[1] for me and her bairns to bless her great household activity.

She was not long deposited in her place of rest till I had occasion to find her loss. All my things were kept by her in a most perjinct[2] and excellent order, but they soon fell into an amazing confusion, for, as she often said to me, I had a turn for heedlessness; insomuch, that although my daughter Janet was grown up, and able to keep the house, I saw that it would be necessary, as soon as decency would allow, for me to take another wife. I was moved to this chiefly by foreseeing that my daughter would in time be married, and taken away from me, but more on account of the servant lasses, who grew out of all bounds, verifying the proverb,[3] 'Well kens the mouse when the cat's out of the house.' Besides this, I was now far down in the vale of years,[4] and could not expect to be long without feeling some of the penalties of old age, although I was still a hail[5] and sound man. It therefore behoved me to look in time for a helpmate, to tend me in my approaching infirmities.

Upon this important concern I reflected, as I may say, in the watches of the night, and, considering the circumstances of my situation, I saw it would not do for me to look out for an overly young woman, nor yet would it do for one of my ways to take an elderly maiden, ladies of that sort being liable to possess strong-set particularities. I therefore resolved that my choice should lie among widows of a discreet age; and I had a glimmer in my mind of speaking to Mrs Malcolm, but when I reflected on the saintly steadiness of her character, I was satisfied it would be of no use to think of her. Accordingly, I bent my brows, and looked towards Irville, which is an abundant trone[6] for widows and other single women; and I fixed my purpose on Mrs Nugent, the relic[7] of a Professor in the University of Glasgow, both because she was a well-bred woman, without any children to plea[8] about the interest of my own two, and likewise because she was held in great estimation by all who knew her, as a lady of a Christian principle.

It was sometime in the summer, however, before I made up my mind to speak to her on the subject; but one afternoon, in the month of August, I resolved to do so, and, with that intent, walked leisurely over to Irville, and after calling on the Rev. Dr Dinwiddie, the minister, I stepped in, as if by chance, to Mrs Nugent's. I could see that she was a little surprised at my visit; however, she treated me with every possible civility, and her servant lass bringing in the tea things, in a most orderly manner, as punctually as the clock was striking, she invited me to sit still, and drink my tea with her; which I did, being none displeased to get such encouragement. However, I said nothing that time, but returned to the Manse, very well content with what I had observed, which made me fain to repeat my visit. So, in the course of the week, taking Janet, my daughter, with me, we walked over in the forenoon, and called at Mrs Nugent's first, before going to any other house; and Janet saying, as we came out to go to the minister's, that she thought Mrs Nugent an agreeable woman, I determined to knock the nail on the head without farther delay.

Accordingly, I invited the minister and his wife to dine with us on the Thursday following; and before leaving the town, I made Janet, while the minister and me were handling a subject, as a sort of thing of common civility, go to Mrs Nugent, and invite her also. Dr Dinwiddie was a gleg[1] man, of a jocose nature; and he, guessing something of what I was ettling[2] at, was very mirthful with me, but I kept my own counsel till a meet season.

On the Thursday, the company, as invited, came, and nothing extraordinary was seen, but in cutting up, and helping a hen, Dr Dinwiddie put one wing on Mrs Nugent's plate, and the other wing on my plate, and said, there have been greater miracles than these two wings flying together, which was a sharp joke, that caused no little merriment, at the expence of Mrs Nugent and me. I, however, to show that I was none daunted, laid a leg also on her plate, and took another on my own, saying, in the words of the Reverend Doctor, there have been greater miracles than that these two legs should lie in the same nest, which was thought a very clever come off; and at the same time, I gave Mrs Nugent a kindly nip on her sonsy[1] arm, which was breaking the ice in as pleasant a way as could be. In short, before any thing passed between ourselves on the subject, we were set down for a tristed pair; and this being the case, we were married as soon as a twelvemonth and a day had passed from the death of the second Mrs Balwhidder; and neither of us have had occasion to rue the bargain. It is, however, but a piece of justice due to my second wife to say, that this was not a little owing to her good management; for she had left such a well plenished house, that her successor said, we had nothing to do but to contribute to one another's happiness.

In this year nothing more memorable happened in the parish, saving that the cotton-mill dam burst, about the time of the Lammas flood, and the waters went forth like a deluge of destruction, carrying off much victual, and causing a vast of damage to the mills that are lower down the stream. It was just a prodigy to see how calmly Mr Cayenne acted on that occasion; for being at other times as crabbed as a wud[2] terrier, folk were afraid to tell him, till he came out himself in the morning, and saw the devastation; at the sight of which he gave only a shrill whistle, and began to laugh at the idea of the men fearing to take him the news, as if he had not fortune and philosophy enough, as he called it, to withstand much greater misfortunes.

CHAPTER XXXVIII · YEAR 1797

*Mr Henry Melcomb comes to the parish to see his
uncle, Mr Cayenne · From some jocular behaviour
on his part, Meg Gaffaw falls in love with him ·
The sad result of the adventure when he is married*

━━━━━━━━

WHEN I have seen, in my walks, the irrational creatures of
God, the birds and the beasts, governed by a kindly instinct
in attendance on their young, often has it come into my head,
that love and charity, far more than reason or justice, formed
the tie that holds the world, with all its jarring wants and woes,
in social dependance and obligation together; and, in this
year, a strong verification of the soundness of this notion, was
exemplified in the conduct of the poor haverel[1] lassie Meg
Gaffaw, whose naturality[2] on the occasion of her mother's
death, I have related at length in this chronicle.

In the course of the summer, Mr Henry Melcomb, who
was a nephew to Mr Cayenne, came down from England to
see his uncle. He had just completed his education at the
College of Christ Church, in Oxford, and was the most perfect
young gentleman that had ever been seen in this part of the
country.

In his appearance he was a very paragon, with a fine manly
countenance, frank-hearted, blithe, and, in many points of
character, very like my old friend the Lord Eglesham, who
was shot. Indeed, in some respects, he was even above his
lordship, for he had a great turn at ready wit, and could joke
and banter in a most agreeable manner. He came very often
to the Manse to see me, and took great pleasure in my company, and really used a freedom that was so droll, I could

scarcely keep my composity and decorum with him. Among others that shared in his attention, was daft Meg Gaffaw, whom he had forgathered with one day in coming to see me, and after conversing with her for some time, he handed her, as she told me herself, over the kirk-stile, like a lady of high degree, and came with her to the Manse-door linking by the arm.[1]

From the ill-timed daffin[2] of that hour, poor Meg fell deep in love with Mr Melcomb, and it was just a play-acting to see the arts and antics she put in practice to win his attention. In her garb, she had never any sense of a proper propriety, but went about the country asking for shapings of silks and satins, with which she patched her duds,[3] calling them by the divers names of robes and negligées. All hitherto, however, had been moderation, compared to the daffadile of vanity which she was now seen, when she had searched, as she said, to the bottom of her coffer. I cannot take it upon me to describe her, but she kithed[4] in such a variety of cuffs and ruffles, feathers, old gumflowers,[5] painted paper knots, ribbans, and furs, and laces, and went about gecking[6] and simpering with an old fan in her hand, that it was not in the power of nature to look at her with sobriety.

Her first appearance in this masquerading, was at the kirk on the Sunday following her adventure with Mr Melcomb, and it was with a sore difficulty that I could keep my eyes off her, even in prayer; and when the kirk skailed,[7] she walked before him, spreading all her grandeur to catch his eye in such a manner as had not been seen or heard of since the prank that Lady Macadam played Miss Betty Wudrife.

Any other but Mr Melcomb would have been provoked by the fool's folly, but he humoured her wit, and, to the amazement of the whole people, presented her his hand, and allemanded[8] her along in a manner that should not have been seen in any street out of a king's court, and far less on the Lord's day. But alas! this sport did not last long. Mr Melcomb had come from England to be married to his cousin, Miss Virginia Cayenne, and poor daft Meg never heard of it till the banns for their purpose of marriage was read out by Mr Loremore on the Sabbath after. The words were scarcely out of his mouth, when the simple and innocent natural gave a loud shriek, that terrified the whole congregation, and ran out of the kirk demented. There was no more finery for poor Meg; she went and sat opposite to the windows of Mr Cayenne's house, where Mr Melcomb was, with clasped hands and beseeching eyes, like a monumental statue in alabaster, and no entreaty could drive her away. Mr Melcomb sent her money, and the bride many a fine thing, but Meg flung them from her, and clasped her hands again, and still sat. Mr Cayenne would have let loose the house-dog on her, but was not permitted.

In the evening it began to rain, and they thought that and the coming darkness would drive her away, but when the servants looked out before barring the doors, there she was in the same posture. I was to perform the marriage ceremony at seven o'clock in the morning, for the young pair were to go that night to Edinburgh; and when I went, there was Meg sitting looking at the windows with her hands clasped. When she saw me she gave a shrill cry, and took me by the hand, and wised[1] me to go back, crying out in a heart-breaking voice, 'O, sir! No yet—no yet! He'll maybe draw back, and think of a far truer bride.' I was wae for her, and very angry with the servants for laughing at the fond folly of the ill-less[2] thing.

When the marriage was over, and the carriage at the door, the bridegroom handed in the bride. Poor Meg saw this, and jumping up from where she sat, was at his side like a spirit, as he was stepping in, and taking him by the hand, she looked in his face so piteously, that every heart was sorrowful, for she could say nothing. When he pulled away his hand, and the door was shut, she stood as if she had been charmed to the spot, and saw the chaise drive away. All that were about the door then spoke to her, but she heard us not. At last she gave a deep sigh, and the water coming into her eye, she said, 'The worm—the worm is my bonny bridegroom, and Jenny with the many feet[1] my bridal maid. The mill-dam water's the wine o' the wedding, and the clay and the clod shall be my bedding. A lang night is meet for a bridal, but none shall be langer than mine.' In saying which words, she fled from among us, with heels like the wind. The servants pursued, but long before they could stop her, she was past redemption in the deepest plumb of the cotton-mill dam.

Few deaths had for many a day happened in the parish, to cause so much sorrow as that of this poor silly creature. She was a sort of household familiar among us, and there was much like the inner side of wisdom in the pattern of her sayings, many of which are still preserved as proverbs.[2]

CHAPTER XXXIX · YEAR 1798

*A dearth · Mr Cayenne takes measures to mitigate
the evil · he receives kindly some Irish refugees · his
daughter's marriage*

THIS was one of the heaviest years in the whole course of my ministry. The spring was slow of coming, and cold and wet when it did come; the dibs[1] were full, the roads foul, and the ground that should have been dry at the seed time, was as claggy as clay and clung to the harrow. The labour of man and beast was thereby augmented, and all nature being in a state of sluggish indisposition, it was evident to every eye of experience that there would be a great disappointment to the hopes of the husbandman.

Foreseeing this, I gathered the opinion of all the most sagacious of my parishioners, and consulted with them for a provision against the evil day, and we spoke to Mr Cayenne on the subject, for he had a talent by common in matters of mercantile management. It was amazing, considering his hot temper, with what patience he heard the grounds of our apprehension, and how he questioned and sifted the experience of the old farmers, till he was thoroughly convinced that all similar seed-times were ever followed by a short crop. He then said, that he would prove himself a better friend to the parish than he was thought. Accordingly, as he afterwards told me himself, he wrote off that very night to his correspondents in America to buy for his account all the wheat and flour they could get, and ship it to arrive early in the fall; and he bought up likewise in countries round the Baltic great store of victual, and brought in two cargos to Irville on purpose for the

parish, against the time of need, making for the occasion a
garnel of one of the warehouses of the cotton-mill.

The event came to pass as had been foretold; the harvest
fell short, and Mr Cayenne's cargos from America and the
Baltic came home in due season, by which he made a terrible
power of money, clearing thousands on thousands by post
after post—making more profit, as he said himself, in the
course of one month, he believed, than ever was made by any
individual within the kingdom of Scotland in the course of
a year.—He said, however, that he might have made more if
he had bought up the corn at home, but being convinced by us
that there would be a scarcity, he thought it his duty as an
honest man to draw from the stores and granaries of foreign
countries, by which he was sure he would serve his country
and be abundantly rewarded. In short, we all reckoned him
another Joseph[1] when he opened his garnels[2] at the cotton-
mill, and, after distributing a liberal portion to the poor and
needy, selling the remainder at an easy rate to the generality
of the people. Some of the neighbouring parishes, however,
were angry that he would not serve them likewise, and called
him a wicked and extortionate forestaller;[3] but he made it
plain to the meanest capacity that if he did not circumscribe
his dispensation to our own bounds it would be as nothing.
So that, although he brought a wonderful prosperity in by the
cotton-mill, and a plenteous supply of corn in a time of famine,
doing more in these things for the people than all the other
heritors had done from the beginning of time, he was much
reviled; even his bounty was little esteemed by my people,
because he took a moderate profit on what he sold to them.
Perhaps, however, these prejudices might be partly owing to
their dislike of his hasty temper, at least I am willing to think
so, for it would grieve me if they were really ungrateful for
a benefit that made the pressure of the time lie but lightly on
them.

The alarm of the Irish rebellion[4] in this year was likewise another source of affliction to us, for many of the gentry coming over in great straights, especially ladies and their children, and some of them, in the hurry of their flight having but little ready money, were very ill off. Some four or five families came to the Cross Keys in this situation, and the conduct of Mr Cayenne to them was most exemplary. He remembered his own haste with his family from Virginia, when the Americans rebelled; and immediately on hearing of these Irish refugees, he waited on them with his wife and daughter, supplied them with money, invited them to his house, made ploys to keep up their spirits, while the other gentry stood back till they knew something of the strangers.

Among these destitute ladies was a Mrs Desmond and her two daughters, a woman of a most august presence, being indeed more like one ordained to reign over a kingdom, than for household purposes. The Miss Desmonds were only entering their teens, but they also had no ordinary stamp upon them. What made this party the more particular, was on account of Mr Desmond, who was supposed to be a united man with the rebels, and it was known his son was deep in their plots; yet although this was all told to Mr Cayenne, by some of the other Irish ladies who were of the loyal connexion, it made no difference with him, but, on the contrary, he acted as if he thought the Desmonds the most of all the refugees entitled to his hospitable civilities. This was a wonderment to our strait-laced narrow lairds, as there was not a man of such strict government principles in the whole country-side as Mr Cayenne: but he said he carried his political principles only to the camp and the council. 'To the hospital and the prison,' said he, 'I take those of a man'—which was almost a Christian doctrine, and from that declaration Mr Cayenne and me began again to draw a little more cordially together; although he had still a very imperfect sense of religion, which I attributed to his being born in America, where even as yet, I am told, they have but a scanty sprinkling of grace.

But before concluding this year, I should tell the upshot of the visitation of the Irish, although it did not take place until some time after the peace with France.

In the putting down of the rebels Mr Desmond and his son made their escape to Paris, where they staid till the Treaty was signed, by which, for several years after the return to Ireland of the grand lady and her daughters, as Mrs Desmond was called by our commonality, we heard nothing of them. The other refugees repaid Mr Cayenne his money with thankfulness, and on their restoration to their homes, could not sufficiently express their sense of his kindness. But the silence and seeming ingratitude of the Desmonds vexed him; and he could not abide to hear the Irish rebellion mentioned without flying into a passion against the rebels, which every body knew was owing to the ill return he had received from that family. However, one afternoon, just about half an hour before his wonted dinner hour, a grand equipage, with four horses and outriders, stopped at his door, and who was in it but Mrs Desmond and an elderly man, and a young gentleman with an aspect like a lord. It was her husband and son. They had come from Ireland in all their state on purpose to repay with interest the money Mr Cayenne had counted so long lost, and to express in person the perpetual obligation which he had conferred upon the Desmond family, in all time coming. The lady then told him, that she had been so straightened in helping the poor ladies that it was not in her power to make repayment till Desmond, as she called her husband, came home; and not choosing to assign the true reason, lest it might cause trouble, she rather submitted to be suspected of ingratitude than do an improper thing.

Mr Cayenne was transported with this unexpected return, and a friendship grew up between the families which was afterwards cemented into relationship by the marriage of the young Desmond with Miss Caroline Cayenne: Some in the parish objected to this match, Mrs Desmond being a papist; but as Miss Caroline had received an Episcopalian education, I thought it of no consequence, and married them after their family chaplain from Ireland, as a young couple, both from beauty and fortune, well matched, and deserving of all conjugal felicity.

*My Daughter's marriage · Her large portion ·
Mrs Malcolm's death*

⸻

THERE are but two things to make me remember this year; the first was the marriage of my daughter Janet with the Reverend Dr Kittleword of Swappington, a match in every way commendable, and on the advice of the third Mrs Balwhidder, I settled a thousand pounds down, and promised five hundred more at my own death, if I died before my spouse, and a thousand at her death, if she survived me; which was the greatest portion ever minister's daughter had in our country side. In this year, likewise, I advanced fifteen hundred pounds for my son in a concern in Glasgow,—all was the gathering of that indefatigable engine of industry the second Mrs Balwhidder, whose talents her successor said were a wonder, when she considered the circumstances in which I had been left at her death, and made out of a narrow stipend.

The other memorable was the death of Mrs Malcolm. If ever there was a saint on this earth she was surely one. She had been for some time bedfast, having all her days from the date of her widowhood been a tender[1] woman; but no change made any alteration on the Christian contentment of her mind. She bore adversity with an honest pride, she toiled in the day of penury and affliction with thankfulness for her earnings, although ever so little. She bent her head to the Lord in resignation when her first-born fell in battle; nor was she puffed up with vanity when her daughters were married, as it was said, so far above their degree, though they shewed it was but into their proper sphere by their demeanour after. She lived to see her second son, the Captain, rise into affluence, married, and with a thriving young family; and she had the very great satisfaction, on the last day she was able to go to church, to see her youngest son, the Clergyman, standing in my pulpit, a doctor of divinity, and the placed minister of a richer parish than mine. Well indeed might she have said on that day, 'Lord, let thy servant depart in peace, for mine eyes have seen thy salvation.'

For some time it had been manifest to all who saw her that her latter end was drawing nigh; and therefore, as I had kept up a correspondence with her daughters, Mrs Macadam and Mrs Howard, I wrote them a particular account of her case, which brought them to the clachan. They both came in their own carriages, for Col. Macadam was now a general, and had succeeded to a great property by an English uncle, his mother's brother; and Capt. Howard, by the death of his father, was also a man, as it was said, with a lord's living. Robert Malcolm, her son the captain, was in the West Indies at the time, but his wife came on the first summons, as did William the minister.

They all arrived about four o'clock in the afternoon, and at seven a message came for me and Mrs Balwhidder to go over to them, which we did, and found the strangers seated by the heavenly patient's bedside. On my entering she turned her eyes towards me and said, 'Bear witness, sir, that I die thankful for an extraordinary portion of temporal mercies. The heart of my youth was withered like the leaf that is seared with the lightning, but in my children I have received a great indemnification for the sorrows of that trial.' She then requested me to pray, saying, 'No, let it be a thanksgiving. My term is out, and I have nothing more to hope or fear from the good or evil of this world. But I have had much to make me grateful; therefore, sir, return thanks for the time I have been spared, for the goodness granted so long unto me, and the gentle hand with which the way from this world is smoothed for my passing.'

There was something so sweet and consolatory in the way she said this, that although it moved all present to tears, they were tears without the wonted bitterness of grief. Accordingly, I knelt down and did as she had required, and there was a great stillness while I prayed; at the conclusion we looked to the bed, but the spirit had in the meantime departed, and there was nothing remaining but the clay tenement.

It was expected by the parish, considering the vast affluence of the daughters, that there would have been a grand funeral, and Mrs Howard thought it was necessary; but her sister, who had from her youth upward a superior discernment of propriety, said, 'No, as my mother has lived so shall be her end.' Accordingly, every body of any respect in the clachan was invited to the funeral; but none of the gentry, saving only such as had been numbered among the acquaintance of the deceased. But Mr Cayenne came unbidden, saying to me, that although he did not know Mrs Malcolm personally, he had often heard she was an amiable woman, and therefore he thought it a proper compliment to her family, who were out of the parish, to shew in what respect she was held among us; for he was a man that would take his own way, and do what he thought was right, heedless alike of blame or approbation.

If, however, the funeral was plain, though respectable, the ladies distributed a liberal sum among the poor families; but before they went away, a silent token of their mother's virtue came to light, which was at once a source of sorrow and pleasure. Mrs Malcolm was first well provided by the Macadams, afterwards the Howards settled on her an equal annuity, by which she spent her latter days in great comfort. Many a year before, she had repaid Provost Maitland the money he sent her in the day of her utmost distress, and at this period he was long dead, having died of a broken heart at the time of his failure. From that time his widow and her daughters had been in very straightened circumstances, but unknown to all but herself, and HIM from whom nothing is hid, Mrs Malcolm from time to time had sent them, in a blank letter, an occasional note to the young ladies to buy a gown. After her death, a bank bill for a sum of money, her own savings, was found in her scrutoire, with a note of her own writing pinned to the same, stating, that the amount being more than she had needed for herself, belonged of right to those who had so generously provided for her, but as they were not in want of such a trifle, it would be a token of respect to her memory, if they would give the bill to Mrs Maitland and her daughters, which was done with a most glad alacrity; and, in the doing of it, the private kindness was brought to light.

Thus ended the history of Mrs Malcolm, as connected with our Parish Annals. Her house was sold, and is the same now inhabited by the mill-wright, Mr Periffery, and a neat house it still is, for the possessor is an Englishman, and the English have an uncommon taste for snod[1] houses and trim gardens; but, at the time it was built, there was not a better in the town, though it's now but of the second class. Yearly we hear both from Mrs Macadam and her sister, with a five-pound note from each to the poor of the parish, as a token of their remembrance; but they are far off, and were any thing ailing me, I suppose the gift will not be continued. As for Captain Malcolm, he has proved, in many ways, a friend to such of our young men as have gone to sea. He has now left it off himself, and settled at London, where he latterly sailed from, and I understand is in a great way as a ship-owner. These things I have thought it fitting to record, and will now resume my historical narration.

CHAPTER XLI · YEAR 1800

*Return of an inclination towards political
tranquillity · Death of the Schoolmistress*

━━━━━

THE same quietude and regularity that marked the progress of the last year, continued throughout the whole of this. We sowed and reaped in tranquillity, though the sough of distant war came heavily from a distance. The cotton-mill did well for the company, and there was a sobriety in the minds of the spinners and weavers, which shewed that the crisis of their political distemperature was over;—there was something more of the old prudence in men's reflections; and it was plain to me that the elements of reconciliation were coming together throughout the world. The conflagration of the French Revolution was indeed not extinguished, but it was evidently burning out; and their old reverence for the Grand Monarque was beginning to revive among them, though they only called him a Consul.[1] Upon the king's fast I preached on this subject; and when the peace was concluded, I got great credit for my foresight, but there was no merit in't. I had only lived longer than the most of those around me, and had been all my days a close observer of the signs of the times; so that what was lightly called prophecy and prediction, were but a probability that experience had taught me to discern.

In the affairs of the parish, the most remarkable generality (for we had no particular catastrophe) was a great death of old people in the spring. Among others, Miss Sabrina, the school-mistress, paid the debt of nature, but we could now better spare her than we did her predecessor; for at Cayenneville there was a broken manufacturer's wife, an excellent teacher, and a genteel and modernized woman, who took the better order of children; and Miss Sabrina having been long frail (for she was never stout), a decent and discreet carlin,[1] Mrs M'Caffie, the widow of a custom-house officer, that was a native of the parish, set up another for plainer work. Her opposition, Miss Sabrina did not mind, but she was sorely displeased at the interloping of Mrs Pirn at Cayenneville, and some said it helped to kill her—of that, however, I am not so certain, for Dr Tanzey had told me in the winter, that he thought the sharp winds in March would blow out her candle, as it was burnt to the snuff; accordingly, she took her departure from this life, on the twenty-fifth day of that month, after there had, for some days prior, been a most cold and piercing east wind.

Miss Sabrina, who was always an oddity and aping grandeur, it was found, had made a will, leaving her gatherings to her favourites, with all regular formality. To one she bequeathed a gown, to another this, and a third that, and to me, a pair of black silk stockings. I was amazed when I heard this; but judge what I felt, when a pair of old marrowless[2] stockings, darned in the heel, and not whole enough in the legs to make a pair of mittens to Mrs Balwhidder, were delivered to me by her executor, Mr Caption, the lawyer. Saving, however, this kind of flummery, Miss Sabrina was a harmless creature, and could quote poetry in discourse, more glibly than texts of Scripture —her father having spared no pains on her mind; as for her body, it could not be mended; but that was not her fault.

After her death, the Session held a consultation, and we agreed to give the same salary that Miss Sabrina enjoyed to Mrs M'Caffie; which angered Mr Cayenne, who thought it should have been given to the head mistress; and it made him give Mrs Pirn, out of his own pocket, double the sum. But we considered that the parish funds were for the poor of the parish, and therefore, it was our duty to provide for the instruction of the poor children. Saving, therefore, those few notations, I have nothing further to say concerning the topics and progress of this Ann. Dom.

CHAPTER XLII · YEAR 1801

An Account of Colin Mavis, who becomes a poet

━━━━━━━━

I T is often to me very curious food for meditation, that as the parish increased in population, there should have been less cause for matter to record. Things that in former days would have occasioned great discourse and cogitation, are forgotten, with the day in which they happen; and there is no longer that searching into personalities which was so much in vogue during the first epoch of my ministry, which I reckon the period before the American war; nor has there been any such germinal changes among us, as those which took place in the second epoch, counting backward from the building of the cotton-mill that gave rise to the town of Cayenneville. But still we were not, even at this era, of which this Ann. Dom. is the beginning, without occasional personality, or an event that deserved to be called a germinal.

Some years before, I had noted among the callans at Mr Loremore's school, a long soople[1] laddie, who, like all bairns that grow fast and tall, had but little smeddum.[2] He could not be called a dolt, for he was observant and thoughtful, and given to asking sagacious questions; but there was a sleepiness about him, especially in the kirk, and he gave, as the master said, but little application to his lessons, so that folk thought he would turn out a sort of gaunt-at-the-door,[3] more mindful of meat than work. He was, however, a good-natured lad; and, when I was taking my solitary walks of meditation, I sometimes fell in with him, sitting alone on the brae by the water-side, and sometimes lying on the grass, with his hands under his head, on the sunny green knolls where Mr Cylindar, the English engineer belonging to the cotton-work, has built the bonny house that he calls Dairyhill Cottage. This was when Colin Mavis was a laddie at the school, and when I spoke to him, I was surprised at the discretion of his answers, so that gradually I began to think and say, that there was more about Colin than the neighbours knew. Nothing, however, for many a day, came out to his advantage; so that his mother, who was by this time a widow woman, did not well know what to do with him, and folk pitied her heavy handful of such a droud.[1]

By and by, however, it happened that one of the young clerks at the cotton-mill shattered his right-hand thumb by a gun bursting; and, being no longer able to write, was sent into the army to be an ensign, which caused a vacancy in the office; and, through the help of Mr Cayenne, I got Colin Mavis into the place, where, to the surprise of every body, he proved a wonderful eydent and active lad, and, from less to more, has come at the head of all the clerks, and deep in the confidentials of his employers. But although this was a great satisfaction to me, and to the widow woman his mother, it somehow was not so much so to the rest of the parish, who seemed, as it were, angry that poor Colin had not proved himself such a dolt as they had expected and foretold.

Among other ways that Colin had of spending his leisure, was that of playing music on an instrument, in which it was said he made a wonderful proficiency; but being long and thin, and of a delicate habit of body, he was obligated to refrain from this recreation; so he betook himself to books, and from reading, he began to try writing; but, as this was done in a corner, nobody jealoused[2] what he was about, till one evening in this year, he came to the Manse, and asked a word in private with me. I thought that perhaps he had fallen in with a lass, and was come to consult me anent matrimony; but when we were by ourselves, in my study, he took out of his pocket a number of the Scots Magazine, and said, 'Sir, you have been long pleased to notice me more than any other body, and when I got this, I could not refrain from bringing it, to let you see 't. Ye maun ken,[1] sir, that I have been long in secret given to trying my hand at rhyme, and, wishing to ascertain what others thought of my power in that way, I sent, by the post, twa three[2] verses to the Scots Magazine, and they have not only inserted them, but placed them in the body of the book, in such a way, that I kenna[3] what to think.' So I looked at the Magazine, and read his verses, which were certainly very well made verses, for one who had no regular education. But I said to him, as the Greenock magistrates said to John Wilson, the author of Clyde, when they stipulated with him to give up the art, that poem-making was a profane and un-profitable trade, and he would do well to turn his talent to something of more solidity, which he promised to do; but he has since put out a book, whereby he has angered all those that had foretold he would be a do-nae-gude. Thus has our parish walked sidy for sidy[4] with all the national improvements, having an author of its own, and getting a literary character in the ancient and famous republic of letters.

*The political condition of the world felt in the
private concerns of individuals · Mr Cayenne comes
to ask my advice, and acts according to it*

'EXPERIENCE teaches fools,' was the first moral apothegm
that I wrote in small text, when learning to write at the school,
and I have ever since thought it was a very sensible reflection.
For assuredly, as year after year has flown away on the swift
wings of time, I have found my experience mellowing, and
my discernment improving; by which I have, in the afternoon
of life, been enabled to foresee what kings and nations would
do, by the symptoms manifested within the bounds of the
society around me. Therefore, at the beginning of the spring
in this Ann. Dom., I had misgivings at the heart, a fluttering
in my thoughts, and altogether a strange uneasiness as to the
stability of the peace and harmony that was supposed to be
founded upon a stedfast foundation between us and the French
people. What my fears principally took the rise from, was
a sort of compliancy, on the part of those in power and
authority, to cultivate the old relations and parts between
them and the commonalty. It did not appear to me that this
proceeded from any known or decided event, for I read the
papers at this period daily, but from some general dread and
fear, that was begotten, like a vapour, out of the fermentation
of all sorts of opinions; most people of any sagacity, thinking
that the state of things in France being so much of an antic,
poetical, and play-actor like guise, that it would never obtain
that respect, far less that reverence from the world, which is
necessary to the maintenance of all beneficial government.
The consequence of this was a great distrust between man

and man, and an aching restlessness among those who had their bread to bake in the world. Persons possessing the power to provide for their kindred, forcing them, as it were, down the throats of those who were dependent on them in business, a bitter morsel.

But the pith of these remarks chiefly applies to the manufacturing concerns of the new town of Cayenneville, for in the clachan we lived in the lea of the dike,[1] and were more taken up with our own natural rural affairs, and the markets for victual, than the craft of merchandize. The only man interested in business, who walked in a steady manner at his old pace, though he sometimes was seen, being of a spunkie[2] temper, grinding the teeth of vexation, was Mr Cayenne himself.

One day, however, he came to me at the Manse. 'Doctor,' says he, for so he always called me, 'I want your advice. I never choose to trouble others with my private affairs, but there are times when the word of an honest man may do good. I need not tell you, that when I declared myself a Royalist in America, it was at a considerable sacrifice. I have, however, nothing to complain of against government on that score, but I think it damn'd hard that those personal connections, whose interests I preserved, to the detriment of my own, should, in my old age, make such an ungrateful return. By the steps I took prior to quitting America, I saved the property of a great mercantile concern in London. In return for that, they took a share with me, and for me, in the cotton-mill; and being here on the spot, as manager, I have both made and saved them money. I have, no doubt, bettered my own fortune in the meantime. Would you believe it, doctor, they have written a letter to me, saying, that they wish to provide for a relation, and requiring me to give up to him a portion of my share in the concern— a pretty sort of providing this, at another man's expence. But I'll be damn'd if I do any such thing. If they want to provide for their friend, let them do so from themselves, and not at my cost—What is your opinion?'

This appeared to me a very weighty concern, and not being versed in mercantile dealing, I did not well know what to say; but I reflected for some time, and then I replied, 'As far, Mr Cayenne, as my observation has gone in this world, I think that the giffs and the gaffs[1] nearly balance one another; and when they do not, there is a moral defect on the failing side. If a man long gives his labour to his employer, and is paid for that labour, it might be said that both are equal, but I say no. For it's in human nature to be prompt to change; and the employer, having always more in his power than his servant or agent, it seems to me a clear case, that in the course of a number of years, the master of the old servant is the obligated of the two; and, therefore, I say, in the first place, in your case there is no tie or claim, by which you may, in a moral sense, be called upon to submit to the dictates of your London correspondents; but there is a reason, in the nature of the thing and case, by which you may ask a favour from them—So, the advice I would give you would be this, write an answer to their letter, and tell them, that you have no objection to the taking in of a new partner, but you think it would be proper to revise all the copartnery, especially as you have, considering the manner in which you have advanced the business, been of opinion, that your share should have been considerably enlarged.'

I thought Mr Cayenne would have louped[2] out of his skin with mirth at this notion, and being a prompt man, he sat down at my scrutoire, and answered the letter which gave him so much uneasiness. No notice was taken of it for some time; but, in the course of a month, he was informed, that it was not considered expedient at that time to make any change in the Company. I thought the old man was gone by himself[3] when he got this letter. He came over instantly in his chariot,[4] from the cotton-mill office, to the Manse, and swore an oath, by some dreadful name, that I was a Solomon. However, I only mention this to shew how experience had instructed me, and as a sample of that sinister provisioning of friends that was going on in the world at this time—all owing, as I do verily believe, to the uncertain state of governments and national affairs.

Besides these generalities, I observed another thing working to effect—mankind read more, and the spirit of reflection and reasoning was more awake than at any time within my remembrance. Not only was there a handsome bookseller's shop in Cayenneville, with a London newspaper daily, but Magazines, and Reviews, and other new publications.

Till this year, when a chaise was wanted, we had to send to Irville; but Mr Toddy of the Cross-keys being in at Glasgow, he bought an excellent one at the second hand, being a portion of the effects of a broken merchant, by which, from that period, we had one of our own; and it proved a great convenience, for I, who never but twice in my life before hired that kind of commodity, had it thrice during the summer, for a bit jaunt with Mrs Balwhidder, to divers places and curiosities in the county, that I had not seen before, by which our ideas were greatly enlarged; indeed, I have always had a partiality for travelling, as one of the best means of opening the faculty of the mind, and giving clear and correct notions of men and things.

CHAPTER XLIV · YEAR 1803

*Fear of an invasion · Raising of volunteers in the
parish · The young ladies embroider a stand of
colours for the regiment*

═══════════

DURING the tempestuous times that ensued, from the death
of the King of France, by the hands of the executioner, in
1793, there had been a political schism among my people
that often made me very uneasy. The folk belonging to the
cotton-mill, and the muslin-weavers in Cayenneville, were
afflicted with the itch of jacobinism,[1] but those of the village
were staunch and true to King and Country; and some of the
heritors were desirous to make volunteers of the young men
of them, in case of any thing like the French anarchy and confusion rising on the side of the manufacturers. I, however,
set myself, at that time, against this, for I foresaw that the
French business was but a fever which would soon pass off,
but no man could tell the consequence of putting arms in the
hands of neighbour against neighbour, though it was but in
the way of policy.[2]

But when Bonaparte gathered his host fornent[3] the English
coast, and the government at London were in terror of their
lives for an invasion, all in the country saw that there was
danger, and I was not backward in sounding the trumpet to
battle. For a time, however, there was a diffidence among
us somewhere. The gentry had a distrust of the manufacturers,
and the farming lads were wud[4] with impatience, that those
who should be their leaders would not come forth. I, knowing
this, prepared a sermon suitable to the occasion, giving out
from the pulpit myself, the Sabbath before preaching it, that

it was my intent, on the next Lord's day, to deliver a religious and political exhortation on the present posture of public affairs. This drew a vast congregation of all ranks.

I trow that the stoor[1] had no peace in the stuffing[2] of the pulpit in that day, and the effect was very great and speedy, for, next morning the weavers and cotton-mill folk held a meeting, and they, being skilled in the ways of committees and associating together, had certain resolutions prepared, by which a select few was appointed to take an enrolment of all willing in the parish to serve as volunteers in defence of their King and country, and to concert with certain gentlemen named therein, about the formation of a corps, of which, it was an understood thing, the said gentlemen were to be the officers. The whole of this business was managed with the height of discretion, and the weavers, and spinners, and farming lads, vied with one another who should be first on the list. But that which the most surprised me, was the wonderful sagacity of the committee in naming the gentlemen that should be the officers. I could not have made a better choice myself, for they were the best built, the best bred, and the best natured, in the parish. In short, when I saw the bravery that was in my people, and the spirit of wisdom by which it was directed, I said in my heart, the Lord of Hosts is with us,[3] and the adversary shall not prevail.

The number of valiant men which at that time placed themselves around the banners of their country was so great, that the government would not accept of all who offered; so, like as in other parishes, we were obligated to make a selection, which was likewise done in a most judicious manner, all men above a certain age being reserved for the defence of the parish, in the day when the young might be called to England, to fight the enemy.

When the corps was formed, and the officers named, they made me their chaplain, and Dr Marigold their doctor. He was a little man with a big belly, and was as crouse[4] as a bantum

cock; but it was not thought he could do so well in field exercises, on which account he was made the doctor, although he
had no repute in that capacity, in comparison with Dr Tanzey,
who was not however liked, being a stiff-mannered man, with
a sharp temper.

All things having come to a proper head, the young ladies
of the parish resolved to present the corps with a stand[1] of
colours, which they embroidered themselves, and a day was
fixed for the presentation of the same. Never was such a day
seen in Dalmailing. The sun shone brightly on that scene of
bravery and grandeur, and far and near the country folk came
flocking in, and we had the regimental band of music hired
from the soldiers that were in Ayr barracks. The very first
sound o't made the hair on my old grey head to prickle up,
and my blood to rise and glow, as if youth was coming again
in to my veins.

Sir Hugh Montgomery[2] was the commandant, and he came
in all the glory of war, on his best horse, and marched at the
head of the men, to the green-head. The doctor and me were
the rear-guard, not being able, on account of my age, and his
fatness, to walk so fast as the quick-step of the corps. On the
field, we took our place in front, near Sir Hugh, and the ladies
with the colours; and, after some salutations according to the
fashion of the army, Sir Hugh made a speech to the men, and
then Miss Maria Montgomery came forward, with her sister
Miss Eliza, and the other ladies, and the banners were un-
furled, all glittering with gold, and the King's arms in needle-
work. Miss Maria then made a speech, which she had got by
heart, but she was so agitated, that it was said she forgot the
best part of it; however, it was very well considering.[3] When
this was done, I then stepped forward, and laying my hat on
the ground, every man and boy taking off theirs, I said a
prayer, which I had conned most carefully, and which
I thought the most suitable I could devise, in unison with
Christian principles, which are averse to the shedding of

blood; and I particularly dwelt upon some of the specialities of our situation.

When I had concluded, the volunteers gave three great shouts, and the multitude answered them to the same tune, and all the instruments of music sounded, making such a bruit, as could not be surpassed for grandeur—a long, and very circumstantial account of all which may be read in the newspapers of that time.

The volunteers, at the word of command, then shewed us the way they were to fight with the French, in the doing of which a sad disaster happened; for when they were charging bayonets, they came towards us like a flood, and all the spectators ran, and I ran, and the doctor ran, but being laden with his belly, he could not run fast enough, so he lay down, and being just before me at the time, I tumbled over him, and such a shout of laughter shook the field, as was never heard.

When the fatigues of the day were at an end, we marched to the cotton-mill, where, in one of the warehouses, a vast table was spread, and a dinner, prepared at Mr Cayenne's own expence, sent in from the Cross-keys, and the whole corps, with many of the gentry of the neighbourhood, dined with great jollity, the band of music playing beautiful airs all the time. At night, there was a universal dance, gentle and semple[1] mingled together. All which made it plain to me, that the Lord, by this unison of spirit, had decreed our national preservation; but I kept this in my own breast, lest it might have the effect to relax the vigilance of the kingdom. And I should note, that Colin Mavis, the poetical lad, of whom I have spoken in another part, made a song for this occasion, that was very mightily thought of, having in it a nerve of valiant genius, that kindled the very souls of those that heard it.

CHAPTER XLV · YEAR 1804

*The Session agrees that church censures shall be
commuted with fines · Our parish has an opportunity
of seeing a turtle, which is sent to Mr Cayenne · Some
fears of popery · Also about a preacher of universal
redemption · Report of a French ship appearing in
the west, which sets the volunteers astir*

IN conformity with the altered fashions of the age, in this
year the Session came to an understanding with me, that we
should not inflict the common church censures[1] for such as
made themselves liable thereto; but we did not formally
promulge[2] our resolution as to this, wishing as long as possible
to keep the deterring rod over the heads of the young and
thoughtless. Our motive, on the one hand, was the disregard
of the manufacturers in Cayenneville, who were, without the
breach of truth, an irreligious people, and, on the other, a
desire to preserve the ancient and wholesome admonitory and
censorian[3] jurisdiction of the minister and elders. We therefore laid it down as a rule to ourselves, that, in the case of
transgressions on the part of the inhabitants of the new
district of Cayenneville, we should subject them rigorously to
a fine; but that for the farming lads, we would put it to their
option to pay the fine, or stand in the kirk.

We conformed also in another matter to the times, by con-
senting to baptize occasionally in private houses. Hitherto
it had been a strict rule with me only to baptize from the
pulpit. Other places, however, had long been in the practice
of this relaxation of ancient discipline.

But all this, on my part, was not done without compunction

of spirit; for I was of opinion, that the principle of Presbyterian integrity should have been maintained to the uttermost.
Seeing, however, the elders set on an alteration, I distrusted
my own judgment, and yielded myself to the considerations
that weighed with them; for they were true men, and of a
godly honesty, and took the part of the poor in all contentions
with the heritors, often to the hazard and damage of their own
temporal welfare.

I have now to note a curious thing, not on account of its
importance, but to shew to what lengths a correspondence
had been opened in the parish with the farthest parts of the
earth. Mr Cayenne got a turtle-fish[1] sent to him from a Glasgow merchant, and it was living when it came to Wheatrig-
house, and was one of the most remarkable beasts that had
ever been seen in our country side. It weighed as much as
a well-fed calf, and had three kinds of meat in its body, fish,
flesh, and fowl, and it had four water-wings, for they could
not be properly called fins; but what was little short of a
miracle about the creature, happened after the head was
cutted off, when, if a finger was offered to it, it would open its
mouth and snap at it, and all this after the carcase was divided
for dressing.

Mr Cayenne made a feast on the occasion to many of the
neighbouring gentry, to the which I was invited, and we
drank lime-punch as we ate the turtle, which, as I understand,
is the fashion in practice among the Glasgow West Indy
merchants, who are famed as great hands with turtles and
lime-punch. But it is a sort of food that I should not like to
fare long upon. I was not right the next day; and I have heard
it said, that, when eaten too often, it has a tendency to harden
the heart, and make it crave for greater luxuries.

But the story of the turtle is nothing to that of the Mass,
which, with all its mummeries and abominations, was brought
into Cayenneville by an Irish priest of the name of Father
O'Grady, who was confessor to some of the poor deluded

Irish labourers about the new houses and the cotton-mill. How he had the impudence to set up that memento of Satan, the crucifix, within my parish and jurisdiction, was what I never could get to the bottom of; but the soul was shaken within me, when, on the Monday after, one of the elders came to the Manse, and told me, that the old dragon of Popery, with its seven heads and ten horns, had been triumphing in Cayenneville on the foregoing Lord's day! I lost no time in convening the Session to see what was to be done; much, however, to my surprise, the elders recommended no step to be taken, but only a zealous endeavour to greater Christian excellence on our part, by which we should put the beast and his worshippers to shame and flight. I am free to confess, that, at the time, I did not think this the wisest counsel which they might have given; for, in the heat of my alarm, I was for attacking the enemy in his camp. But they prudently observed, that the days of religious persecution were past, and it was a comfort to see mankind cherishing any sense of religion at all, after the vehement infidelity that had been sent abroad by the French Republicans; and to this opinion, now that I have had years to sift its wisdom, I own myself a convert and proselyte.

Fortunately, however, for my peace of mind, there proved to be but five Roman Catholics in Cayenneville; and Father O'Grady, not being able to make a living there, packed up his Virgin Marys, saints, and painted Agnuses in a portmanteau, and went off in the Ayr Fly one morning for Glasgow, where I hear he has since met with all the encouragement that might be expected from the ignorant and idolatrous inhabitants of that great city.

Scarcely were we well rid of Father O'Grady, when another interloper entered the parish. He was more dangerous, in the opinion of the Session, than even the Pope of Rome himself; for he came to teach the flagrant heresy of Universal Redemption, a most consolatory doctrine to the sinner that is loth to repent, and who loves to troll his iniquity like a sweet morsel under his tongue. Mr Martin Siftwell, who was the last ta'en on elder, and who had received a liberal and judicious education, and was, moreover, naturally possessed of a quick penetration, observed, in speaking of this new doctrine, that the grossest papist sinner might have some qualms of fear after he had bought the Pope's pardon, and might thereby be led to a reformation of life; but that the doctrine of universal redemption was a bribe to commit sin, the wickedest mortal, according to it, being only liable to a few thousand years, more or less, of suffering, which, compared with eternity, was but a momentary pang, like having a tooth drawn for the toothache. Mr Siftwell is a shrewd and clear-seeing man in points of theology, and I would trust a great deal to what he says, as I have not, at my advanced age, such a mind for the kittle[1] crudities[2] of polemical investigation that I had in my younger years, especially when I was a student in the Divinity-Hall of Glasgow.

It will be seen from all I have herein recorded, that, in the course of this year, there was a general resuscitation of religious sentiments; for what happened in my parish was but a type and index to the rest of the world. We had, however, one memorable that must stand by itself; for although neither death nor bloodshed happened, yet was it cause of the fear of both.

A rumour reached us from the Clyde, that a French man of war had appeared in a Highland loch, and that all the Greenock volunteers had embarked in merchant-vessels to bring her in for a prize. Our volunteers were just jumping and yowling, like chained dogs, to be at her too; but the colonel, Sir Hugh, would do nothing without orders from his superiors. Mr Cayenne, though an aged man, above seventy, was as bold as a lion, and came forth in the old garb of an American huntsman, like, as I was told, a Robin Hood in the play[3] is; and it was just a sport to see him, feckless man, trying to march so crously[1] with his lean shaking shanks. But the whole affair proved a false alarm, and our men, when they heard it, were as well pleased that they had been constrained to sleep in their warm beds at home, instead of lying on coils of cables, like the gallant Greenock sharp-shooters.

CHAPTER XLVI · YEAR 1805

Retrenchment of the extravagant expences usual at burials · I use an expedient for putting even the second service out of fashion

―――――――

FOR some time I had meditated a reformation in the parish, and this year I carried the same into effect. I had often noticed with concern, that, out of a mistaken notion of paying respect to the dead, my people were wont to go to great lengths at their burials,[1] and dealt round short-bread and sugar biscuit, with wine and other confections, as if there had been no ha'd[2] in their hands; which straightened many a poor family, making the dispensation of the Lord a heavier temporal calamity than it should naturally have been. Accordingly, on consulting with Mrs Balwhidder, who has a most judicious judgment, it was thought that my interference would go a great way to lighten the evil. I therefore advised with those whose friends were taken from them, not to make that amplitude of preparation which used to be the fashion, nor to continue handing about as long as the folk would take, but only at the very most to go no more than three times round with the service. Objections were made to this, as if it would be thought mean; but I put on a stern visage, and told them, that if they did more I would rise up and rebuke and forbid the extravagance. So three services became the uttermost modicum at all burials. This was doing so much, but it was not all that I wished to do.

I considered that the best reformations are those which proceed step by step, and stop at that point where the consent to what has been established becomes general; and so I governed myself, and therefore interfered no farther; but I was determined to set an example. Accordingly, at the very next draigie,[1] after I partook of one service, I made a bow to the servitors and they passed on, but all before me had partaken of the second service; some, however, of those after me did as I did, so I foresaw that in a quiet canny way I would bring in the fashion of being satisfied with one service. I therefore, from that time, always took my place as near as possible to the door, where the chief mourner sat, and made a point of nodding away the second service, which has now grown into a custom, to the great advantage of surviving relations.

But in this reforming business I was not altogether pleased with our poet; for he took a pawkie[2] view of my endeavours, and indited a ballad on the subject, in the which he makes a clattering[3] carlin describe what took place, so as to turn a very solemn matter into a kind of derision. When he brought his verse and read it to me, I told him that I thought it was overly natural; for I could not find another term to designate the cause of the dissatisfaction that I had with it; but Mrs Balwhidder said that it might help my plan if it were made public, so upon her advice we got some of Mr Loremore's best writers to make copies of it for distribution, which was not without fruit and influence. But a sore thing happened at the very next burial. As soon as the nodding away of the second service began, I could see that the gravity of the whole meeting was discomposed, and some of the irreverent young chiels[4] almost broke out into even-down[5] laughter, which vext me exceedingly. Mrs Balwhidder, however, comforted me by saying, that custom in time would make it familiar, and by and by the thing would pass as a matter of course, until one service would be all that folk would offer; and truly the thing is coming to that, for only two services are now handed round, and the second is regularly nodded by.

CHAPTER XLVII · YEAR 1806

*The death-bed behaviour of Mr Cayenne · A schism
in the parish, and a subscription to build a meeting
house*

━━━━━

MR CAYENNE of Wheatrig having for several years been in a declining way, partly brought on by the consuming fire of his furious passion, and partly by the decay of old age, sent for me on the evening of the first Sabbath of March in this year. I was surprised at the message, and went to the Wheatrig-house directly, where, by the lights in the windows as I gaed up through the policy¹ to the door, I saw something extra-ordinary was going on. Sambo, the blackamoor servant, opened the door, and without speaking shook his head; for it was an affectionate creature, and as fond of his master as if he had been his own father. By this sign I guessed that the old gentleman was thought to be drawing near his latter end, so I walked softly after Sambo up the stair, and was shewn into the chamber where Mr Cayenne, since he had been confined to the house, usually sat. His wife had been dead some years before.

Mr Cayenne was sitting in his easy chair, with a white cotton night-cap on his head, and a pillow at his shoulders to keep him straight. But his head had fallen down on his breast, and he breathed like a panting baby. His legs were swelled, and his feet rested on a footstool. His face, which was wont to be the colour of a peony rose, was of a yellow hue, with a patch of red on each cheek like a wafer,² and his nose was shirpet³ and sharp, and of an unnatural purple. Death was evidently fighting with Nature for the possession of the body. 'Heaven have mercy on his soul,' said I to myself, as I sat me down beside him.

When I had been seated some time, the power was given him to raise his head as it were ajee,[1] and he looked at me with the tail of his eye, which I saw was glittering and glassy. 'Doctor,' for he always called me doctor, though I am not of that degree, 'I am glad to see you,' were his words, uttered with some difficulty.

'How do you find yourself, sir?' I replied in a sympathising manner.

'Damned bad,' said he, as if I had been the cause of his suffering. I was daunted to the very heart to hear him in such an unregenerate state; but after a short pause I addressed myself to him again, saying, that 'I hoped he would soon be more at ease, and he should bear in mind that the Lord chasteneth[2] whom he loveth.'

'The devil take such love,' was his awful answer, which was to me as a blow on the forehead with a mell.[3] However, I was resolved to do my duty to the miserable sinner, let him say what he would. Accordingly, I stooped towards him with my hands on my knees, and said in a compassionate voice, 'It's very true, sir, that you are in great agony, but the goodness of God is without bound.'

'Curse me if I think so, doctor,' replied the dying uncircumcised Philistine. But he added at whiles, his breathlessness being grievous, and often broken by a sore hiccup, 'I am however no saint, as you know, doctor; so I wish you to put in a word for me, doctor; for you know that in these times, doctor, it is the duty of every good subject to die a Christian.'

This was a poor account of the state of his soul, but it was plain I could make no better o't, by entering into any religious discourse or controversy with him, he being then in the last gasp; so I knelt down and prayed for him with great sincerity, imploring the Lord, as an awakening sense of grace to the dying man, that it would please him to lift up, though it were but for the season of a minute, the chastening hand which was laid so heavily upon his aged servant; at which Mr Cayenne, as if indeed the hand had been then lifted, cried out, 'None of that stuff, doctor; you know that I cannot call myself his servant.'

Was ever a minister in his prayer so broken in upon by a perishing sinner! However, I had the weight of a duty upon me, and made no reply, but continued, 'Thou hearest, O Lord! how he confesses his unworthiness—Let not thy compassion, therefore, be withheld, but verify to him the words that I have spoken in faith, of the boundlessness of thy goodness, and the infinite multitude of thy tender mercies.' I then calmly, but sadly, sat down, and presently, as if my prayer had been heard, relief was granted; for Mr Cayenne raised his head, and, giving me a queer look, said, 'that last clause of your petition, doctor, was well put, and I think, too, it has been granted, for I am easier,'—adding, 'I have, no doubt, doctor, given much offence in the world, and oftenest when I meant to do good; but I have wilfully injured no man, and as God is my judge, and His goodness, you say, is so great, He may perhaps take my soul into His holy keeping.' In saying which words, Mr Cayenne dropped his head upon his breast, his breathing ceased, and he was wafted away out of this world with as little trouble as a blameless child.

This event soon led to a change among us. In the settling of Mr Cayenne's affairs in the Cotton-mill Company, it was found that he had left such a power of money, that it was needful to the concern, in order that they might settle with the doers under his testament, to take in other partners. By this Mr Speckle came to be a resident in the parish, he having taken up a portion of Mr Cayenne's share. He likewise took a tack[1] of the house and policy[2] of Wheatrig. But although Mr Speckle was a far more conversible man than his predecessor, and had a wonderful plausibility in business, the affairs of the Company did not thrive in his hands. Some said this was owing to his having owre[1] many irons in the fire; others, to the circumstances of the times; in my judgment, however, both helped; but the issue belongs to the events of another year. In the meanwhile, I should here note, that in the course of this current Ann. Dom. it pleased Heaven to visit me with a severe trial; the nature of which I will here record at length—the upshot I will make known hereafter.

From the planting of inhabitants in the cotton-mill town of Cayenneville, or, as the country folk, not used to such lang-nebbit[2] words, now call it, Canaille, there had come in upon the parish various sectarians among the weavers, some of whom were not satisfied with the gospel as I preached it, and endeavoured to practise it in my walk and conversation;[3] and they began to speak of building a kirk for themselves, and of getting a minister that would give them the gospel more to their own ignorant fancies. I was exceedingly wroth and disturbed when the thing was first mentioned to me; and I very earnestly, from the pulpit, next Lord's day, lectured on the growth of new-fangled doctrines; which, however, instead of having the wonted effect of my discourses, set up the theological weavers in a bleeze,[4] and the very Monday following they named a committee, to raise money by subscription, to build a meeting-house. This was the first overt-act of insubordination, collectively manifested in the parish; and it was conducted with all that crafty dexterity, with which the infidel and jacobin spirit of the French Revolution had corrupted the honest simplicity of our good old hameward[5] fashions. In the course of a very short time, the Canaille folk had raised a large sum, and seduced not a few of my people into their schism, by which they were enabled to set about building their kirk; the foundations thereof were not, however, laid till the following year, but their proceedings gave me a het[6] heart, for they were like an open rebellion to my authority, and a contemptuous disregard of that religious allegiance which is due from the flock to the pastor.

On Christmas day, the wind broke off the main arm of our Adam and Eve pear-tree, and I grieved for it more as a type and sign of the threatened partition, than on account of the damage, though the fruit was the juiciest in all the country-side.

CHAPTER XLVIII · YEAR 1807

Numerous marriages · Account of a pay-wedding,
made to set up a shop .

═══════

THIS was a year to me of satisfaction, in many points, for a greater number of my younger flock married in it, than had done for any one of ten years prior. They were chiefly the offspring of the marriages that took place at the close of the American war; and I was pleased to see the duplification of well-doing, as I think marrying is, having always considered the command, to increase and multiply, a holy ordinance, which the circumstances of this world but too often interfere to prevent.

It was also made manifest to me, that in this year there was a very general renewal in the hearts of men, of a sense of the utility, even in earthly affairs, of a religious life: In some, I trust it was more than prudence, and really a birth of grace. Whether this was owing to the upshot of the French Revolution, all men being pretty well satisfied in their minds, that uproar and rebellion make but an ill way of righting wrongs, or that the swarm of unruly youth, the offspring, as I have said, of the marriages after the American war, had grown sobered from their follies, and saw things in a better light, I cannot take upon me to say. But it was very edifying to me, their minister, to see several lads, who had been both wild and free in their principles, marrying with sobriety, and taking their wives to the kirk, with the comely decorum of heads of families.

But I was now growing old, and could go seldomer out among my people than in former days, so that I was less a partaker of their ploys and banquets, either at birth, bridal, or burial. I heard, however, all that went on at them, and I made it a rule, after giving the blessing at the end of the ceremony, to admonish the bride and bridegroom to ca' canny,[1] and join trembling[2] with their mirth. It behoved me on one occasion, however, to break through a rule, that age and frailty had imposed upon me, and to go to the wedding of Tibby Banes, the daughter of the betherel,[3] because she had once been a servant in the Manse, besides the obligation upon me from her father's part, both in the kirk and kirk-yard. Mrs Balwhidder went with me, for she liked to countenance the pleasantries[4] of my people; and, over and above all, it was a pay-wedding,[5] in order to set up the bridegroom in a shop.

There was, to be sure, a great multitude, gentle and semple,[6] of all denominations, with two fiddles and a bass, and the volunteers' fife and drum, and the jollity that went on was a perfect feast of itself, though the wedding-supper was a prodigy of abundance. The auld carles kecklet[7] with fain-ness,[8] as they saw the young dancers; and the carlins[9] sat on forms,[10] as mim[11] as May puddocks,[12] with their shawls pinned apart, to shew their muslin napkins. But, after supper, when they had got a glass of the punch, their heels shewed their mettle, and grannies danced with their oes,[13] holding out their hands as if they had been spinning with two rocks.[14] I told Colin Mavis, the poet, that an *Infare*[15] was a fine subject for his muse, and soon after, he indited an excellent ballad under that title, which he projects to publish with other ditties by subscription; and I have no doubt a liberal and discerning public will give him all manner of encouragement, for that is the food of talent of every kind, and without cheering, no one can say what an author's faculty naturally is.

CHAPTER XLIX · YEAR 1808

*Failure of Mr Speckle, the proprietor of the
cotton-mill · the melancholy end of one of the
overseers and his wife*

———

THROUGH all the wars that have raged from the time of the
King's accession to the throne, there has been a gradually
coming nearer and nearer to our gates, which is a very alarming
thing to think of. In the first, at the time he came to the crown,
we suffered nothing. Not one belonging to the parish was
engaged in the battles thereof, and the news of victories,
before they reached us, which was generally by word of mouth,
were old tales. In the American war, as I have related at length,
we had an immediate participation, but those that suffered
were only a few individuals, and the evil was done at a distance,
and reached us not until the worst of its effects were spent.
And during the first term of the present just and necessary
contest for all that is dear to us as a people, although, by the
offswarming of some of our restless youth, we had our part
and portion in common with the rest of the Christian world;
yet still there was at home a great augmentation of prosperity,
and every thing had thriven in a surprising manner; somewhat, however, to the detriment of our country simplicity.
By the building of the cotton-mill, and the rising up of the new
town of Cayenneville, we had intromitted so much with
concerns of trade, that we were become a part of the great web
of commercial reciprocities, and felt in our corner and
extremity, every touch or stir that was made on any part of the
texture. The consequence of this I have now to relate.

Various rumours had been floating about the business of

the cotton manufacturers not being so lucrative as it had been; and Bonaparte, as it is well known, was a perfect limb of Satan against our prosperity, having recourse to the most wicked means and purposes to bring ruin upon us as a nation. His cantrips,[1] in this year, began to have a dreadful effect.

For some time it had been observed in the parish, that Mr Speckle, of the cotton-mill, went very often to Glasgow, and was sometimes off at a few minutes warning to London, and the neighbours began to guess and wonder at what could be the cause of all this running here, and riding there, as if the littlegude[2] was at his heels. Sober folk augured ill o't; and it was remarked, likewise, that there was a haste and confusion in his mind, which betokened a foretaste of some change of fortune. At last, in the fulness of time, the babe was born.

On a Saturday night, Mr Speckle came out late from Glasgow; on the Sabbath he was with all his family at the kirk, looking as a man that had changed his way of life; and on the Monday, when the spinners went to the mill, they were told that the company had stopped payment. Never did a thunderclap daunt the heart like this news, for the bread in a moment was snatched from more than a thousand mouths. It was a scene not to be described, to see the cotton-spinners and the weavers, with their wives and children, standing in bands along the road, all looking and speaking as if they had lost a dear friend or parent. For my part, I could not bear the sight, but hid myself in my closet, and prayed to the Lord to mitigate a calamity, which seemed to me past the capacity of man to remedy; for what could our parish fund do in the way of helping a whole town, thus suddenly thrown out of bread.

In the evening, however, I was strengthened, and convened the elders at the Manse to consult with them on what was best to be done, for it was well known that the sufferers had made no provision for a sore foot.[3] But all our gathered judgments could determine nothing; and therefore we resolved to wait the issue, not doubting but that HE who sends the night, would bring the day in His good and gracious time, which so fell out. Some of them who had the largest experience of such vicissitudes, immediately began to pack up their ends and their awls,[1] and to hie them in to Glasgow and Paisley in quest of employ; but those who trusted to the hopes that Mr Speckle himself still cherished, lingered long, and were obligated to submit to sore distress. After a time, however, it was found that the company was ruined, and the mill being sold for the benefit of the creditors, it was bought by another Glasgow company, who, by getting it a good bargain, and managing well, have it still, and have made it again a blessing to the country. At the time of the stoppage, however, we saw that commercial prosperity, flush as it might be, was but a perishable commodity, and from thence, both by public discourse and private exhortation, I have recommended to the workmen to lay up something for a reverse; and shewed that, by doing with their bawbees[2] and pennies, what the great do with their pounds, they might in time get a pose[3] to help them in the day of need. This advice they have followed, and made up a Savings Bank, which is a pillar of comfort to many an industrious head of a family.

But I should not close this account of the disaster that befell Mr Speckle, and the cotton-mill company, without relating a very melancholy case that was the consequence. Among the overseers, there was a Mr Dwining,[4] an Englishman from Manchester, where he had seen better days, having had himself there of his own property, once as large a mill, according to report, as the Cayenneville mill. He was certainly a man above the common, and his wife was a lady in every point; but they held themselves by themselves, and shunned all manner of civility, giving up their whole attention to their two little boys, who were really like creatures of a better race than the callans of our clachan.

On the failure of the company, Mr Dwining was observed by those who were present, to be particularly distressed, his salary

being his all; but he said little, and went thoughtfully home. Some days after he was seen walking by himself with a pale face, a heavy eye, and slow step—all tokens of a sorrowful heart. Soon after he was missed altogether; nobody saw him. The door of his house was however open, and his two pretty boys were as lively as usual, on the green before the door. I happened to pass when they were there, and I asked them how their father and mother were. They said they were still in bed, and would not waken, and the innocent lambs took me by the hand, to make me waken their parents. I know not what was in it, but I trembled from head to foot, and I was led in by the babies, as if I had not the power to resist. Never shall I forget what I saw in that bed   *   *   *   *   *   *
I found a letter on the table; and I came away, locking the door behind me, and took the lovely prattling orphans home. I could but shake my head and weep, as I gave them to the care of Mrs Balwhidder, and she was terrified, but said nothing. I then read the letter. It was to send the bairns to a gentleman, their uncle, in London. Oh it is a terrible tale, but the winding-sheet and the earth is over it. I sent for two of my elders. I related what I had seen. Two coffins were got, and the bodies laid in them; and the next day, with one of the fatherless bairns in each hand, I followed them to the grave, which was dug in that part of the kirk-yard where unchristened babies are laid. We durst not take it upon us to do more, but few knew the reason, and some thought it was because the deceased were strangers, and had no regular lair.[1]

I dressed the two bonny orphans in the best mourning at my own cost, and kept them in the Manse till we should get an answer from their uncle, to whom I sent their father's letter. It stung him to the quick, and he came down all the way from London, and took the children away himself. O he was a vext[2] man, when the beautiful bairns, on being told he was their uncle, ran into his arms, and complained that their papa and mamma had slept so long, that they would never waken.

*Opening of a Meeting-house · The elders come to the
Manse, and offer me a helper*

════════

As I come towards the events of these latter days, I am surprised to find myself not at all so distinct in my recollection
of them, as in those of the first of my ministry; being apt to
confound the things of one occasion with those of another,
which Mrs Balwhidder says is an admonishment to me to
leave off my writing. But, please God, I will endeavour to fulfil
this as I have through life tried, to the best of my capacity,
to do every other duty; and with the help of Mrs Balwhidder,
who has a very clear understanding, I think I may get through
my task in a creditable manner, which is all I aspire after; not
writing for a vain world, but only to testify to posterity anent
the great changes that have happened in my day and generation—a period which all the best informed writers say, has not
had its match in the history of the world, since the beginning
of time.

By the failure of the cotton-mill company, whose affairs
were not settled till the spring of this year, there was great
suffering during the winter; but my people, those that still
adhered to the establishment, bore their share of the dispensation with meekness and patience, nor was there wanting edifying monuments of resignation even among the strayvaggers.[1]

On the day that the Canaille Meeting-house was opened,
which was in the summer, I was smitten to the heart to see the
empty seats that were in my kirk, for all the thoughtless, and
some that I had a better opinion of, went to hear the opening
discourse. Satan that day had power given to him to buffet me

as he did Job of old; and when I looked around and saw the empty seats, my corruption[1] rose, and I forgot myself in the remembering prayer; for when I prayed for all denominations of Christians, and worshippers, and infidels, I could not speak of the schismatics with patience, but entreated the Lord to do with the hobbleshow[2] at Cayenneville, as he saw meet in his displeasure, the which, when I came afterwards to think upon, I grieved at with a sore contrition.

In the course of the week following, the elders, in a body, came to me in the Manse, and after much commendation of my godly ministry, they said, that seeing I was now growing old, they thought they could not testify their respect for me in a better manner, than by agreeing to get me a helper. But I would not at that time listen to such a proposal, for I felt no falling off in my powers of preaching; on the contrary, I found myself growing better at it, as I was enabled to hold forth, in an easy manner, often a whole half hour longer than I could do a dozen years before. Therefore nothing was done in this year anent my resignation; but during the winter, Mrs Balwhidder was often grieved, in the bad weather, that I should preach, and, in short, so worked upon my affections, that I began to think it was fitting for me to comply with the advice of my friends. Accordingly, in the course of the winter, the elders began to cast about for a helper, and during the bleak weather in the ensuing spring, several young men spared me from the necessity of preaching. But this relates to the concerns of the next and last year of my ministry. So I will now proceed to give an account of it, very thankful that I have been permitted, in unmolested tranquillity, to bring my history to such a point.

CHAPTER LI · YEAR 1810

Conclusion · I repair to the church for the last time · Afterwards receive a silver server from the parishioners · And still continue to marry and baptize

————

MY tasks are all near a close; and in writing this final record of my ministry, the very sound of my pen admonishes me that my life is a burden on the back of flying time, that he will soon be obliged to lay down in his great store-house, the grave. Old age has, indeed, long warned me to prepare for rest, and the darkened windows of my sight shew that the night is coming on, while deafness, like a door fast barred, has shut out all the pleasant sounds of this world, and inclosed me, as it were, in a prison, even from the voices of my friends.

I have lived longer than the common lot of man, and I have seen, in my time, many mutations and turnings, and ups and downs, notwithstanding the great spread that has been in our national prosperity. I have beheld them that were flourishing like the green bay trees,[1] made desolate, and their branches scattered. But, in my own estate, I have had a large and liberal experience of goodness.

At the beginning of my ministry I was reviled and rejected, but my honest endeavours to prove a faithful shepherd, were blessed from on high, and rewarded with the affection of my flock. Perhaps, in the vanity of doting old age, I thought in this there was a merit due to myself, which made the Lord to send the chastisement of the Canaille schism among my people, for I was then wroth without judgment, and by my heat hastened into an open division the flaw that a more considerate manner might have healed. But I confess my fault, and submit my cheek to the smiter; and I now see that the finger of Wisdom was in that probation, and it was far better that the weavers meddled with the things of God, which they could not change, than with those of the king, which they could only harm. In that matter, however, I was like our gracious monarch in the American war; for though I thereby lost the pastoral allegiance of a portion of my people, in like manner as he did of his American subjects; yet, after the separation, I was enabled so to deport myself, that they shewed me many voluntary testimonies of affectionate respect, and which it would be a vain glory in me to rehearse here. One thing I must record, because it is as much to their honour as it is to mine.

When it was known that I was to preach my last sermon, every one of those who had been my hearers, and who had seceded to the Canaille meeting, made it a point that day to be in the parish kirk, and to stand in the crowd, that made a lane of reverence for me to pass from the kirk door to the back-yett[1] of the Manse. And shortly after a deputation of all their brethren, with their minister at their head, came to me one morning, and presented to me a server of silver, in token, as they were pleased to say, of their esteem for my blameless life, and the charity that I had practised towards the poor of all sects in the neighbourhood; which is set forth in a well-penned inscription, written by a weaver lad that works for his daily bread. Such a thing would have been a prodigy at the beginning of my ministry, but the progress of book learning and education has been wonderful since, and with it has come a spirit of greater liberality than the world knew before, bringing men of adverse principles and doctrines, into a more humane communion with each other, shewing, that it's by the mollifying influence of knowledge, the time will come to pass, when the tiger of papistry shall lie down with the lamb of reformation, and the vultures of prelacy be as harmless as the presbyterian doves; when the independent, the anabaptist, and every other order and denomination of Christians, not forgetting even these poor wee wrens of the Lord, the burghers and anti-burghers,[1] who will pick from the hand of patronage, and dread no snare.

On the next Sunday, after my farewell discourse, I took the arm of Mrs Balwhidder, and with my cane in my hand, walked to our own pew, where I sat some time, but owing to my deafness, not being able to hear, I have not since gone back to the church. But my people are fond of having their weans still christened by me, and the young folk, such as are of a serious turn, come to be married at my hands, believing, as they say, that there is something good in the blessing of an aged gospel minister. But even this remnant of my gown I must lay aside, for Mrs Balwhidder is now and then obliged to stop me in my prayers, as I sometimes wander—pronouncing the baptismal blessing upon a bride and bridegroom, talking as if they were already parents. I am thankful, however, that I have been spared with a sound mind to write this book to the end; but it is my last task, and, indeed, really I have no more to say, saving only to wish a blessing on all people from on High, where I soon hope to be, and to meet there all the old and long-departed sheep of my flock, especially the first and second Mrs Balwhidders.

FINIS

APPENDIX

———

I. GALT TO BLACKWOOD[1]

London 27 Feb.ᵧ 1821

My dear Sir

I have both your obliging favours of the 17th & 22d—and I now return '*the Annals*'. I think the simplicity of the altered title better than mine—I have adopted some of the alterations but I am very reluctant to part with what is objected to in 1765, 1766, 1773, and 1774—Some of them are characteristic of the garrulous humour of the old doited author, and the others are such events as are long remembered in country parishes besides they have all a vague reference to real events which happened about the time in Ayrshire —and are calculated, as I conceive, to give that degree of reality to the story that may induce *some* to think there has actually been an original chronicle—I mean to write a dedicatory epistle to the King in the character of the Session Clerk. However I am not very tenacious, and I trust much to yourself even with respect to these things that I may myself wish retained.

I was in hopes that you would have given me £100 however I shall be contented with the sixty Gˢ The fact is that by my confidence in a connection last year I was brought into trouble and obliged to borrow a thousand pounds which I am anxious to repay and every little helps, on this account the sooner you can send me the note it will be a favour—

By the way it strikes me that you do not advertise enough in London. . . .

I remain my dear Sir
Truly Yours
John Galt.

[1] Excerpted by courtesy of the National Library of Scotland. N.L.S. MS. 4006, ff. 223-4 and 235.

London 10th April 1821

My dear Sir,

Yesterday I received your two parcels the MS & the sheets & the latter I have read entirely over and I am much satisfied with the omissions. I had begun to question in my own mind the strength of some of the incidents as being out of keeping with the general tone of the work. The printing is surprisingly correct from a manuscript of mine: had the proofs been revised by myself they would in all probability not have been so much so. I am glad the work is to be a little shortened. It is not a subject that can bear a great deal and the interest will be improved by the condensation.

Upon reflection no introductory matter is required, but if *you* think fit I would inscribe it to Henry Mackenzie in the following manner—

To
Henry Mackenzie Esqr
author of the man of feeling.
A small acknowledgment
for the pleasure derived
In early life
from the perusal of his simple
and beautiful tales
by the author—. . . .[1]

I remain my Dear Sir
faithfully Yours
[unsigned]

---

[1] Blackwood did not think fit to allow this dedication. His decision was prudent. Five years later Lady Louisa Scott heard *The Man of Feeling* (1771) read in company: 'I am afraid I perceived a sad change in it, or myself—which was worse; and the effect altogether failed. Nobody cried, and at some of the passages, the touches that I used to think so exquisite—Oh Dear! they laughed. . . . Yet I remember so well its first publication, my mother and sisters crying over it . . . and when I read it, as I was a girl of 14 not yet versed in sentiment, I had a secret dread I should not cry enough to gain the credit of proper sensibility' (Sir Walter Scott, *Letter Books*).

II. GALT ON THE *ANNALS*[1]

AFTER my return from Gibraltar,[2] the work subsequently published under the title of the Annals of the Parish was my first
production. It was undertaken in the summer of 1813. . . .

When very young, I wished to write a book that would be for
Scotland what the Vicar of Wakefield is for England, and early
began to observe and to conjecture in what respects the minister
of a rural parish differed from the general inhabitants of the
country. The study was not, however, pursued with any particular
intensity, the opportunity being wanting, for our town was large,
and the clergymen in it too urbane to furnish a model. The *beau
idéal* of a rural pastor never presented itself to me; but I heard
from others descriptions of the characters of individuals, by which
I was furnished with many hints. The original of Micah Balwhidder
was minister of Saltcoats in my youth; I never saw him, though
from boyhood intimate with members of his family.[3]

One Sunday, happening to take a walk to the neighbouring
village to Greenock, Innerkip,[4] I observed, that from the time I
had been there, some progress had been made by Sir John Shaw
Stewart in turning it inside out. While looking at the various improvements around, my intention of writing a minister's sedate
adventures returned upon me, as if the mantle of inspiration had
suddenly dropped upon my shoulders, and I resolved to make the
schoolmaster of the village the recorder of a register. A specimen of
what I then designed is introduced into Eben Erskine;[5] but I did not
proceed with that intention, and it was not till after my marriage
that I altered my plan into the Annals of the Parish, nor did I then
quite complete it, as I was informed that Scottish novels would

[1] *Literary Life, and Miscellanies*, 1834, i. 152-7.
[2] In 1811.
[3] Saltcoats was, at this time, a town of about 2,000 people in Ardrossan parish.
Here Ardrossan kirk was transferred in 1744 (rebuilt in 1774; the manse rebuilt in
the late 1780s—cf. *Annals*, ch. xxvii, 1786). Until two years before the Galts left
Irvine for Greenock, the minister of Ardrossan was Robert Dow (1707-87). It is
worth noting, however, that his successor John Duncan (1749-1819) was presented
by the patron, the Earl of Eglinton, in 1788— like Mr Balwhidder, against the
opposition of a mob; and that during Duncan's ministry two secession churches
and a meeting-house were erected in Saltcoats (cf. *Annals*, chs. xlvii-l).
[4] Inverkip, Renfrewshire, on the Firth of Clyde.
[5] 1833, i. 71.

not succeed (Waverley was not then published); and in consequence I threw the manuscript aside.[1]

Years after, I found it among my papers, and read it over as an entire stranger, when several passages struck me as having some merit, and as they produced the same effect on my friend Mr O——, who that day dined with me, I sent the manuscript to Mr Blackwood of Edinburgh, by whom it was published.

Some of the individuals who have been the models of the characters, were, on the publication, at once recognised, which tended to corroborate the favourable opinion I had myself formed of the work; but although the story was suggested by the improvements of Innerkip, the scene is laid in the whereabouts of the village of Dreghorn.[2]

I have been told, when the book first came out, Lady M. recognised her aunt Lady B. C.[3] in Lady Macadam. There was some shrewdness in the guess, for although of the eccentricities of the old lady I have but a schoolboy's recollection, she certainly was present to my imagination in the conception of the character, arising from local circumstances connected with Dreghorn. The actual model was a Mrs P——, of St. Peter's, Isle of Thanet. . . .

I am led from many circumstances to conclude that this simple work is considered the best of my productions; but although willing to regard it among the most original, I do not myself think so. No doubt it has what my own taste values highly, considerable likeliness, if the expression may be used, but it is so void of any thing like a plot, that it lacks in the most material feature of the novel.

To myself it has ever been a kind of treatise on the history of society in the West of Scotland during the reign of King George the Third; and when it was written, I had no idea it would ever have been received as a novel. Fables are often a better way of illustrating philosophical truths than abstract reasoning; and in this class of compositions I would place the Annals of the Parish;

---

[1] The draft of *Annals* was rejected by Constable. Scott 'threw together' the first part of *Waverley* 'about the year 1805', but set it aside and forgot it. He turned the manuscript up years later, and Constable published the novel in 1814.

[2] A village near Irvine, with only sixty inhabitants in 1810. The manse was rebuilt in 1789, when the Galts left the district.

[3] Possibly Lady Elisabeth Montgomery (1707-1800), wife of Sir John Cuninghame of Caprington, to the south-east of Dreghorn; sister to Archibald, 11th Earl of Eglinton, and so aunt to Lady Mary Montgomery (b. 1787).

but the public consider it as a novel, and it is of no use to think of altering the impression with which it has been received. . . .

But the conception of the work is now an old story, and I have had, since it was written, something else to do than to think much about it. Indeed, it is full ten years since I looked into it, nor was I aware, till I did so to-day . . . that it affords so many exact specimens of the kind of art which I have indifferently studied. In turning over the leaves, I see, in almost every page, proofs of those kind of memorials to which I have been most addicted—things of which the originals are, or were, actually in nature, but brought together into composition by art. I will give some of them, that the reader may see why I deny to memory that honour which is so freely granted, while I admit that my portfolio possessed scarcely more than her sketches. . . .[1]

---

[1] Galt's illustrations are quoted in the Explanatory Notes, *infra*.

TEXTUAL NOTES

21, 22: the editions of 1821, 1822

Page	Line	
11	4	well-water 22: well water 21
13	3	hedge 22: hedge, 21
13	8	conek 22: conck 21
14	23	cotters' 22: cotter's 21
22	19	Skim-milk, 22: Skim-milk 21
22	35	Inns 22: Inn 21
23	10	time in 22: time would do in 21
23	11	or in a 22: or a 21
29	18	interment, 22: interment 21
31	13	thir] their 22
32	5	me, we were] me were 22
35	9	panic laugh 22: panic of laugh 21
36	11	skreighing 22: searching 21 (*perhaps misreading of* screeching *in MS.*)
37	12	Gorbyholm] Galyholm 21
37	15	near-begun 22: near-begoing 21
41	17	was, 22: was 21
43	16	school 22: score 21 (*perhaps misinterpretation of MS.: see O.E.D.* score, *sb. 3. b*)
54	27	came 22: come 21
56	22	declaring] declared 22
59	31	made 22: took 21
60	6	Katy] Katty 21
66	3 ff.	crap (*Scots*) 22: crop 21
70	9	serge 22: sage 21
73	24	who 22: who, 21
75	6	spring, though . . . and was 22: spring, which, though . . . was 21
76	11 ff.	Wudrife 22: Wadrife 21
77	33	the enemy] my enemy 22
81	1–3	—from . . . —soldiers 22: from . . . soldiers 21
84	7–8	preached a sermon 22: preached to them a sermon 21
85	15	frosty 22: pretty 21

Page	Line	
85	22	ramplor 22 : rampler 21
94	27	working 22 : waking 21
102	18	herried 22 : harried 21
104	16	his gleg] gleg 22
107	20	smashery 22 : smashing 21
108	*heading*	XXIII] XXII 21
111	6	ramplor 22 : rampler 21
116	10	As there was 22 : There being 21 (*note* being *in next line*)
117	19	connect 22 : correct 21
120	2	puddock (*Scots*) 22 : paddock 21
121	22	overly 22 : everly 21
124	18	grozet (*Scots*) 22 : goose 21
124	32	Martinmas] Martimas 21
133	9	was 22 : were 21
143	9	afar 22 : far 21
143	11	the Heavens 22 : Heaven 21
144	12	starns 22 : stones 21
153	2–3	delighteth . . . passeth 22 : delights . . . passes 21
155	7	Dinwiddie] Dunwiddie 21
156	4	than that these 22 : than these 21
160	8	but long 22 : but o'er long 21
161	5	clung 22 : dung 21
162	6–7	post after post 22 : port after port 21
168	1	which the . . . world is smoothed 22 : which I feel the . . . world smoothed 21
171	1–2	frail (. . . stout), 22 : frail, (. . . stout) 21
171	13	Miss] Mrs 21
172	9	those 22 : these 21
177	11	it's] its 21 22
180	7	ways 22 : way 21
182	6	bruit 22 : show 21
182	20	expence, sent 22 : expence, was sent 21
182	25	unison 22 : union 21
184	18	called 22 : said to be 21
184	26	Indy (*Scots*) 22 : India 21
185	11	Christian] christian 21 22
185	31	O'Grady] O'Graddy 21
187	1	shanks] hands 22
187	4	on coils 22 : on the coils 21
188	6	there 22 : these 21
191	5	glassy 22 : glossy 21
193	1	owre (*Scots*) 22 : o'er 21
193	33	het (*Scots*) 22 : hot 21

Page	Line	
195	16	make *22*: is *21*
196	30	cheering *22*: it *21*
200	3	and slow step *22*: and a slow pace *21* (*note preceding* pale face)
200	12	not the power *22*: not power *21*
202	17	than I *22*: than what I *21*
205	2	wee (*Scots*) *22*: little *21*

EXPLANATORY NOTES

━━━

ABBREVIATIONS

Ayrshire   *Ayrshire at the Time of Burns*, ed. John Strawhorn, Collections of the Ayrshire Archaeological and Natural History Society, v, 1959.

Graham   H. G. Graham, *The Social Life of Scotland in the Eighteenth Century* (1899), 1950.

Hamilton   Henry Hamilton, *An Economic History of Scotland in the Eighteenth Century*, 1963.

Literary Life   Galt, *Literary Life, and Miscellanies*, 3 vols., 1834.

Mitchell   John Mitchell, D.D., *Memories of Ayrshire about 1780*, ed. W. K. Dickson, *Miscellany of the Scottish History Society*, vi, 1939.

Plant   Marjorie Plant, *The Domestic Life of Scotland in the Eighteenth Century*, 1952.

Scottish Costume   S. Maxwell and R. Hutchison, *Scottish Costume 1550–1850*, 1958.

Statistical Account   Sir John Sinclair, *The Statistical Account of Scotland*, 21 vols., 1791–8.

Page 1. (1) *set by*: put aside.

(2) *I was obliged*, etc.: see ch. L.

(3) *Session*: parish court of minister and elders.

Page 2. *burly*: tumult, uproar. On patronage in the Kirk of Scotland, see p. 5, note 2.

Page 3. (1) *the tribulation . . . of their forefathers*: in the religious persecutions of the seventeenth century.

(2) *they ate the bread of carefulness*: cf. Ezek. xii. 18–19.

(3) *thole*: endure.

(4) *the divine right of resistance*: in contrast to the Anglican doctrine of divine right and the obedience of the subject. See G. R. Cragg, *From Puritanism to the Age of Reason*, 1950, ch. viii. On Calvinistic resistance to

absolutism, see J. T. McNeill, *The History and Character of Calvinism*, 1957, ch. xxiv.

(5) *our right hand forget its cunning*: cf. Ps. cxxxvii. 5.

Page 4. (1) *like Lazarus*: Luke xvi. 19–31.

(2) *the session-house*: the meeting-room of the session (see p. 1, note 3).

(3) *back-yett*: back gate between kirk and manse. Cf. p. 204.

Page 5. (1) 'The account of "the placing" of Mr Balwhidder is derived from a description, which I perfectly recollect, of some similar ceremony that my grandmother had witnessed. At a placing which happened in Greenock, I heard myself a weaver . . . pronounce the very words I have ascribed to Thomas Thorl. . . . The account of "laying the hands" was a joke ascribed to Mr Thom, the minister of Govan, at the placing of a neighbouring minister. The interview with Thomas Thorl is founded on an account given by my grandmother. . . . The whole story of Mrs Malcolm and her family, is an invention, though I am inclined to think it is indebted to some hints of the same ingenious carlin, for her maiden name was Malcolm' (*Literary Life*, i. 157–8).

(2) *put in by the patron*: By the Patronage Act of 1712 the right of presenting ministers to vacant parishes was restored to the lay patrons who were heirs of the original donors of ecclesiastical properties. This violated the Act of Security (1707) which protected the polity of the Presbyterian Kirk at the Union of the Parliaments. Patronage was accepted by the 'Moderate' core of the Kirk. But the issue caused a secession in 1732 when the Assembly gave power of election to heritors (see note 5 below) whenever the patron failed to exercise his right; and it remained a persistent source of trouble. See Burns's poem, *The Ordination*.

(3) *the presbytery*: the court of ministers and representative elders holding jurisdiction over a group of parishes.

(4) *clash of glar*: fistful of mud.

(5) *heritors*: landed proprietors, who contribute to the upkeep of the kirk.

Page 6. (1) *yellyhooing*: bellowing, shouting.

(2) *Verily, verily*, etc.: John x. 1.

(3) *outstrapolous*: obstreperous; eighteenth-century form.

(4) *laying of the hands*: during the minister's induction.

(5) *Irville*: for Galt's birthplace, the royal burgh of Irvine, at this time a busy seaport of about 4,000 inhabitants.

(6) *brae*: hill.

(7) *Mess-John*: minister. *Mess*: master (of arts).

Page 7. (1) *almous deed*: alms.

(2) *gorbies*: fledglings.

(3) *mair . . . observe*: more . . . observation.

(4) *egg*: urge.

(5) *genty*: courteous; neat.

(6) *lint*: flax.

Page 8. (1) *bit and drap*: food and drink.

(2) *daunrin' bye*: strolling by.

(3) *greeting*: weeping.

(4) *clachan*: village (usually with a church).

(5) *huxtry-shop*: huckstery, general store.

(6) *silly*: weak, delicate.

(7) *get the turn*: pass the crisis.

(8) *cast up*: made a reproach.

Page 9. (1) *lend . . . soom*: loan . . . sum.

(2) *Yillcogie*: i.e. 'Ale-jug'.

(3) *ta'en a notion of*: fancied.

Page 10. *tent*: out-door pulpit, used in the great inter-parochial communion services and preachings. For a satiric account of the custom, see Burns's *Holy Fair*.

Page 11. (1) 'The Second Chapter owes much to my recollection of hearing of the smuggling days at the Troon, in Ayrshire, the same place where the Duke of Portland, since my boyhood time, has built a town. The story of the Chelsea pensioner is an invention; but the surreptitious tea-drinking in the garden is beholden to the "venerable parent". What ensues, the dust of forgetfulness hides. . . . I think that Nanse Galt, whom I have denominated Nanse Banks, kept a school in Irvine, and my description . . . was taken from that peering personage. The story anent her is a contrivance. The Irvine dancingmaster was a Mr Banks, but Macskipnish is a caricature of one that afterwards taught me to walk minuets at Greenock. His story, however, is a fiction' (*Literary Life*, i. 158-9).

(2) *the Laigh Lands . . . Loans*: the low country round the coastal promontory of Troon and the hamlet of Loans, both in Dundonald parish.

(3) *wastrie*: reckless extravagance.

(4) *cadgers*: hawkers.

(5) *sclate stones*: thin slates. Cf. p. 33.

Page 12. (1) *Chelsea Hospital*: modelled on Louis XIV's Hotel des Invalides; opened in 1694 to house army pensioners.

(2) *art and part in*: '*ope et consilio*. . . . By *art* is understood, the mandate, instigation, or advice, that may have been given towards committing the crime; *part* expresses the share that one takes to himself in it, by . . . aid or assistance' (Erskine, *Institute of the Law of Scotland* [1773], 1828, ii. 1024). Cf. p. 52.

(3) *tea*: imported into England by the East India Company in the seventeenth century. But it was a luxury in Scotland a century later and,

though it replaced whisky and ale as morning drinks, it was the subject of some moral debate. See Plant, pp. 113-15, 138-42.

(4) *heritors*: see p. 5, note 5.

(5) *ploys*: parties, junketings.

(6) *bye-places*: out-of-the-way places.

(7) *lang syne*: long since, long ago.

(8) *possets*: hot milk curdled with liquor.

(9) *galravitchings*: drinking bouts.

(10) *pint-stoup*: pint tankard.

(11) *caps and luggies*: wooden drinking dishes. The *luggie* was made up of staves, hooped, with handles.

Page 13. (1) *dawner*: stroll.

(2) *carlins*: old women.

(3) *bohea*: 'a species of tea, of higher colour, and more astringent taste, than green tea' (Johnson, *Dictionary*, 1755).

(4) *conek*: French brandy distilled from Cognac wine.

(5) *pen-guns*: pop-guns made from quills. 'Pen-guns are made and fired at the season when the turnip first comes to market; which turnip, cut in thin slices and bored through with the quill, forms the charge' (*Blackwood's Magazine*, August 1821). Cf. Scott, *The Heart of Midlothian*, 1818, ch. xvii, 'This mad quean . . . cracking like a pen-gun'.

(6) *host*: cough.

(7) *skailed the bike*: dispersed the hive.

(8) *truck-pots*: bits of crockery, odds and ends.

(9) *callans*: lads.

(10) *clachan*: see p. 8, note 4.

(11) *grulshy*: fat, clumsy.

(12) *cotters*: tenants.

(13) *biggit*: built.

(14) *sclate-house*: house with a slated roof.

Page 14. (1) *bleer eyn*: enflamed eyes.

(2) *tholing the dule*: enduring the trouble.

(3) *trigness*: neatness, smartness.

(4) *anent*: concerning.

(5) *bearing*: fruition.

Page 15. (1) *cartel*: ship commissioned to exchange prisoners of hostile powers.

(2) *a dancing-school at Irville*: cf. Burns's attendance 'to give my manners a brush' at 'a country dancing school' in 1779; 'My father had an un-accountable antipathy against these meetings; and my going was, what to this hour I repent, in absolute defiance of his commands' (*Letters*, ed. J. DeL. Ferguson, 1931, i. 109).

(3) *siller*: silver, money.

(4) *loan*: open ground near a farmhouse, where the cows are milked.

(5) *linking and louping*: tripping and jumping.

(6) *tappit-hen*: hen with a top-knot.

(7) *a droll cockit thing*: countrymen wore the Kilmarnock bonnet; 'hats of English fabric were . . . used wholly by the upper and wealthier classes of society' (Mitchell, p. 264).

(8) *petty suppers*: informal repasts.

(9) *one Madam Pompadour*: the Marquise de Pompadour (1721–64), mistress of Louis XV from 1745.

(10) *scrutoire*: escritoire, writing desk.

Page 16. (1) *the action sermon*: preached at the administration of the half-yearly sacrament; the preaching on the preceding Saturday was called the 'preparation sermon'.

(2) *birr*: energy, violence.

(3) *tirled . . . rigging*: stripped the thatch from the roof (ridging).

(4) *smashing*: devastation; cf. *smashery*, p. 107.

Page 17. (1) *income*: infirmity without apparent cause.

(2) *the Tobacco trader*: one of the ships at this time bringing great wealth into Glasgow; see Hamilton, pp. 18–21, 255 ff.

(3) *the coal-trade with Ireland*: the basis of Irvine's prosperity, amounting to 20,000 tons a year and employing about 300 local sailors by 1790 (*Statistical Account*: see *Ayrshire*, pp. 55–56).

(4) *weans*: children.

Page 18. (1) *begreeten*: tear-stained.

(2) *yett*: gate.

(3) *hirpling*: limping.

(4) *bachle*: old shoe.

(5) *freats*: omens, presages.

(6) *howdies*: midwives.

(7) *set*: leased.

(8) *nabob*: one returned rich from India.

(9) *narrow*: parsimonious.

(10) *scrimpetest*: stingiest.

(11) *policy*: grounds around the house (Lat. *policies*, elegancy).

(12) *tack*: (period of) lease.

(13) *kent*: knew.

Page 19. (1) *a bit and a drap*: something to eat and drink.

(2) *birky*: sharp.

(3) *dark*: *daurg*, day's labour.

Page 20. (1) *possets*: see p. 12, note 8.

(2) *tozy and cosh*: tipsy and happy.

(3) *masking*: mashing, brewing.

Page 21. (1) *hoggits*: hogsheads; casks of differing capacity.

(2) *puncheons*: casks of about 100 gallons.

(3) *creditable*: worthy, considerable. Port Glasgow was founded to take sea-going ships in 1668, and expanded with the tobacco trade.

(4) *cocker-nut*: the seventeenth-century form of coconut (Dutch *koker-noot*).

(5) *callant*: lad, stripling.

(6) *his leaful lane*: lonely and alone.

Page 22. (1) 'The incident of the limes is true, and was performed by a boy that I well knew' (*Literary Life*, i. 159).

(2) *gied a skraik*: gave a screech.

(3) *dirl*: ring, rattle.

(4) *boyne*: broad flat dish into which the milk-pail is emptied.

(5) *birth*: berth.

(6) *jointure house*: house settled upon a woman for life on the death of her husband.

(7) *the Cross Keys Inns*: see p. 123. The plural form 'inns' is not recorded in English after 1603.

Page 23. (1) *doited*: crazed, enfeebled.

(2) *precentor*: the leader of congregational praise, often occupying a pulpit below the minister's. By an act of 1696 a schoolmaster was appointed in every parish 'by advice of the heritors and ministers'; and down to modern times the offices of schoolmaster and session-clerk (see p. 1, note 3) have, in rural districts, been commonly combined.

(3) *lint-mill*: factory for breaking flax.

Page 24. (1) *sarking*: shirting material.

(2) *dwining*: declining, failing.

(3) *Hogmanae*: the last day of the year (apparently from French *aguillanneuf*, a gift given at *l'an neuf*, New Year). Cf. E. K. Chambers, *The Mediaeval Stage*, 1963, i. 254.

(4) *uncanny*: imprudent.

(5) *anent*: concerning.

Page 25. (1) *nae daub in my aught*: no adept in my estimation.

(2) *sin' syne*: since then.

(3) *vaunty*: vain.

Page 26. (1) *posey*: 'poesy', poetical epitaph.

(2) 'The two first lines of the epitaph are taken from an inscription in the West Kirkyard of Greenock, written by the Reverend Mr Buist, an antiburgher minister, on the tomb of his first wife. The third, somewhat altered, is from a very common epitaph in the Brighton churchyard. It is

engraved on my memory by an exclamation of a soldier . . . meditating among the tombs. . . . "D—n it, Jack, here's that there pale consumption again!" The rest of the epitaph is Mr Balwhidder's own composition' (*Literary Life*, i. 159–60).

Page 27. (1) *nerve*: feeling.

(2) *warsle*: struggle.

(3) *eirie*: melancholy.

Page 28. (1) *the Slough of Despond*: 'the descent whither the scum and filth that attends conviction for sin doth continually run . . . for still as the sinner is awakened about his lost condition, there ariseth in his soul many fears and doubts' (Bunyan, *The Pilgrim's Progress*, 1900 ed., p. 17).

(2) *for a constancy*: as a permanent preoccupation.

(3) *the hypochonderies*: melancholy.

(4) *layeth up no store*: cf. Ps. xxxiii. 7, Matt. vi. 19–20.

(5) *connect*: connected, systematic.

(6) *wastered*: wasted.

(7) *galravitching*: high living, extravagance.

Page 29. (1) *douce*: grave, prudent, worthy.

(2) *mint*: venture, hint.

(3) *jealoused*: suspected, surmised.

(4) *clash*: tittle-tattle.

(5) *latheron*: slattern. Cf. p. 112.

(6) *obligated to stand in the kirk*: The kirk session took over the duties of the medieval consistory, retaining the stool of repentance—'the vera tassel o' the breeks o' Popery'—for the punishment of fornicators. The culprit, 'arrayed in the black sackcloth gown of fornication', stood on a pedestal before the pulpit 'three Sundays successively, his face uncovered, and the awful scourge of unpardoning divinity hung over him' (R. H. Cromek, *Remains of Nithsdale and Galloway Song*, 1810, appendix D). See Graham, pp. 321 ff.; cf. Keats's letter of 6 July 1818.

Page 30. (1) *change-house*: alehouse (probably so named because post-horses were changed there). The innkeeper takes his name from the quarter-pint Scots measure.

(2) *howf*: shelter.

Page 31. (1) *coal-heughs . . . shanked*: coal-pits . . . sunk ('shafted'). Doura is 4 miles north-east of Irvine, on the Glasgow road.

(2) *thir*: these.

(3) *gowk*: fool (cuckoo).

(4) *gowpins*: double handfuls. A *gowpan* is the hollow formed by the two hands held together.

(5) *incoming*: income.

(6) *Kibbock*: named from *kebbuck*, a home-made cheese.

EXPLANATORY NOTES 221

Page 32. (1) *geni*: natural aptitude, bent.

(2) *rookit and herrit*: despoiled and plundered.

(3) *a booming of the meikle wheel*: 'When very young I had great delight and wonderment in looking at a woman spinning wool on . . . "the muckle wheel", turning the periphery round most majestically with one hand, and drawing the thread out from the *rowan* with the other, gradually stretching her arm as she drew out the thread walking backwards. The employment stands in my fancy as the most sublime and mystical of human avocations' (*Literary Life*, i. 52).

(4) *birring*: whirring.

(5) *organ kist*: pipe-organ loft. The episcopalian organ was derisively known as 'a kist o' whistles'.

(6) *kirning*: churning.

Page 33. (1) *huxtry*: huckstery, general store.

(2) *tot*: sum.

(3) *making siller like sclate stones*: cf. p. 11, 'the money came in like sclate stones'.

(4) *grumphies*: pigs.

(5) *wabs*: webs, fabric.

(6) *end's errand*: 'anes-errand', errand with a single purpose.

(7) *beak*: toast.

Page 34. (1) *a thrashing . . . bells*: vain labour. *Bells*: bubbles. Cf. Tomson, *Sermons of M. John Calvin*, 1579, p. 988: 'As we say in a common prouerbe, to beate the water, Saint Paule saith to beate the ayre.' On the agricultural 'improvers', typified by Mr Kibbock, see J. E. Handley, *Scottish Farming in the Eighteenth Century*, 1953, chs. vi–vii; *Ayrshire*, pp. 37–41.

(2) *tack ran*: lease went on.

(3) *stabs*: posts.

(4) *stake and rice*: hedges made of boughs (*rice*) stretched between stakes.

(5) *trig*: neat, smart.

(6) *Vennel*: narrow lane, wynd. Cf. pp. 41–43.

(7) *mortification*: charitable bequest (legal term).

Page 35. (1) *infused or masket*: brewed. A whimsical conjunction of the vernacular and (still current) latinate terms.

(2) *low*: blaze. 'The burning of the Breadland, is somewhat indebted to a similar calamity that befell a cousin's house. She was herself, however, rescued from the flames, with her watch and her tea-pot. I remember giving great offence by a pathetic letter I wrote to condole with her on the occasion' (*Literary Life*, i. 160).

(3) *rigging*: ridging, roof.

(4) *lum*: chimney.

(5) *killogie*: kiln for drying corn before milling.

(6) *course*: pace.

(7) *forenent*: near to.

Page 36. (1) *cast up*: turned up.

(2) *skreighing*: screaming, screeching.

(3) *claught*: laid hold of.

(4) *atomy*: remains.

(5) *flaught*: flurry of fear.

Page 37. (1) *tack*: lease.

(2) *Mr Coulter*: an 'improver'; cf. p. 34, note 1.

(3) *rugget*: pulled, torn.

(4) *near-begun*: 'nearby-going', close-fisted, stingy.

(5) *rigs*: ridges.

(6) *braird*: first shoots of grain.

Page 38. (1) *big*: build.

(2) *argol-bargling*: disputation.

Page 39. (1) *keepit*: restrained.

(2) *tinklers*: tinkers.

(3) *blackaviced*: swarthy.

(4) *squattling*: nestling down.

(5) *herrit*: despoiled.

(6) *clecking*: litter.

Page 41. (1) *coal-heughs . . . Douray*: see p. 31, note 1.

(2) *The king's highway*: see p. 34.

(3) *middens*: dung-heaps.

(4) *reested*: stopped, held up.

(5) *laired*: bogged down.

Page 42. (1) *sappy*: rich and wet.

(2) *loup*: leap.

(3) *couped*: overturned.

(4) *discreet*: polite.

Page 43. (1) *steadings*: sites, plots.

(2) *fewed off*: divided into feus, pieces of land held in perpetuity for a fixed annual payment to the owner. The commonest kind of tenure in Scotland.

(3) *sairly*: sorely.

(4) *warsled with poortith*: struggled with poverty.

(5) *shed*: cottage.

(6) *maun*: must.

(7) *thole*: endure.

Page 44. (1) *am wae . . . Session*: would be distressed to go on parish relief.
(2) *alane*: alone.
(3) *pick and drap*: food and drink.
(4) *gloaming*: twilight.
(5) *vacance*: vacation.

Page 45. (1) *Macabaw*: snuff from Macouba, Martinique, scented with attar of roses.
(2) *sough*: rush of wind; rumour.
(3) *down-lying*: lying-in.
(4) *howdie*: midwife.

Page 46. (1) *loun*: serene.
(2) *buirdly*: stalwart, well set-up.

Page 47. (1) *been out of his time*: served his apprenticeship.
(2) *a bit nota bene*: a little footnote.

Page 48. (1) *warsle*: struggle.
(2) *canary-headed*: spirited; perhaps from 'canary', a lively Spanish dance.
(3) *gatherings*: savings.
(4) *but within our lip*: only as long as our breath; uncertain, passing. Cf. p. 119.

Page 49. (1) *stramash*: disturbance, uproar.
(2) *howff*: shelter.
(3) *ogling and gogling*: making eyes and staring.
(4) *Sabrina*: Milton, *Comus*, ll. 824 ff.
(5) *mantua-making*: dressmaking. *Mantua*: loose gown. Cf. Miss Mitford's 'young mantua-making school-mistresses', *The Village*, 1824, i. 287.
(6) *the silken plaidie*: worn by ladies of quality in the early decades of the century and passing into general use; giving way to hooded cloaks of English duffel, which had also, by the 1770s, become common among country women and servants. Cf. *Scottish Costume*, pp. 93–95; Mitchell, pp. 265–6.
(7) *bravery*: finery.

Page 50. (1) *snood*: fillet, hair-band, worn by unmarried women since the early seventeenth century.
(2) *snod*: trim.
(3) *bees-cap*: in the shape of a *skep*, beehive.
(4) *mutches*: close-fitting white linen or muslin caps with a gathered or trimmed border; in their traditional form worn only, in the 1770s, by the elderly (cf. Mitchell, p. 264; *Scottish Costume*, p. 90), but held in fashion in Dalmailing by 'curious contrivances of French millendery'.
(5) *incomings*: income.

(6) *Candlemas offerings*: gratuities brought to the schoolmistress at Candlemas (2 February); the most generous contributor was awarded a 'Candlemas crown' and the prerogative of granting holidays and remitting punishments.

Page 51. (1) *the toll, or trust-road*: until 1878 roads in Ayrshire were kept up by tolls levied at junctions and at rates fixed by road trustees.

(2) *boss*: hollow.

(3) *yird*: 'earthed', buried.

(4) *nevelled*: beat (lit. with the 'nieve', fist).

(5) *the Scots Magazine*: 1739–1826, 'containing a general view of the religion, politics, entertainment, etc., in Great Britain, and a succinct account of public affairs, foreign and domestic'; an anthology of extracts from newspapers and books, and the only magazine appearing continuously in Scotland from 1750 until the end of the century.

(6) *deil*: devil.

(7) *sough*: breath of wind; rumour.

Page 52. (1) *the Americas . . . were snapping their fingers*: see J. Steven Watson, *The Reign of George III*, 1960, ch. vii. The American War was still six years off.

(2) *Modewort*: i.e. 'the mole'.

(3) *art and part*: see p. 12, note 2.

Page 53. (1) *deals*: planks of pine or fir.

(2) *the canal . . . Forth and Clyde*: completed in 1790, after more than a century of discussion and projection. See Hamilton, pp. 234–8.

(3) *overly*: excessively, too.

(4) *down-lying*: lying-in.

Page 54. (1) *stand*: set.

(2) *host*: cough.

(3) *kittling*: tickling.

(4) *gleg . . . quean*: sprightly, sharp . . . lass.

(5) *Spunkie*: will o' the wisp; mettlesome, lively.

Page 55. (1) *douce*: grave, prudent, worthy.

(2) *they who put their trust*, etc.: cf. Ps. xl. 4, Prov. xxix. 25.

Page 56. (1) *bars*: sandbars.

(2) *lown*: quiet, peaceful.

(3) *gowans*: daisies.

(4) *tent*: see p. 10, note.

Page 57. (1) *the fair*: for contemporary accounts (and moral criticism) of Ayrshire fairs, see *Ayrshire*, pp. 71–75, 75–77.

(2) *mountebanks and Merry Andrews*: itinerant quacks and clowns.

(3) *daffing*: frolic.

(4) *hobble-shows*: unruly gatherings, uproars.

(5) *change-houses*: see p. 30, note 1.

(6) *Punch's opera*: the Italian puppet show introduced into England at the Restoration.

(7) *napped*: knocked, struck.

Page 58. (1) *kythe*: show itself, become manifest.

(2) *the cards . . . sinful pastime*: described by one of Burns's *Twa Dogs* as 'the devil's pictur'd beuks' (l. 226).

(3) *the Douglas cause*: the most celebrated civil trial of the day (1762-9), on 'that great principle of law—*filiation*' (Boswell). Archibald, Duke of Douglas, died in 1761, and the title was claimed by the survivor of twins born in Paris to the duke's sister, Lady Jane Douglas, when she was fifty. This claim was contested on behalf of the Duke of Hamilton; it was argued that the twins were spurious. The Court of Session found for Hamilton, but its decision was reversed by the House of Lords on appeal. See A. F. Steuart, *The Douglas Cause*, 1901.

Page 59. (1) *singing Italian songs, and . . . for the music . . . to instruct Kate*: cf. Henry Mackenzie, *Anecdotes and Egotisms 1745-1831*, ed. H. W. Thompson, 1927, p. 80: 'I have lived long enough to see a progressive change . . . in performance from singing plain Scots songs without accompaniment to singing Italian music accompanied, and now bravuras with loud accompaniments that "rowze as with a rattling peal of thunder".'

(2) *Vauxhall*: 'that excellent place of publick amusement . . . there being a mixture of curious shew,—gay exhibition,—musick, vocal and instrumental, not too refined for the general ear' (Boswell, *Life of Johnson*, 1934 ed., iii. 308).

(3) *trinkum-trankum*: trivially decorative. Cf. p. 60.

(4) *sough*: hint.

Page 60. *gum-flowers*: artificial flowers.

Page 61. (1) *trysted*: engaged.

(2) *neither to bind nor to hold*: beyond control.

Page 62. (1) *nose of wax*: weak, flexible fellow. Originally used of distortions of scripture.

(2) *stramash*: altercation.

(3) *tack*: spell.

(4) *mart*: a fattened beast killed at the end of the year to provide salted meat over the winter (Gaelic).

Page 63. (1) *as a mustard-seed . . . tree*: Matt. xiii. 31-32.

(2) *fact*: moral offence.

(3) *tutor in Sir Hugh Montgomerie's family*: a hint of historicity. Col. Hugh Montgomerie of Coylfield (born 1739), later 12th Earl of Eglinton (1796), was an infantry officer at the time the minister records. He was two years dead when the *Annals* appeared. Cf. p. 105, note 1; p. 181.

(4) *check*: 'bite', snack.

Page 64. (1) *donsie*: hapless, ill-fortuned.

(2) *in fault*: guilty of fornication, and due for public chastisement in the kirk. Cf. p. 29, note 6.

(3) *crying*: labour pains.

(4) *oil cast upon a burning coal*: a creative mixture of metaphors.

(5) *threapit*: 'maintain[ed] by dint of assertion' (Burns).

Page 65. (1) *douce*: grave, prudent, quiet.

(2) *Muscovy duck*: i.e. musk-duck, 'so called from a supposed musky smell . . . a native of Africa' (Goldsmith, *History of Animated Nature*, 1776, VI. 130).

(3) *bowly*: crooked, bow.

Page 66. (1) *stravaggers*: wanderers.

(2) *crap*: crop.

(3) *kyte*: belly.

(4) *muckle jock*: great gander. Cf. the 'turkey-jock' or 'bubbly-jock'.

(5) *tympathy*: i.e. tympany, tumour; apparently meant as the minister's error.

(6) *cleck*: hatch.

(7) *mutchkin stoup*: quarter-pint flagon. (A Scots gallon = 3 English gallons.)

Page 67. *a plea getting to a head*, etc.: the heritors (see p. 5, note 5) being, by parish law, liable for maintenance of the school.

Page 68. (1) *advised*: judicious, well-considered.

(2) *pock-nook*: corner at the bottom of a money-bag; private resources.

(3) *discretion*: civility.

(4) *weighty sentences . . . I was pleased to hear*: but see p. 132, note 2.

Page 69. *boss*: hollow, empty.

Page 70. (1) *clecking*: litter.

(2) *dule*: woe.

(3) *Jenny Gaffaw, and her idiot daughter*: On the Scottish parish idiot, 'imperfectly intelligent, but often perfectly cunning', see Dean Ramsay, *Reminiscences of Scottish Life and Character*, ch. vi (1872 ed., pp. 188–200). Meg Gaffaw displays the standard 'admixture of cunning, observation, craziness, and sentiment' (D. S. Meldrum), and in the end something of the distracted lyricism of Scott's defectives. See *infra*, p. 160, and the minister's obituary comment.

(4) *hap*: covering.

(5) *mair . . . claes*: more . . . clothes.

Page 71. (1) *gear*: accoutrements, impedimenta.

(2) *Glaikit*: i.e. foolish, frivolous.

(3) *jo*: sweetheart.

Page 72. (1) *limmer*: jade, whore.

(2) *from less to more*: with increasing argument.

(3) *firelock*: a musket with a lock in which the priming was ignited by sparks.

(4) *the play*: leave from school.

Page 73. *tap of tow*: head of flax on the distaff.

Page 74. (1) *jealoused*: suspected.

(2) *cagey and meikle taken up*: affectionately cheerful and quite delighted.

(3) *inoculation*: practised in England from about 1720. Cf. the minister of Kilwinning's account, in the *Statistical Account* (xi. 142), of an outbreak of smallpox in the parish in 1791, when 90 children were affected and 'more than one half of them died. . . . Inoculation . . . is only practised here in two or three families. From ignorance, and the most superstitious prejudice, the parents, regardless, or insensible of consequences, instead of inoculating their children, crowd into those houses in which the disease is of the most malignant nature. . . .'

(4) *faculty*: medical school.

Page 75. *Pace*: Pasch, Easter.

Page 76. (1) *prelatic*: see p. 58.

(2) *vogie*: vain.

(3) *flagrant*: flaring, gaudy.

Page 77. (1) *bravery*: finery.

(2) *duds*: clothes.

(3) *haverels*: garrulous half-wits.

(4) *the stool of repentance*: see p. 29, note 6.

(5) *antics linking*: clowns tripping.

Page 78. (1) *betheral*: beadle, church officer. He usually acted as bellman and—as the name 'Howking' indicates—gravedigger. Galt's *Miscellanies* (1834) include *The Betheral; or, The Autobiography of James Howkings*.

(2) *They twa*: these two.

(3) *adversary*: Devil. Cf. 1 Peter v. 8.

(4) *Synod*: ecclesiastical court intermediate between presbytery and General Assembly.

(5) *endless*: infinitely resourceful.

Page 79. (1) *playrife*: full of fun.

   (2) *swatch*: sample.

   (3) *assoilzied*: absolved.

   (4) *put to the wall*: driven to extremity.

Page 80. (1) *fired into open war*: with the American declaration of independence in July 1776.

   (2) *foregathered . . . doited tawpy*: taken up . . . senseless girl.

   (3) *cleeding*: clothing.

   (4) *change-house*: see p. 30, note 1.

   (5) *wally wallying*: crying of 'waly', lamentation.

Page 81. (1) *black-cuffs*: dragoons, in the seventeenth-century religious persecutions.

   (2) *weans*: children.

   (3) *cess*: tax, imposition.

   (4) *cadger*: hawker.

   (5) *plagues*: i.e. family.

   (6) *preeing*: trial, proof.

   (7) *ramplor*: unsettled, restless.

Page 82. (1) *eydent*: diligent.

   (2) *ettling*: trying.

   (3) *a bit and a brat*: food and clothing.

   (4) *canty*: cheerful.

   (5) *playocks*: toys.

   (6) *callans*: lads.

   (7) *Marymas*: the festival of the Assumption of the Blessed Virgin Mary.

   (8) *cauldrife*: cold.

   (9) *tow*: flax prepared for spinning.

   (10) *no a bodle*: not tuppence.

   (11) *Rachel weeping for her children*: Jer. xxxi. 15.

   (12) *rattling*: loquacious, lively.

Page 83. (1) *overly perjinct*: too rigid, precise.

   (2) *the play*: a holiday.

   (3) *ploy*: junketing, merry time.

   (4) *fantastical*: grotesque, extravagant fancy.

   (5) *out of the body*: beside herself, transported.

Page 84. *kithed*: turned out.

Page 85. (1) *sound*: word.

   (2) *bruited*: rumoured, reported.

   (3) *beild*: shelter, dwelling.

   (4) *ramplor*: restless.

   (5) *croon*: muttering, moan.

Page 86. (1) *aiblins*: perhaps.

(2) *couldna warsle*: could not struggle.

(3) *thole*: endure.

Page 87. (1) *cauld*: cold.

(2) *greeting*: crying.

(3) *douce*: prudent, sober.

(4) *o'ercome*: shock, attack.

Page 88. (1) *tawpy*: silly girl.

(2) *rank and file*: 'Ranks and files, are the horizontal and vertical lines of soldiers when drawn up for service' (James, *Military Dictionary*, 1802); but the minister's 'both' suggests that he took the phrase to mean officers and men.

(3) *grat*: wept.

(4) *a newspaper twice a-week*: In fact, the Edinburgh papers of this time—the *Caledonian Mercury*, *Advertiser*, and *Evening Courant*—came out three times a week. A *Journal* and *Mercury* appeared weekly. The other publications were literary magazines.

(5) *callans*: lads.

(6) *girs*: iron hoops.

Page 89. (1) *shintys*: balls used in shinty, a game resembling hockey.

(2) *sicklike*: such.

(3) *holms*: low grounds.

(4) *speat*: spate.

(5) *like the war-horse . . . might*: Job xxxix. 21.

(6) *lade*: mill-race.

(7) *looting*: bending.

(8) *mutch*: see p. 50, note 4.

Page 90. (1) *corking pins*: long pins.

(2) *toupee*: topknot of natural or false hair.

Page 91. (1) *bygane*: past (year).

(2) *mailing*: arable land, small-holding.

(3) *cutters*: small single-masted vessels used by the Revenue.

(4) *gaugers*: excisemen.

Page 92. (1) *dealing*: trading.

(2) *Pawkie*: i.e. crafty, sly.

(3) *laigh*: low, coastal.

(4) *huxtry*: store.

(5) *parliament-cakes*: thin crisp rectangular cakes of gingerbread.

(6) *back-bitten*: slandered.

(7) *jealoused*: suspected.

(8) *Sir Hugh Montgomerie*: see p. 63, note 3. The real Hugh Montgomerie's father was Alexander.

(9) *queer*: roguish.

(10) *coothy*: sociable, affable.

(11) *overly gleg*: too sharp-sighted.

(12) *waught*: draught, swig.

Page 93. (1) *clecking*: 'bringing forth'.

(2) *howdies*: midwives.

(3) *trance-door*: door between the kitchen and the *trance* or passage inside the outer door of a cottage.

(4) *stoups*: flagons.

(5) *chaff-bed*: '. . . the softness of a feather bed was comparatively seldom enjoyed; except in the wealthier and genteeler houses. . . . Of mattresses there were none:— the . . . family slept either upon straw smoothly spread out with a sheet above it, upon the boards . . . or upon a large tick bag filled like the accompanying bolsters with chaff' (Mitchell, pp. 261-2).

(6) *tikeing*: ticking; the case for the bed-chaff.

(7) *graining*: groaning.

(8) *dead thraws*: throes of death.

(9) *sorner*: sponger, vagabond taking advantage of hospitality.

(10) *divor*: bankrupt, ne'er-do-well.

(11) *gang*: go.

(12) *not canny*: unfavourable, ill-omened. Cf. Scott, *Waverley*, 1814, ch. lxvii: 'At these unsonsy [dangerous] hours the glen has a bad name—there's something no that canny about auld Janet Gellatley.'

(13) *down*: hangdog, guilty.

(14) *looted*: bent.

Page 94. (1) *rode on the top of*: took advantage of.

(2) *rabiator*: violent, noisy bully.

(3) *the wicked . . . troubling*: a charitable application of Job iii. 17.

(4) *a chosen vessel*: description of Paul in Acts ix. 15.

(5) *cess*: tax, burden.

Page 95. (1) *twenty pounds*: almost as much as a schoolmaster's annual income (*Statistical Account*, xi. 168-9).

(2) *off-hand*: without reflection, casually.

(3) *foreign*: outside the parish or district; someone else's (*alienus*).

Page 96. (1) *General Assembly*: the annual supreme court of the Kirk.

(2) *fly*: 'flier', stage-coach.

(3) *caddy*: 'a very useful Black-guard, who attends the Coffee-Houses and publick Places to go of Errands; and though they are wretches, that in Rags lye upon the Stairs, and in the Streets at Night, yet are they often considerably trusted' (E. Burt, *Letters from the North of Scotland* (*c*. 1730), 1754, i. 26). Cf. Smollett, *Humphry Clinker*, 1771, Melford's letter of 8 August.

(4) *the Covenanters' Close*: on the south side of the High Street, between St. Giles' and the Tron Church.

(5) *uncos*: persons unknown to her (and therefore proposing to pay for lodging).

(6) *gawsy furthy*: buxom, forthcoming.

(7) *cagey*: delighted.

Page 97. (1) *that more sanctified place*: in the Canongate.

(2) *the Commissioner*: the king's representative at the Assembly.

(3) *kentspeckle*: conspicuous, remarked.

(4) *sure and steadfast earth*: imitating Shakespeare's echo (*Macbeth*, II. i. 56) of Ps. xciii. 2.

(5) *coggly*: shaky, unsteady.

Page 98. (1) *I described*, etc.: drawing on Rev. xvii–xviii.

(2) *sough*: sigh, murmur.

Page 100. (1) *flaunty*: giddy, capricious.

(2) *aught*: consequence.

Page 102. (1) *lown*: shelter.

(2) *Lord George Gordon*: (1751–93), president of a protestant association formed against the Roman Catholic relief act of 1778; tried for high treason after the anti-papist riots of June 1780; and acquitted.

(3) *herried*: harried, plundered.

Page 103. (1) *bit hole*: little mean cottage.

(2) *doups*: stumps.

(3) *linking*: skipping.

Page 104. (1) *a rod of iron*: Ps. ii. 9; Rev. ii. 27, xii. 5.

(2) *pointer dogs*: introduced into England about the beginning of the eighteenth century.

(3) *fay*: doomed. 'The Scots call a Man *Fay* when he alters his Conditions, and Humours, which they think a sign of Death' (Kelly, *Scottish Proverbs*, 1721, p. 333).

(4) *gleg*: lively, active.

(5) *no canny*: see p. 93, note 12.

(6) *dree*: suffer.

(7) *madam . . . Miss*: whore.

Page 105. (1) *sure enough it so happened*, etc.: There is some correspondence in name and interest between the minister's Lord Eglesham and Alexander, 10th Earl of Eglinton (1723–69), who was recognized in Galt's boyhood as 'the reviver of agriculture in Ayrshire'; and Eglesham's death at the hands of Mungo Argyle is based on the shooting of Eglinton by the Highland exciseman, Mungo Campbell, on 24 October 1769. Eglinton came upon Campbell, whom he had previously admonished for poaching, and ordered him to surrender his gun. Campbell answered 'that he would sooner part with his life; desiring his Lordship to keep off, if he regarded his own. Lord Eglintoun replying, that he could use a gun as well as he, ordered one of the servants to fetch his fowling-piece from the carriage. In the meantime he kept still advancing and gaining on Campbell, circling and winding to avoid the muzzle of the gun. Campbell retired backwards, till he stumbled on a stone and fell. In rising, he fired at Lord Eglintoun, then within three or four yards of him, and lodged the whole charge in the left side of his belly.' Eglinton died the next day, having said that 'he had intended no harm to Campbell, as his gun . . . was not loaded' (Douglas, *The Peerage of Scotland*, 1813, i. 506–7).

(2) *the valley of Jehoshaphat in the latter day*: Joel iii. 2.

(3) *hips and haws*: the fruit of the dog-rose and hawthorn.

Page 106. *thrown*: distorted.

Page 107. (1) *stickit*: without a charge. Cf. Galt, *Sir Andrew Wylie*, 1822, ch. i: 'Dominie Tannyhill, one of those meek and modest novices of the Scottish priesthood, who, never happening to meet with any such stroke of good fortune as the lot of a tutor in a laird's family, wear out the even tenor of their blameless days in the little troubles of a village school'.

(2) *camstrairy*: unmanageable, riotous.

(3) *Thomas Howkings, the betherel*: see p. 78, note 1.

(4) *smashery*: devastation.

Page 108. *a victory over the French fleet*: the decisive victory of Rodney and Hood over de Grasse in the Battle of the Saints, 12 April 1782.

Page 109. *kail-blades*: leaves of borecole, green kale.

Page 110. *Howl ye ships of Tarshish*, etc.: Isa. xxiii. 1.

Page 111. (1) *in the bank more than a thousand pounds*: He had been able to go on, as the second Mrs Balwhidder made possible in 1765, putting away the 'whole tot' of his stipend. The average stipend of the ministry was £52 (see Graham, pp. 361–2).

(2) *ramplor*: restless, active.

(3) *straighted*: laid out.

(4) *a plate of earth and salt*: cf. Pennant, *A Tour in Scotland; MDCCLXIX*, 1774, p. 98: 'On the death of a Highlander . . . the friends lay on the breast of the deceased a wooden platter, containing a small quantity of salt and earth, separate and unmixed; the earth, an emblem of the corruptible body; the salt, an emblem of the immortal spirit.' The practice survives.

(5) *kimmers*: gossips, neighbours.

(6) *gane*: gone.

(7) *bein*: comfortable, well-stocked.

(8) *brittle bail*: brief, temporary release.

Page 112. (1) *mess or mell we the lathron lasses*: keep company with the slatternly girls.

(2) *maun dree*: must suffer.

(3) *maunnering*: incoherent babbling.

(4) *late wake*: lykewake, vigil kept until burial.

Page 113. (1) *unco*: notable, wonder.

(2) *fash*: trouble, put out.

Page 114. (1) *Judith*: the heroic widow of the Apocrypha. But the comparison is extravagant.

(2) *gowans*: daisies.

Page 115. (1) *a Mr Cayenne*: Returned colonists, with fortunes to invest in estates and industry, were familiar in Galt's Ayrshire—among them Claud Alexander of Ballochmyle who founded Catrine and its cotton works, Robert Hamilton of Bourtreehill, Captain John Morrice of Craig, John Fergusson of Doonholm, Governor Macrae of Orangefield, and Dr. William Fullarton of Rosemount.

(2) *etter-cap . . . spunkie*: spider, ill-tempered fellow . . . man of fire.

Page 116. (1) *tap of tow*: head of flax on the distaff.

(2) *fash*: worry, fret.

(3) *clagged*: clogged.

(4) *wud*: enraged, beside himself.

(5) *stottit against*: bounced, rebounded from.

Page 117. (1) *truly a thorn in our side*: cf. Num. xxxiii. 55, 'those which ye let remain of them shall be . . . thorns in your sides, and shall vex you in the land wherein ye dwell'.

(2) *sederunt*: meeting ('there were sitting').

(3) *occasion*: communion.

(4) *Keekie*: i.e. 'Peep'.

(5) *kittle*: difficult, awkward.

(6) *connect*: logical.

(7) *old stoops*: well-tried supports.

Page 118. (1) *hand-ball*: used in an organized game with goals, a familiar village sport.

(2) *stotting on*: rebounding from.

(3) *the old proverb*: see M. P. Tilley, *Dictionary of the Proverbs in England*, 1950, D 563.

Page 119. (1) *long-headed*: cf. Madame D'Arblay, *Diary* (1815), 1876, iv. 301, 'a woman that the Scotch would call long-headed; she was sagacious, penetrating, and gifted with strong humour'.

(2) *but in my lip*: see p. 48, note 4.

Page 120. (1) *cobbling*: patching up.

(2) *sarking*: lining of boards between rafters and slates.

(3) *frush*: brittle, rotten.

(4) *puddock*: toad.

(5) *a sepulchre full of rottenness*: (and not to be purified by whitening). Matt. xxiii. 27; cf. Acts xxiii. 3.

(6) *wright*: carpenter.

(7) *pawkie*: sly.

(8) *cast*: reckoned.

Page 121. (1) *big*: build.

(2) *draughtiness*: artfulness, cunning.

(3) *the fifteen Lords of Edinburgh*: the judges of the Court of Session, which developed from a committee of the Privy Court. 'A nobleman was called a Lord of State. The Senators of the College of Justice were termed Lords of Seat, or of the Session' (Scott, *The Heart of Midlothian*, 1818, ch. iv).

(4) *cess*: tax, burden.

Page 122. (1) *tiends*: tithes. Cf. p. 125.

(2) *gorbie*: fledgling; minister. Cf. p. 7.

(3) *mailing*: small-holding, property.

Page 123. (1) *jointure-house*: cf. p. 22 and note 6.

(2) *flitting*: moving.

(3) *Toddy*: see p. 150, note 2.

(4) *set*: let.

Page 124. (1) *kail-stocks*: borecole, green kale.

(2) *grozet and berry*: gooseberry and other fruit.

(3) *fasherie*: bother.

Page 125. (1) *[tythe-]boll*: a measure of grain, rather more than 4 bushels. Traditionally the minister's stipend was paid in kind and sent in on horseback, each horse carrying a boll (see Graham, pp. 281–2).

(2) *chimlay-lug*: side wall of the chimney recess, chimney-corner.

(3) *the widow's creuse*: 1 Kings xvii. 8–16.

(4) *garnel-kests*: granary bins.

(5) *tume*: empty.

(6) *corn . . . oil . . . wine*: cf. Deut. xi. 14, 2 Chron. xxxii. 28, Joel ii. 19.

Page 126. (1) *lofts*: galleries.

(2) *Hogmanay*: see p. 24, note 3.

Page 127. (1) *a cotton-mill*: cf. the mill at Catrine, in Sorn parish, which 'is entirely a new creation, and owes its existence to the flourishing state of the cotton manufacture in Great Britain. In the year 1787, Mr. Alexander of Ballochmyle, the proprietor of the village, in partnership with the patriotic Mr. Dale of Glasgow, built a cotton twist-mill . . . with a fall of water . . . of 46 feet. A jeanie [jenny, spinning machine] factory and a corn-mill are drove by the same fall. . . . Three hundred and one persons, old and young, are just now employed, in carding, roving, and in spinning, with an overseer and two clerks: Clock-makers, smiths, mill-wrights, and other mechanics, amount to 15 more. . . . Children are not admitted into the work unless 9 years old, and they all lodge with their parents or friends. . . . Few examples of so rapid an increase of population are to be found; for in the year 1787, two or three thatched houses occupied the place where this thriving village now stands [1795; pop. over 1,600]. In such a multi-tude, collected from different parts of the kingdom, we may reasonably expect to find some of very exceptionable morals. . . . The persons who work in the twist-mill and jeanie factory, are obliged to pay unwearied attention in their different departments; which, perhaps, has no small influence in counteracting the bad habits they may have acquired in an idler scene of life' (Rev. Robert Steven, minister of Catrine; *Statistical Account*, xx. 176-80).

(2) *serpent plague*: cf. Num. xxi. 5-9, Jer. viii. 17.

Page 128. (1) *tambouring*: embroidery on circular frames.

(2) *turretted houses*: the baronial style fashionable until the mid-seventeenth century.

(3) *by common*: out of the ordinary.

Page 129. (1) *topping*: excellent.

(2) *the boughs . . . fowler's snare*: cf. Luke xiii. 19, Ps. xci. 3.

(3) *pinch*: critical occasion.

Page 130. (1) *observe*: observation.

(2) *upsetting*: misfortune.

(3) *divors*: bankrupts.

Page 131. On the improved communications between Ayrshire and Glasgow see *Ayrshire*, p. 158.

Page 132. (1) *fleeching*: coaxing.

(2) *thought his language rather too Englified*: He inclined to the 'New Licht' or 'Moderate' fashion, which was ethical and rational rather than evangelical: his first publication is a book of moral essays 'lacking somewhat of . . . birr and smeddum' (see below, note 4). Cf. Burns, *The Holy Fair*, sts. xiv-xv, on a Moderate's 'cauld harangues / On *practice* and on *morals*':

> What signifies his barren shine,
>   Of *moral pow'rs* an' *reason*?
> His English style, an' gesture fine,
>   Are a' clean out o' season. .

> Like Socrates or Antonine,
> Or some auld pagan heathen,
> The *moral man* he does define,
> But ne'er a word o' *faith* in
> That's right that day.

(3) *stoop*: support.

(4) *birr and smeddum*: force and spirit.

Page 133. (1) *pouncet-boxes*: perfume-boxes with perforated lids. (*O.E.D.* wrongly says that this 'Shaksperian term (*1 Henry IV*, 1. iii. 38]' was 'revived by Scott'.)

(2) *a patent lamp*: an advance on the *crusie*, a boat-shaped iron lamp with a rush wick, made by the blacksmith, and hung from a nail on the wall.

(3) *Castile soap*: used in England since the early seventeenth century, and available in Scottish towns. But the country housewife made her own soap (see Plant, p. 148).

Page 134. (1) *whawp*: curlew.

(2) *Corresponding Societies*: begun in 1792 for the discussion of constitutional reform, and inevitably suspected of being subversive.

(3) *Esculapian*: healer. Both doctors are named from plants with some medicinal properties; but while tansy is functional, the marigold is also decorative.

Page 135. (1) *speat*: spate.

(2) *Boney*: Napoleon Bonaparte.

(3) *purer . . . tried*: cf. Ps. xii. 6, Dan. xii. 10.

Page 136. *But although there was no doubt*, etc.: For a fuller view of Glasgow in the 1770s, 'the pride of Scotland' that 'might pass for an elegant and flourishing city in any part of Christendom', see Smollett, *Humphry Clinker*, 1771, Melford's letter of 3 September and Matthew Bramble's following.

Page 137. (1) *levelling*: radical, revolutionary.

(2) *black-neb*: one disaffected to the government.

Page 138. *bittle*: pound with a mallet.

Page 139. (1) *as the smoke that mounteth up*: cf. Isa. ix. 18.

(2) *fashed*: troubled.

Page 140. *gled*: kite.

Page 141. (1) *cantily*: cheerfully.

(2) *cheeks*: side pieces of the frames.

(3) *roans*: roof guttering.

Page 143. *the news came*, etc.: Louis XVI was executed on 21 January 1793.

Page 144. *starns*: stars.

Page 146. (1) *jacobins*: supporters of the French Revolution (the name of a political club formed in 1789 in the Jacobin—Dominican—convent in Paris).

(2) *crouse*: merry, cocky.

Page 147. (1) *the sun . . . unjust*: adapting Matt. v. 45.

(2) *man . . . beasts that perish*: Ps. xlix. 12.

(3) *Utilitarians*: holding, with Jeremy Bentham, that 'it is the greatest happiness of the greatest number that is the measure of right and wrong' (*A Fragment on Government*, 1776), and judging morality by utility. Bentham used the term 'utilitarian' in the 1780s, but later gave it up for the 'greatest happiness principle'; but it was recovered by John Stuart Mill from *Annals of the Parish*, and he adopted it as a 'sectarian appellation' 'with a boy's fondness for a name and a banner' (*Autobiography*, 1873, pp. 79–80; *Utilitarianism*, 1863, p. 9, n.)

Page 148. (1) *spunk*: spark.

(2) *bounty*: gratuity paid to recruits.

Page 149. (1) *dunt*: stroke, blow.

(2) *gied*: gave.

(3) *Hansel Monday*: the first Monday of the new year, on which handsel, the new-year gift, was given.

(4) *throng*: busy, closely engaged.

(5) *lown*: quiet.

(6) *aloof*: standing at a distance.

Page 150. (1) *thole*: endure.

(2) *toddy*: whisky mixed with hot water and sugar.

(3) *came no speed*: had no luck.

(4) *clanjamfrey*: worthless lot, rabble.

(5) *Their first performance*, etc.: They played the only two Scots eighteenth-century dramas of any note: Allan Ramsay's *Gentle Shepherd*, *A Pastoral Comedy* (1725), and John Home's *Douglas; a Tragedy* (1757).

(6) *cracket*: mad.

(7) *portion*: dowry.

Page 151. (1) *this was a sinful curiosity*: The minister played safe. When Home's *Douglas* was first performed in Edinburgh, the presbytery published 'a solemn admonition' on the moral danger of theatre-going; and despite general ridicule, then censured a number of Home's clerical friends who had attended. The minister of Liberton said, in apology, 'that he attended the representation only *once*, and endeavoured to conceal himself in a corner, to avoid giving offence'. The General Assembly 'passed a declaratory act, prohibiting the clergy from being concerned in, or countenancing, theatrical representations. But the manners overcame the law of the Church', and in 1784 Mrs Siddons was reducing ministerial attendances at the General Assembly (see Henry Mackenzie, *Works of Home*, 1822, i. 39-49; Alexander Carlyle, *Autobiography*, ed. J. H. Burton, 1910, ch. viii).

(2) *duddy betherel*: ragged beadle; scarecrow.

(3) *kail-pot*: soup-pot.

(4) *leather*: one of Ayr's main manufactures at this time.

(5) *whisky*: described by Scott in 1823 as 'that almost forgotten accommodation. . . . Green was . . . its original colour, and it was placed sturdily and safely low upon its little old-fashioned wheels, which bore much less than the usual proportion to the size of the carriage. . . . It had a calash head, which had been pulled up, [and] . . . leathern curtains' (*St. Ronan's Well*, ch. xiv).

Page 152. *mares and scaffold-deals*: trestles and planks.

Page 153. (1) *income*: ailment, pain.

(2) *geer*: wealth.

(3) *eydent*: diligent.

Page 154. (1) *bank and bond*: cash and securities.

(2) *perjinct*: precise.

(3) *the proverb*: see M. P. Tilley, *Dictionary of the Proverbs in England*, 1950, C 175 and M 1239.

(4) *far down . . . years*: cf. Shakespeare, *Othello*, III. iii. 266.

(5) *hail*: hale, healthy.

(6) *trone*: market-place.

(7) *relic*: widow.

(8) *plea*: contend, go to law.

Page 155. (1) *gleg*: quick, sprightly.

(2) *ettling*: aiming.

Page 156. (1) *sonsy*: plump, comely.

(2) *wud*: angry.

Page 157. (1) *haverel*: half-witted.

(2) *naturality*: natural feeling.

Page 158. (1) *linking by the arm*: tripping arm-in-arm.

(2) *daffin*: fooling.

(3) *duds*: clothes.

(4) *kithed*: appeared, displayed herself.

(5) *gumflowers*: artificial flowers.

(6) *gecking*: tossing her head.

(7) *skailed*: dispersed, came out.

(8) *allemanded*: handed with a stately air, as in the German dance.

Page 159. (1) *wised*: tried to entice.

(2) *ill-less*: harmless.

Page 193. (1) *owre*: too.
   (2) *lang-nebbit*: 'long-nosed', polysyllabic, pedantic.
   (3) *conversation*: (in the Pauline (AV) sense) behaviour, conduct.
   (4) *bleeze*: blaze, flame.
   (5) *hameward*: homely.
   (6) *het*: hot.

Page 196. (1) *ca' canny*: go cautiously, gently.
   (2) *trembling*: i.e. the fear of the Lord.
   (3) *betherel*: beadle; see p. 78, note 1.
   (4) *pleasantries*: enjoyments.
   (5) *pay-wedding*: a wedding at which each guest paid for his food and drink, the profits going to the bride and groom.
   (6) *gentle and semple*: cf. p. 182.
   (7) *auld carles kecklet*: old men cackled.
   (8) *fainness*: gladness.
   (9) *carlins*: old women.
   (10) *forms*: benches.
   (11) *mim*: demure, reserved.
   (12) *puddocks*: toads.
   (13) *oes*: grandsons.
   (14) *rocks*: distaffs.
   (15) *Infare*: the bride's coming to her new house, and the feast in celebration.

Page 198. (1) *cantrips*: magic spells.
   (2) *littlegude*: Devil.
   (3) *for a sore foot*: even for trivial misfortunes.

Page 199. (1) *ends and . . . awls*: bits and pieces. Metaphor from shoe-making: the threads and tools used in working leather.
   (2) *bawbees*: halfpennies.
   (3) *pose*: store.
   (4) *Dwining*: i.e. 'declining'.

Page 200. (1) *lair*: grave.
   (2) *vext*: distressed.

Page 201. *strayvaggers*: wanderers, seceders from the Establishment.

Page 202. (1) *corruption*: wrath.
   (2) *hobbleshow*: disorderly rabble.

Page 203. *like the green bay trees*: Ps. xxxvii. 35–36.

Page 204. *back-yett*: back gate.

Page 205. *the burghers and anti-burghers*: the section of the secession church who upheld the Burgess oath, by which a citizen taking office in Edinburgh, Glasgow, or Perth 'professed and allowed the true religion presently professed in this realm and authorised by the laws thereof'; and the section which opposed, as sinful, such recognition of the establishment as 'true'. On this issue the seceders split in 1747; and schism followed schism.

THE WORLD'S CLASSICS

A Select List

SERGEI AKSAKOV: A Russian Gentleman
Translated by J. D. Duff
Edited by Edward Crankshaw

A Russian Schoolboy
Translated by J. D. Duff
With an introduction by John Bayley

Years of Childhood
Translated by J. D. Duff
With an introduction by Lord David Cecil

ROBERT BAGE: Hermsprong
Edited with an introduction by Peter Faulkner

WILLIAM BECKFORD: Vathek
Edited by Roger Lonsdale

JAMES BOSWELL: Life of Johnson
The Hill/Powell edition, revised by David Fleeman
With an introduction by Pat Rogers

FANNY BURNEY: Camilla
Edited by Edward A. Bloom and Lilian D. Bloom

Evelina
Edited by Edward A. Bloom

JOHN CLELAND: Memoirs of a Woman of Pleasure (Fanny Hill)
Edited with an introduction by Peter Sabor

THOMAS DE QUINCEY:
The Confessions of an English Opium-Eater
Edited with an introduction by Grevel Lindop

MARIA EDGEWORTH: Castle Rackrent
Edited by George Watson

JOHN GALT: The Entail
Edited with an introduction by Ian A. Gordon

The Provost
Edited by Ian A. Gordon

WILLIAM GODWIN: Caleb Williams
Edited by David McCracken

JAMES HOGG: The Private Memoirs and
Confessions of a Justified Sinner
Edited by John Carey

MATTHEW LEWIS: The Monk
Edited by Howard Anderson

ANN RADCLIFFE:
The Italian
Edited by Frederick Garber

The Mysteries of Udolpho
Edited by Bonamy Dobrée

SIR WALTER SCOTT: The Heart of Midlothian
Edited by Clare Lamont

Redgauntlet
Edited by Kathryn Sutherland

Waverley
Edited by Claire Lamont

MARY SHELLEY: Frankenstein
Edited by M. K. Joseph

SIDNEY SMITH: Selected Letters
Edited by Nowell C. Smith
With an introduction by Auberon Waugh

LAURENCE STERNE: A Sentimental Journey
Edited with an introduction by Ian Jack

Tristram Shandy
Edited by Ian Campbell Ross

A complete list of Oxford Paperbacks, including The World's
Classics, Twentieth-Century Classics, OPUS, Past Masters,
Oxford Authors, Oxford Shakespeare, and Oxford Paperback
Reference, is available in the UK from the General Publicity
Department (JH), Oxford University Press, Walton Street,
Oxford OX2 6DP.

In the USA, complete lists are available from the Paperbacks
Marketing Manager, Oxford University Press, 200 Madison
Avenue, New York, NY 10016.

Oxford Paperbacks are available from all good bookshops. In
case of difficulty, please order direct from Oxford University
Press Bookshop, 116 High Street, Oxford, Freepost, OX1 4BR,
enclosing full payment. Please add 10% of published price for
postage and packing.